The
Terrible Truth
About Litigation

The Terrible Truth About Litigation

An Insider's Guide How To

Manage Your Litigation

and

Negotiate A Settlement

Nik Lavrinoff

SIGNATURE BOOKS
New York

SIGNATURE BOOKS An imprint of Signature Publishing House LLC
signaturepublishinghouse.com

Library of Congress Control Number: 2024932641

Publisher's Cataloging-in-Publication Data

Names: Lavrinoff, Nik, author.

Title: The terrible truth about litigation : an insider's guide how to manage your litigation and negotiate a settlement / Nik Lavrinoff.

Description: Includes bibliographical references. | New York, NY: Signature Books, an imprint of Signature Publishing House LLC, 2024.

Identifiers: LCCN: 2024932641 | ISBN: 979-8-9898613-0-9 (hardcover) | 979-8-9898613-1-6 (paperback) | 979-8-9898613-2-3 (ebook)

Subjects: LCSH Complaints (Civil procedure)—United States—Popular works. | Actions and defenses—United States—Popular works. | Attorney and client—United States—Popular works. | Liability (Law)—United States—Popular works. | Bankruptcy—United States—Popular works. | Mediation—United States. | Dispute resolution (Law)—United States—Popular works. | Compromise (Law)—United States—Popular works. | Negotiation—United States. | BISAC LAW / General. | LAW / Litigation. | LAW / Bankruptcy & Insolvency. | LAW / Arbitration, Negotiation, Mediation.

Classification: LCC KF8841.L38 2024 | DDC 347.73—dc23

Printed in the United States of America, First Printing

Dedication

§

For my children and the opportunity to raise them:

Yisroel

Rochel Elisheva, husband Yonasan Shlomo, and baby Michal Miriam

Zlota Shira and husband Akiva Eliyahu

Chana Leeba

Paysach Aharon (of blessed memory)

Yehudis

Yerucham Eliyahu

Menachem Mendel

Esther

Ariela Kayla

Table of Contents

§

Preface

§

LITIGATION PRESENTS A FORMIDABLE CHALLENGE FOR CONSUMERS to navigate. Reflecting on my three decades as a real estate developer managing diverse teams of experts, including architects, engineers, consultants, and contractors, I never handed over my trust or relinquished complete control. Even with highly skilled professionals, I maintained a close collaboration, asserting my role as the owner with the authority to steer and amicably veto when necessary. This hands-on, granular approach not only saved time and money but also averted potential problems, ensuring that real estate development ventures stayed on course while minimizing liabilities.

However, managing litigation introduces unique hurdles. Litigators are unaccustomed to clients considering them to be accountable service providers, preferring to interact with clients as they see fit rather than in a more collaborative manner. The concept of being managed by a client is scoffed at, and it can be intimidating for a client to ponder any legal management involvement in their case without an in-depth understanding of the legal system.

I became a journeyman in the legal realm, investing millions of my hard-earned dollars as a consumer defending my interests and also consulting for clients as I endeavored to rein in disputes and manage litigators within a seemingly chaotic system.

This book unfolds as a collection of eye-opening insights into the intricacies of the litigation system. Each chapter imparts valuable, and at times, insider lessons. Together, these insights form an informative roadmap, equipping you with the tools to effectively manage your litigation and potentially save significant sums of money, time, and emotional energy.

Embarking on a journey through the land of litigation, we traverse hostile territory. One hundred twenty chapters await, each offering a distinct lesson, each presenting a landscape with unique terrain and atmosphere. As we move from chapter to chapter, I will share clear survivalist techniques for managing the elements and your destiny. At other times, I offer no concrete solution or tactic, but you will gain an understanding of the field conditions, which is in itself edifying, as you learn about the obstacles and weather conditions ahead. Some chapters flow seamlessly into others, closely related in subject matter, while other times the journey hopscotches suddenly, seemingly to the other side of the world. I hope that the cumulative travels herein will bestow upon you much benefit.

This genre-defying blend of exposé and practical handbook is, to my knowledge, a one-of-a-kind resource. Employ it judiciously and to your advantage!

Introduction

§

IN THE INTRICATE TAPESTRY OF OUR SOCIETY, ONE THREAD STANDS out as deep and enduring: the pursuit of justice. We've clung to the belief that our legal system, with its revered courts, solemn judges, diligent clerks, and adept attorneys, would be the unwavering beacon of fairness and resolution. It's a belief that has shaped generations of minds and an idea deeply rooted in our collective consciousness.

But as we turn the pages of this book, a different narrative begins to unfold—a story of limitations, inefficiencies, and failures that lurk beneath the surface of our revered legal system. *The Terrible Truth About Litigation* is an invitation to join me on an intimate journey, a candid conversation with a seasoned friend in the know, as we expose the world of litigation.

This book isn't a product of ivory tower theories or distant observations. It is forged from the fires of personal experience. For three decades, I've been a real estate developer, a journey that led me to cough up millions of my hard-earned dollars in legal fees to combat business issues and pay litigators. Concurrently, I became the trusted advisor to countless clients, guiding them through the treacherous terrain of litigation and attempting to lead them from the grinding gears of their legal disputes to the solid ground of settling their cases.

Many among us still cling to these comforting myths: that problems find their resolutions in the courtroom, that fairness is the ultimate goal, and that justice waits at the end of the rainbow. I, too, once held these myths close. However, the deeper I ventured into the quagmire of litigation, the more I realized the illusion of these myths.

As you delve into the upcoming chapters, buckle up for a high-speed journey straight to the heart of the matter, but be warned—this is no ordinary expedition. Picture it more like a demolition derby, where courts, judges, clerks, U.S. Trustees, and attorneys are behind the wheel, relentlessly ramming into litigants. Together, we'll strip away the layers of the legal system, revealing its fractures, inefficiencies, and failures. Prepare for a revealing spotlight on the exorbitant costs, deceptive practices, and conflicts of interest that afflict litigants. Above all, we'll face the stark truth that justice, more often than not, remains elusive.

Yet, this book is not a tale of despair or an academic discourse. Instead, it's a roadmap through the legal labyrinth, illuminated by the stark realities of human nature. It's a tool to help you recognize the terrain you navigate. I trust that you'll absorb the strategic essence of this book much like mastering a martial art, where it becomes second nature and your innate defensive and offensive abilities are unlocked, becoming as natural as drawing a breath.

I won't sell you vague notions or empty clichés about hope and change for the legal system. Instead, my goal is to uncover and enhance your understanding of the challenging terrain of conflict and resolution, enabling you to navigate it more skillfully.

This book serves as an unvarnished reminder that the solutions to your legal challenges may not rest solely, if at all, in the hands of litigators. Believing that your attorney holds some magical or systematic panacea for your legal troubles in court is akin to chasing something appetizing that isn't real—like how greyhounds run around in circles racing after a mechanical fake rabbit.

Recognizing the real lay of the land and embracing personal accountability serves as a far more potent catalyst for resolving your predicaments.

Now let me share a groundbreaking truth about the legal industry, a truth that might be overlooked or even offensive to some attorneys: Your attorneys practice law and make a good living thanks to your legal matters, and their interactions with you during working hours are primarily opportunities to support their lifestyle.

Yet, when night falls, it's crickets. It's as if you never existed. Your predicaments are yours alone, and you carry them with you every day and every night, 24/7. Therefore, both the predicament and the solution are yours alone, and attorneys are simply hired tools to be employed when you face a problem that requires the assistance of a particular tool.

The burden of resolving your issues invariably falls on you, even if your challenge involves the complexities of the law. If you have any choice in the matter, entering the world of litigation is not a decision to be made lightly.

Part One

Litigation

Chapter 1

Courthouse Combat: Litigation Defined

§

L ITIGATION, IN THE ROUGH-AND-TUMBLE ARENA OF THE LEGAL world, is the battle cry of disputes. It's when individuals or entities haul their grievances into the courtroom and duke it out, seeking resolution, retribution, or redemption. Think of it as the legal equivalent of a heavyweight boxing match, where opposing sides throw punches in the form of legal arguments, evidence, and persuasion. It's a clash of wills and wits, where each party strives to emerge victorious, whether through a judge's gavel or a jury's verdict.

But make no mistake, litigation is no tea party. It's a high-stakes game where the outcome can profoundly impact lives, fortunes, and futures. It's a realm where the battle lines are drawn, and warriors in suits or robes wage intellectual combat. It's a world of rules, rituals, and rhetoric, where the strongest case, the sharpest legal mind, or the most compelling narrative can all tip the scales of justice. The scales also fluctuate depending on which attorney the judge knows or likes best, which party's narrative aligns most with the judge's personal opinions and worldview, which attorney tells the biggest lies, or which attorney donated to a cause the judge holds dear.

In the end, litigation is the cauldron where disputes are cast and ultimately resolved. It's a journey through the labyrinth of the legal system, where the terrain is treacherous, the costs are steep, and the outcome is often a coin toss. And whether you're a plaintiff seeking justice or a defendant fighting for your rights, one thing is sure—litigation is a no-holds-barred contest, not unlike the World Wide Wrestling Federation's equivalent of a Battle Royale and or an Inferno Match.

The next few chapters lay the groundwork, with essential definitions, for the building blocks of general knowledge that every reader needs. While they might not be the most thrilling read, these definitions are the necessary foundation before I dive into the real-life tales that follow. In these upcoming chapters, we'll explore what is a court of law, the diverse array of court types, and the roles played by litigators and judges. So, fasten your seat belts, because in the world of litigation, it's an all-or-nothing game, and there's no place for the faint of heart.

Chapter 2

Courts to Litigate

§

WOULD YOU BELIEVE IT IF I TOLD YOU THERE ARE MORE TYPES OF courts than you can shake a stick at? Well, it's true, my friends. But here's the deal: I won't subject you to an exhaustive list that'll have you seeing stars. After all, this isn't a textbook; it's more like a thoughtfully compiled collection of litigation insights, poised for you to incorporate into the intricacies of your individual legal scenario.

Now if you're itching for a comprehensive list of every court under the sun, you'll find it in the Appendix. But for now, let's keep our focus sharp and our legal journey finely tuned. We're all about delivering the right information for the right moment—no dizzying propositions here.

Chapter 3

What's a Litigator's Role?

§

Alitigator's job, with zero embellishment, involves representing clients in legal disputes. They manage various aspects of a lawsuit, including case assessment, research, negotiation, and courtroom representation. Their primary objective is to advocate for their clients' interests and work toward resolving disputes within the boundaries of the law.

This entails pretrial preparations, such as evidence and fact gathering and legal strategy formulation, as well as, when necessary, representing the case in court, making or objecting to motions, making legal arguments, questioning witnesses, and seeking a favorable resolution for their clients. A litigator's role is firmly rooted in the practical application of legal knowledge and procedures to navigate and adjudicate conflicts.

So, the rest of this book? Brace yourself for the real deal—it's a lot closer to those lawyer jokes you've heard. Here's one for you:

> *Santa Claus, the tooth fairy, an honest lawyer, and an old drunk spot a hundred-dollar bill on the sidewalk. Who snags it? Surprise, surprise, it's the old drunk. Why? Because the other three are mythical creatures!*[4]

Chapter 4

What's a Judge's Role?

§

AJUDGE IS A LEGAL OFFICIAL APPOINTED OR ELECTED TO PRESIDE over and administer justice within a courtroom and exercise authority to interpret and apply the law, make legal rulings, and ensure that legal procedures are followed during legal proceedings.

They play a crucial role in upholding the law, and their job requires adjudicating disputes and ensuring that the rights of individuals involved in legal cases are protected. Judges can preside over various types of cases, including civil, criminal, family, and administrative matters, and they are responsible for making impartial and fair decisions based on the facts and applicable laws.

Now let's talk turkey. While I've watched judges in some criminal and civil cases follow the playbook of fairness, due process, and wisdom, I've also seen judges presiding over business clashes, family feuds, and bankruptcy battles who have strayed so far off base that they have entered criminal territory and should be behind bars themselves. How does that even happen? The answer, my friend, lies in the joke:

> *What's the difference between G-d and a family court judge?*
> *G-d doesn't think He's a family court judge.*

Chapter 5

The Medical-Legal Industrial Complex Parallel

§

IN THE ARENA OF LIFE, WHERE MEDICINE AND LAW TAKE CENTER stage, there's a curious parallel between these two worlds. But before we dive into this complex intersection, let me make one thing crystal clear: I hold doctors in high regard, recognizing their critical role in healing and saving lives. They're the real-life heroes who mend broken bodies, transplant organs, and fight diseases, and I tip my hat to their dedication and steadfastness in this noble profession of healing, despite the daily pressures of modern medicine and the medical establishment that burden practitioners in so many ways.

Now let's unfurl the curtain and reveal the surprising connection between the medical and legal establishments. At first glance, medicine and law might seem like distant galaxies, but as we delve deeper, the similarities become apparent. When individuals face health or legal issues, they seek help from professionals, expecting solutions to their problems. However, neither profession is inherently designed to tackle the root causes of these issues effectively.

Consider a trip to your doctor's office. You arrive with a health concern, and typically, your doctor responds by prescribing medications, treatments, or procedures aimed at alleviating your symptoms. Rarely do these medical interventions target the underlying cause of your ailment. Why? Two primary reasons.

First, it's baffling that medical schools dedicate a mere eight hours of their curriculum to nutritional training for aspiring doctors. This oversight is astonishing, given the overwhelming evidence showing that proper nutrition can prevent, improve, or even reverse a plethora of diseases— and not just the lesser ones, but the real big ones, like high blood pressure, type 2 diabetes, and coronary heart disease. Imagine if doctors handed out prescriptions that read "Consume whole, unprocessed foods" instead of for pills. It's a straightforward solution, so why isn't it happening?

The second reason is as clear as day: it's all about the money. The medical/pharmaceutical industrial complex thrives on promulgating medications, treatments, and procedures, not dietary advice. Shifting the focus to nutrition would jeopardize profits, and so the medical industrial complex, some argue, prioritizes financial gain over your well-being, leaving you suffering needlessly.

Surprisingly, the legal system mirrors this approach. When you're embroiled in a quagmire of disputes, you turn to a lawyer in the hope of resolving your issue. However, litigators aren't trained core problem solvers; they operate within a system designed to administer lengthy legal procedures and battles that can consume your time, money, emotions, and energy. Litigators are trained to litigate.

Depending on your location and the level of litigation, you might pay anywhere from $350 to $2,500 per hour per attorney on your case over multiple years with no solution in sight. It's a taxing and expensive journey, and yet, it's often the only path litigators can offer. Sharing similarities with the medical/pharmaceutical industrial complex, the legal establishment isn't equipped to address the root problem; each profession is geared up to serve as perpetual service providers rather than genuine core problem solvers.

Litigators' financial interests align with prolonged legal battles, and swift settlements would disrupt their lucrative income stream. Some may argue, "But lawyers settle cases all the time."

True, but often it's on the brink of trial when the litigants, exhausted and disheartened, seek resolution, realizing the flaws in the system and the uncertainty of the outcome. Their attorneys, like hungry hyenas, laughed all the way to the bank and have already feasted on much of their clients' resources, and the litigants are now more receptive to promulgating settlement.

In both medicine and law, the wrong tools are often employed for the task at hand. Many medical doctors gratuitously medicate, and doctors of jurisprudence gratuitously litigate. Seeking the help of doctors may not necessarily lead to true health, and turning to lawyers and litigation may not lead to effective resolutions.

So, always bear in mind this cardinal rule: assuming primary responsibility for any aspect of your life, be it your health or legal matters, will propel you much further toward achieving your goals of overall wellness and resolution compared to solely relying on professionals.

Chapter 6

The Legal Establishment: No Justice, No Peace

§

When there are too many policemen, there can be no liberty. When there are too many soldiers, there can be no peace. Where there are too many lawyers, there can be no justice.

Grand Master Lin Yutang, Chinese Inventor, Scholar, Philosopher

IN THE UNITED STATES, THERE ARE OVER 1.3 MILLION LICENSED attorneys.[1] Each year, more than 100 million cases flood into state trial courts, with another 400,000 cases making their way to federal trial courts. While we have approximately 30,000 state judges, we count 1,700 federal judges.[2]

Some cases wrap up within a year of being filed, but others linger on for years, and some even stretch past a decade. With a population of 335 million Americans[3], it's conceivable and probable that there may be a backlog of nearly one case for every man, woman, and child in the entire United States. That, my friends, is an abundance of litigation.

Let me take you back thirty-three years to a Saturday night in Newport Beach, California. Picture this: a world-famous rabbi from Jerusalem, a United States Supreme Court Justice, a Hollywood film critic, and I walk into a bar—well, almost. Back then, before I ever spent a dollar on legal fees and while in college for an engineering degree, I crashed a party. A local rabbi had organized a weekend retreat for Jewish, mostly nonobservant lawyers, drawing hundreds for a leisurely weekend that conveniently delivered Bar Association-required yearly continuing education credits. The local rabbi aimed to weave religion into the program casually and entertainingly to inspire his new flock.

On that Saturday night, Michael Medved, the movie critic, hosted what was billed as a debate between Supreme Court Justice Antonin Scalia and Rabbi Adin Steinsaltz, a scholar *Time Magazine* called "a once-in-a-millennium scholar" for his commentary and translation of the entire Talmud. The rabbi and the justice, giants of jurisprudence in their own right, engaged in a friendly conversation rather than a debate. The mood was festive and jovial, and we learned that the rabbi and the justice were long-time friends.

The soft-spoken elderly rabbi explained the Jewish court system, from Moses to the Sanhedrin to the present-day Beth Din, highlighting a system that had worked well for millennia. Then, an audience member posed a question: What does Judaism say about the role of lawyers, as you haven't mentioned courtroom advocacy? The rabbi responded with something akin to: Professional advocates in court, litigators, are looked upon as prostitutes. True justice happens when disputing parties present their issues to the court themselves without legal advocates, and the judges apply the law and decide the case. Advocates corrupt the delivery of justice.

A collective gasp swept through the hundreds of lawyers and their spouses. The woman who had asked the question was visibly shaken and, in a quivering voice, asked a follow-up question: How then, through practicing our craft of litigation, could we bring sanctity to our profession and to G-d? Rabbi Steinsaltz replied instantly in a loud whisper: You can't. That's simply impossible—total mic drop. The room fell silent as the truth settled in. There was no rebuttal. In that interval of silence, the crowd in unison seemed to accept the rabbi's assessment; the reverberation of a shock to hear something so true stated publicly, echoed and etched itself in all of us present.

And so, my friends, I'll leave it up to you to decide if these two scholars, Grand Master Lin Yutang and the honorable Rabbi Adin Steinsaltz, were onto something.

Chapter 7

The Pitch:
Setting the Stage for Legal Representation

§

PICTURE THIS SCENARIO, MY FRIENDS: YOU'RE GRAPPLING WITH A problem that's left you emotionally charged, bewildered, and convinced that only an attorney can untangle the web of complexities before you. You schedule a meeting and enter the attorney's domain. As the secretary ushers you through the door, you're greeted by an impressive collection of legal casebooks adorning the bookshelves, the rich aroma of dark leather chairs, and an aura of gravitas that fills the room.

The attorney exudes a confident yet inviting demeanor, firmly but gently shaking your hand. He radiates warmth and professionalism, hanging on your every word as you pour out your troubles. Seated behind his substantial mahogany desk, he locks eyes with you, his gaze brimming with intent and empathy. You sense that he's carefully assessing the situation, ready to stand by your side. And without fail, Mr. Esquire utters these words:

> Mr. Johnson, you have an incredibly strong case, and I wholeheartedly believe we can secure a victory for you. I'll have a retainer agreement sent to you later tonight. Please take the time to review, sign, and promptly transfer your deposit. Once that's settled, we'll unleash the full might of our firm to champion your cause.

This scene unfolds in countless attorney-client meetings, and it's a pitch that rarely fails to leave an impression. For the uninitiated client, it's a moment of awe and reassurance—the assurance that a formidable ally now stands in their corner, a true champion ready to secure triumph. Even experienced clients who have navigated the legal terrain and felt the sting of disappointment may find themselves emotionally vulnerable in this moment. They silently hope, *Perhaps this attorney is genuinely skilled and competent, distinct from those who in the past overcharged and left me disheartened. Maybe this time, things will be different.*

This pitch marks the opening act of the attorney-client relationship, a complex dance of expectations and aspirations, setting the stage for what's to come. But as we venture deeper into the realm of litigation, we'll uncover the intricacies concealed behind this initial "hook-setting" scene. We'll explore the dynamics shaping the attorney-client relationship, shedding light on the underlying objectives and motivations at play.

Chapter 8

The Hollow Initial Meeting with a Litigator

§

YOU FIND YOURSELF IN A SITUATION WHERE YOU'VE EITHER BEEN served with a lawsuit or are considering taking legal action against another. So, you pick up the phone and set up an appointment with a litigator's office. You walk into that office because you've got a problem that needs addressing. If you're sharp and seasoned, your primary goal is to dive straight into the heart of the matter, discussing the crucial aspects of your case. But here's the thing—the attorney's ability to offer a meaningful assessment of your case is severely limited without the full context and history leading up to the lawsuit.

Now picture a scenario where you're less than laser-focused, and your part of the conversation revolves around the perceived injustice of the situation, the animosity between you and the other party, or the emotional toll it's taken on you. While these aspects may be important and even relevant to the case, they often overshadow the basic facts, the very essence of the matter, which is crucial for a productive discussion.

Moreover, remember that during this typical initial meeting, the attorney's natural inclination is to sell you on hiring their firm and convincing you to write that initial retainer check. You and the litigator are essentially having two different conversations. They're paying close attention to your concerns, maybe grasping vague notions of various puzzle pieces of your case, but it's all part of their strategy to meet their needs—getting you on board for the long run and kick-starting their cash flow.

Whether you end up signing the retainer agreement or not, keep in mind that this attorney probably has ten more introductory meetings lined up, in addition to their existing caseload. Your case details won't linger in their mind rent-free. It's not sinister; it's just a fact of life for anyone offering professional services.

Even as you share what might be highly relevant information, these details only serve as tools to steer their sales pitch, and hardly anything you say will find a permanent place in their memory. They won't invest mental effort into evaluating your case, especially during the actual meeting. Time is money, and they can't wait to conclude the meeting because they're losing money as they speak with you.

It's only after you've hired the litigator that you can begin conveying valuable information to them, allowing them to gradually grasp the essence of your case. Unfortunately, this part of the process is often woefully inefficient and provides ample opportunities for the litigator to rack up billable hours. They'll likely ask you to provide documents and spend many hours in their office retelling your story. They'll listen and construct a narrative they need to put down on paper. Only at this point will they have condensed the essential story and finally have a chance to assess the case's viability.

But guess what? Even if your case is weak and there's little to gain from litigation, they might keep the game going, continue with the hearings and filing pleadings, back and forth like a never-ending volleyball match with opposing counsel. Why? Because that's how they make their money. However, there is an alternative approach that I employ, one that comes with a plethora of benefits.

Chapter 9

Triaging Your Case Before Meeting and Hiring a Litigator

§

T HE BEST PERSON TO NARRATE A CASE'S HISTORY IS OFTEN A KEY player in the dispute. It's practical for you to compile and edit your own story, a meticulous timeline that lists dates on the left-hand side with succinct, narrative paragraphs of events on the right. This chronology will serve as the centerpiece for discussion when evaluating your case's viability and potential defenses in your conversation with a potential litigator.

Start by crafting this chronology. A helpful method to jog your memory is to sift through all your emails and text messages to and from the parties involved in the conflict. Nowadays, our emails and texts serve as a significant repository of most of our written interactions. These communications serve several purposes:

1. They help you recall important events when drafting your chronology.

2. They may contain messages, emails, or attachments that could serve as strong evidence in support of your case.

As you meticulously sift through these communications, imagine yourself as a legal prospector panning for gold. In this pre-discovery sweep, every piece of evidence you uncover is like discovering a hidden nugget—it could be a game changer, either a powerful and beneficial weapon or a potential landmine. Litigation, my friends, can often drag on for years, only to face a cataclysmic revelation during the discovery phase, a found document that undermines your developing narrative, a legal bombshell that can obliterate your entire case. That's why this proactive sweep is invaluable, because your case could be doomed from the outset. So, before you embark on the long journey of a legal battle, where your litigator happily profits from those monthly billing cycles until a case-maiming bomb is discovered, comb through the beach of your communications and documents.

And so, when you stumble upon that email that feels like a "poison pill," don't just let it slide. Include it in your meticulously compiled chronology, an appendix of exhibits that may prove to be your ace in the hole. In the arena of litigation, my friends, it's often the details that make all the difference.

As you go through all your communications, copy and attach any relevant messages or attachments as additional documents in your appendix. You need not be overly formal in your organization.

As you continue with your chronology, when discussing a particular communication or document that you believe is evidentiary, print or copy it and include it on the following page. You can also circle and jot down a brief note or two to direct the reader's attention to the most pertinent part of the document.

Once you've completed your chronology, set it aside and review it the following day. Edit and revise it for clarity and use the checklist below to ensure that it's optimized:

Review all emails, texts, WhatsApp messages, and relevant social media interactions from all parties directly and indirectly involved.

- Go through all your hardcopy files and review all documents.

- Essentially, you will have conducted a pre-discovery exploration, strengthened your initial chronology, and exposed any potential liabilities to your case.

Armed with this chronology, it's wise to share it with a litigator before your meeting. When you do meet, both you and the litigator will be on the same page, and the attorney will have invested their own time in reviewing your case. This way, the client and litigator will have a more meaningful conversation during the initial meeting, making it less hollow.

Notwithstanding that the litigator's prime motivation is to get you to sign a retainer, you will have shifted his focal point to a document with a story. If he doesn't read it before your free consultation, that's an indicator of how prepared he is to handle your case. If he does read it, then you'll have a chance for a more productive meeting. If you're legally savvy, your chronology document can also include potential defenses that you believe are relevant. If not applicable, these suggested defenses can at least serve as food for thought in your discussions with your litigator.

This approach allows you to share the same information as you consult with different litigators and compare their responses. It turns the process into more of a controlled study rather than visiting multiple litigator offices and providing different pieces of the story to each.

Furthermore, you can easily email your case chronology to attorneys who might be beyond your normal geographical reach. This will provide you with a variety of expert opinions, and you can even set up virtual meetings on platforms like Zoom.

By condensing your case into a manageable chronology, you will save time and money. This document will serve as a reference and a foundation for your litigator to proceed with your case after retention without the hassle of you scrambling to provide information in the typical scattered and piecemeal manner. You'll gain some flex and be in control of your destiny and better equipped for intelligent discussions with potential litigators.

Chapter 10

Legal Opinions: Unfiltered Realities

§

LET'S CUT TO THE CHASE: LEGAL OPINIONS OFTEN DON'T SERVE THE purpose you truly need, especially when you're navigating the labyrinth of litigation.

Here's the lowdown. Legal opinions come in two distinct flavors. One delves deep into the nuances of the law, providing an intricate analysis. The other type is all about compliance and due diligence, ensuring your actions play by the regulatory rules. Most of the time, these opinions are just checkboxes to satisfy the demands of title insurance or other transactional components.

But let's talk about what you really want—an opinion that tells you if your legal battle is worth fighting. Now getting that kind of straight talk might not be as easy as it sounds.

Imagine this: You stroll into your attorney's office with a big problem, like defaulting on a hefty mortgage for your downtown Miami office building. You're served a pre-foreclosure notice, and panic is setting in. Your attorney, Mr. Esquire, is gearing up for the retainer deal, ready to tell you that your case is airtight, and he's itching for the courtroom showdown.

But, hang on. What if Mr. Esquire gave you the most brutally honest but completely accurate response? It might sound something like this: "Mr. Hansen, you borrowed a cool fifty million bucks, and you've got to pay it back. The lender is dead set on foreclosing, and legally speaking, you're holding an empty bag. Now if you need some time to hatch an exit plan—

maybe a refinancing or a sale—I can help you drag out the legal process. But anything approaching winning in court? That's a pipe dream."

Now that kind of candid advice is a rare breed among attorneys. It's a sign that your best interests are their top priority. But let's face it; when emotions escalate and the stakes are sky-high, there's something oddly appealing about a legal gladiator who promises victory, even when it's not really in the cards.

People tend to be drawn to the charismatic sales pitch rather than guided toward what they genuinely need. So, it's no wonder that many folks gravitate toward attorneys who promise miraculous triumph. It's akin to offering a lifeline to someone drowning in pressure and adversity, and that's precisely what most people yearn for—a savior.

My advice? Buck the trend. The next time you're in the hot seat, opt for level-headed, no-nonsense representation. Seek out attorneys and advisors who don't sugarcoat things, those who don't sell you on their prowess or expertise, and those who won't push you into signing a retainer.

Go for the lawyer who talks to you in simple, straightforward terms. And remember, it all starts with how you frame your request—skip asking about the legal opinion, and ask about the legal viability of your case instead. This shift in perspective can be a game changer.

Chapter 11

The Pitch 2.0:
A Curve Ball to the Sophisticated Client

§

AH, THE PITCH 2.0, FOLKS. LET ME BREAK IT DOWN FOR YOU. You're no legal rookie; you've waltzed through the litigation arena before. Those leather chairs, the litigator's empathy, eye contact, and firm handshake won't dazzle you. No, you're seasoned and sharp as a tack. You've got one question on your mind: What's this lawyer's legal artillery for your battle?

Initially, the litigator played the empathy card, reassuring you about your strong case. But now they've shifted gears. It's all about flaunting their legal prowess, boasting their brilliance, expertise, and valor. They've unveiled their secret weapon argument to slay your legal dragon.

This salesman's confidence flows like a fire hose, and it's hard not to be impressed. Maybe you've shopped around and spoken to other attorneys, but this one, this one seems to have the golden ticket. The winning argument.

By now most experienced litigation clients are hooked. This litigator has set themselves apart from the rest. They're the obvious choice. What could possibly go wrong, right?

So, you sign that retainer, months or even years pass, and reality hits. That once-brilliant legal theory? Well, it's springing leaks, and you've poured a fortune into legal bills. It's a mess, and it's your mess, not theirs. Your time, your money, your fight—all down the drain. You've even got new liabilities, thanks to the ongoing litigation.

Here's some practical advice: When you're considering a litigator's legal theory, don't stop at the surface. Ask for the specific precedent court cases that back up their argument. You may not be a lawyer, but if you can read and you've played "Spot the Difference" as a kid, you've got the tools to compare and evaluate your case, the legal theory, and the provided case law.

In your next conversation with the attorney, be ready to walk away if you spot significant differences or if the litigator dismisses your concerns, insisting everything aligns perfectly. You've played the game of detecting differences successfully in the past—don't lose your marbles now that you are an adult. Trust your discerning eye.

That litigator is out there hunting for their next meal ticket, and they're working hard to close the deal. Don't let their bravado blind you to your observations!

Witness the audacity of a prominent NYC litigator as he persistently pushed for a deal. My client faced a mortgage default on a commercial piece of real estate, and this attorney resorted to smoke and mirrors, attempting to convince him of a mythical defense solution. He offered explanations and cited case law that crumbled under scrutiny. The litigator's conduct was egregious, and he was well aware of it, yet he clung to his sales pitch. Below is his final email to my client, along with my dissection and comments included for clarity sent to my client:

All,

Here is a recent case where I succeeded in enjoining a foreclosure of a $74 million leasehold mortgage by Fannie Mae.

> *Comment: Hold on a second, this claim needs closer inspection.*

Not true. Enjoining is the verb form of getting an injunction. The court didn't grant an injunction against a Fannie Mae foreclosure because there was none on record. There wasn't even a Fannie Mae default notice.

... and sought injunctive relief with respect to a default notice served on Fannie Mae and a concomitant threat of acceleration and foreclosure by Fannie Mae.

Comment: This doesn't add up either.

There seemingly was no such threat.

As you can see, the court declared the default notice to be ineffective and void—a result that would be appropriate in your matter.

Comment: A complete misdirection.

You have a lender default notice. The default in the case was concerning a lease. A different animal altogether!

Time is of the essence if you want to proceed as we discussed. Please get back to me ASAP.

Comment: False urgency to try and seal the deal.

Not so fast! Hold your horses!

This is costly, dangerous, and malicious legal advice proffered only to excite a potential client with an offer of salvation so that the litigator can bag another client and secure a hefty retainer, even though it would lead to a legal dead end. Happens every day!

Chapter 12

Conflict of Interest: Signing the Retainer— Open-Ended Billing Dilemma

§

FOLKS, LET'S DIVE INTO THE LEGAL WHIRLWIND, WHERE OUR TALE kicks off with a classic conflict of interest that's sure to get your wheels turning. It all starts the moment you ink that retainer agreement and open the floodgates, allowing the attorney or firm to charge those eye-popping hourly rates without a finish line in sight.

Now picture this: You agree to foot the bill for your litigator's services at an astounding rate of $1,000 per hour, and there's no cap on the hours they can bill. They're raking in a cool $17 a minute in a contract without an upper limit of hours as part of the deal and no time clock to punch. Your attorney pencils in his own hours!

The attorney is then off to the races, not unlike the driver in that vintage video game, Crazy Taxi, who maneuvers his taxi recklessly over land, air, and sea, pedal to the metal with abandon, as his meter accrues astronomically high customer charges.

It's not about sinister plots or secret schemes; it's just plain human nature. You see, when there's money on the table, even the nicest, smartest, and most empathetic lawyers can get caught up in the world of billable hours. They've got a knack for stretching a five-minute chat into an epic saga, and why? Well, the longer you're on the line, the fatter their paycheck gets.

Just think about it—making that kind of money for drafting documents, making phone calls, and the occasional courtroom appearance or deposition. It might just be the easiest and most addictive money-making game in town. It's like that monkey in a cage, constantly pulling the lever for another hit, only this time, the lawyers are hitting the "billable hours" button.

Now it's not about the lawyers getting high; it's about all of us feeding their habit by letting them burn through our hard-earned cash without limit. We can certainly take steps to rein in those hourly charges, but let's face it, this is a systemic issue that's deeply ingrained in the legal landscape.

And this isn't just about one lawyer trying to hit the jackpot. It's woven right into the legal billing system. Hourly billing is the name of the game, and it inadvertently encourages delaying and dragging things out instead of wrapping them up.

So, there you are, stuck in a system where time is money, and your wallet takes the hit. It's not some grand conspiracy; it's just how things roll in the legal world. As we dig deeper into the wild world of litigation, we'll uncover more sinews of this twisty tale. But, understanding this fundamental conflict of interest is like taking a peek at the opening act of a legal drama that's been playing out for eons in the land of the free and the home of the billable hour.

Chapter 13

Outsmarting the High-Priced Attorney: Negotiating a Retainer Deal

$

YOU FIND YOURSELF FACING A MONUMENTAL LEGAL CASE, ONE WHERE hiring a top-tier attorney will set you back a jaw-dropping $1,500 per hour. Drawing inspiration from the previous chapter, you're feeling rather shrewd, and you're determined to keep costs in check while outsmarting the soon-to-be-hired legal heavyweight.

You decide to insert a clause into his retainer agreement that reads something like, "All non-partner level work shall be delegated to the appropriate-level staff for the task at hand." You believe this maneuver will circumvent your attorney's ability to bill you the full $1,500 per hour for all the legal work your case entails, delegating much of the work to lower-level and lower-cost staff.

A sense of pride washes over you as you picture yourself as the mastermind who has appointed your litigator as the Legal Tom Brady, tasked with managing your case and assigning most of the work to lower-cost staff. However, this quarterback attorney is no rookie. He agrees to your retainer stipulation and comfortingly informs you that a significant portion of the work will be handled by his associate, billing at $750 per hour. While not exactly cheap, it's certainly a welcome reduction from the original $1,500 per hour. You sign the retainer agreement and walk away feeling like Robert Kraft, the owner of the New England Patriots.

But when the bill arrives, you're met with a shock. The sheer number of billable hours leaves you bewildered. You might even contemplate taking legal action against your renowned top-tier attorney for overcharging, although finding another attorney willing to take on a fellow practitioner seems like a long shot. You may even consider representing yourself in the case to confront the top gun. It appears straightforward, but you're mistaken.

The top-tier attorney will have a rationale to justify his billing practices. I've seen this movie before. He can successfully argue that due to the tight timeline you imposed and the pressure to get the job done, Tom Brady needed to delegate and guide the less experienced staff to expedite the work. So, instead of billing you the full $1,500 per hour for his services, as he delegated the work to a junior associate billing at $750 per hour, he also had to invest half an hour collaborating with the associate for every hour of work he performed. Consequently, the $750-per-hour associate effectively costs you not just his hourly rate but also half an hour of the top gun's hourly rate, resulting in a total blended rate of $1,500 per hour.

If it weren't bordering on legal larceny, you might almost admire the quarterback litigator's fancy footwork.

Chapter 14

The Wildly High Hourly Rate:
A Question of Justification

§

Ladies and gentlemen, let's talk about the elephant in the room—those sky-high hourly rates charged by attorneys. Sure, lawyers go through the rigors of law school, but what truly justifies these exorbitant fees?

Think about it: Meetings with clients are typically straightforward, conversations between legal peers are hardly rocket science, and making phone calls is par for the course. These days, drafting legal documents has become a breeze with the aid of templates, previously filed documents for reference, and the magic of AI. It's like having a supercharged assistant at their fingertips.

Now don't get me wrong; there's undeniable skill involved in depositions, some hearings, and certainly during a full-blown trial. But get this—a staggering 97 percent[5] of all cases settle before they even reach the trial stage. So, in the life of your average litigator, a trial is more like a solar eclipse—highly anticipated but very infrequent.

So, let's dissect the piggy bank here. These billing rates might seem baffling and downright costly for the folks footing the bill, but for the attorneys, it's a pretty sweet gig, isn't it? Let's take a closer look at what's really driving these rates and what's hidden behind the legal fee shell game.

Chapter 15

The Billing Lifecycle of a Case: Navigating the Costly Maze

$

IMAGINE THIS SCENARIO: YOU'RE SHELLING OUT A WHOPPING $1,000 an hour for partner-level legal work, another $500 an hour for the paralegal's assistance, and don't forget the $3 a page for printing. It's enough to make anyone wish for a swift resolution. But here's where the rub lies: while you're eager to settle your case and put an end to the financial drain, your attorney, well, they're not exactly on the same page.

You see, your attorney is not trained to settle your case swiftly or to resolve your problem. No, their training is focused on the art of litigation, a process that, by definition, involves a ton of work stretched over multiple years, all with the ultimate goal of duking it out in court at a trial or final hearing.

So, while you're looking for that off-ramp to resolution, your attorney is often cruising down the litigation highway, billing hours and racking up expenses along the way. It's a disconnect that can leave you feeling like you're fodder on a collision course with a never-ending legal bill.

Chapter 16

Why Are You Heading to Trial?

§

DEPENDING ON THE SPECIFICS OF YOUR CASE, THE MULTI-MILLION-dollar question—yes, you read that right—is this: Why in the world would you dedicate years and a fortune to litigate a case with the grand ambition of going to trial, when a jaw-dropping 97 percent of all cases end up settling without going to trial?

Let's get real. You've got a problem that demands a swift solution, and you're not too thrilled about hemorrhaging a grand an hour on legal fees. But on the flip side, your attorney is raking in serious money every hour and has every reason to keep that cash flow flowing like a mighty river.

Their playbook isn't about putting a cap on expenses; it's more like a per-hour constant wind on their back, propelling them down the field, and if they are lucky, they get to earn the touchdown dance in the end zone because the case went to trial, taking another huge bite of the golden apple that is your wallet. The only thing spiking is your temperature and the attorney's income.

So here's the burning question I put to you: Armed with the knowledge that a staggering 97 percent of cases settle before they step into the final courtroom act, why not steer the ship toward settlement sooner rather than later? If you're itching to slam the brakes on the attorney's never-ending billing machine and put an end to your own migraine-inducing legal odyssey, every chat with your legal counsel on your litigation journey should revolve around the potential and strategy to settle your case expeditiously.

Sure, an attorney might argue that court proceedings can sometimes lay the groundwork for settlement, and there's a grain of truth to that. But let's be brutally honest here—a litigator's laser focus is fixed on the trial or final adjudication, where he can garner even more cash flow.

So, let's not kid ourselves; court proceedings don't organically lead to settlement—they rather create an accumulation of pain and disappointment in the litigants, sometimes because of their attorney's poor performance. But even if their attorney's service was stellar, the system is frustrating overall, the time expended is exhaustive, the financial costs exponential over time, and the liabilities created during this lag cumulative. So, the litigants are no longer fired up, trying to get even, looking for justice, wanting of punishing the other side, or believe, as their lawyer told them on day one, that they "have a very good case."

The litigants are pained, have lost the will to fight, and just want the madness to stop.

So, the grueling battle of attrition wears down both the plaintiff and the defendant, and that causes a ground-up movement in the case where these battle-scarred parties essentially force their somewhat hesitant attorneys to broach the topic of settlement with one another.

It's the germinating seed of settlement sprouting in the trenches of litigation. But make no mistake, the attorneys usually feel like they have been robbed of the final curtain call, the pomp and circumstance of running a trial, and the final big cash dividends from the intensive hours involved.

Chapter 17

Litigator Skin in the Game:
The World of Contingency Fees

$

CONTINGENCY FEE ARRANGEMENTS, FOLKS, ARE MOST OFTEN LINKED with personal injury cases like car accidents, slip and falls, medical malpractice, and product liability claims. When folks find themselves in these tough situations, they often lack the financial resources to pay for legal services upfront.

So, what do attorneys do? They say, "You know what? We'll have some skin in the game." They'll agree to represent these folks on a contingency basis, and that usually means they'll take a chunk, around 33 to 40 percent, of the final settlement or award as their fee once they win the case.

Now, it's not just personal injury cases that go this route. Employment law cases, like workplace discrimination and wrongful termination disputes, often play by the same rules. This kind of arrangement lets employees stand up to workplace injustice, even when they might not have the financial muscle to do so. It's like a David vs. Goliath situation, where attorneys step in, ready to fight for justice, and they only get their piece of the pie if they win.

Now, the benefits of these contingency deals are clear. They open the doors of justice to those who might not be able to afford the steep upfront legal fees. The clients can go after what's rightfully theirs without the stress of hourly attorney costs. Plus, the attorney's payment is tied to a successful outcome. This means the attorneys are in the same boat as their clients— rowing hard toward that win. And they're motivated, believe me!

What's more, these cases come with a safety net. If the case doesn't pan out, clients don't have to open their wallets wide for legal fees. It means that justice is served without the financial roadblocks. But, like everything else in life, there's a flip side. You see, the attorneys tend to charge a heftier fee when they win. That 33 to 40 percent chunk they take can be a hefty bite out of the compensation pie. Sometimes it makes clients second-guess settling when they see how much they'll lose.

There is a solution to prevent this sticker shock, and that is to negotiate a sliding fee contingency deal upfront with a litigator, say 35 percent on the first million dollars of a payout reduced to 15 percent on every dollar thereafter.

And here's another twist: sometimes, it's not about justice but about the money. Litigators lean toward cases with fat payouts rather than cases that primarily cry out for justice but have a lesser potential for significant payouts. This cash-driven approach might mean some folks with strong but less financially rewarding claims get left behind. It's a harsh reality.

Plus, clients might start to feel like they've lost control of their own cases. The attorneys are chasing that pot of gold at the end of the rainbow, and that can lead to conflicts and strategy disagreements. So, folks, before you wade into these contingency waters, think long and hard about what you're diving into. It's not always as clear-cut as it seems.

Chapter 18

Settlement Stalemate: It Takes Two to Tango

§

Now, let me lay it out with a real-world story that encapsulates a crucial point. I was knee-deep in trying to settle one of my client's litigation cases. I crafted a solid settlement offer and handed it to my client's attorney with a crystal clear directive: take it to the opposition's counsel. A week later, what I heard left me baffled. "They rejected your offer," my client's attorney declared. Not only was the rejection surprising but there was no sign of any counteroffer—not even a whisper of negotiation.

Something reeked, and in the world of high-stakes litigation, my distrust and paranoia antennae shot through the roof. So, I decided to do some sleuthing. Lucky for me, I had a buddy who was a partner at the law firm of opposing counsel. I called in a favor and asked him to check with his associate to see if they'd received any word from my client's lawyer about settling the matter in the past week. The result? Hold onto your hats— there was radio silence. No communication was transmitted whatsoever.

Based on my experience and keen observation, many lawyers not only avoid kick-starting settlement talks with their own clients but also dodge discussions with opposing counsel about settlement like they're hot potatoes. Plus, they often conveniently brush aside communicating settlement offers, whether they're from their own clients or from opposing counsel.

Now I can hear some of you shouting, "That's downright scandalous! It's unethical!" I'm glad you're saying it, so I don't have to. What I can vouch for is that stories like this play out day in and day out, as common as grains of sand on a beach.

Here's the golden nugget of wisdom: Realize that your attorney's default mode often leans toward steering clear of settlement discussions, even with you, and swatting away settlement offers like pesky flies, whether they're from you or the opposing camp. While there might be ethical obligations to relay any offers to a client, the art of omission or a convenient case of amnesia serves as an all-too-handy alibi, placing their addiction to the cash flow ahead of your well-being.

You might never get concrete proof that your attorney received a settlement offer from the other side, but here's a savvy move if you have an offer to proffer—draft a settlement proposal and hand it over to your attorney. Ask them to shoot it over to opposing counsel with a courtesy copy to you. Some lawyers might think you're hovering, but in this case, a bit of shoulder surfing isn't such a bad thing.

If any dialogue springs forth, make it clear that you'd like a seat at the table for discussions with the opposing attorney, even if you plan to play the role of a silent observer. When it comes to steering the ship toward settling your case, you've got to grab the wheel and take charge.

Chapter 19

Litigators and Lawyers: Different Hats, Different Roles

§

NOT ALL ATTORNEYS ARE CUT FROM THE SAME CLOTH, MY FRIENDS. You see, there's a breed of legal eagles out there that prefers the boardroom to the courtroom, the pen to the sword, if you will. We're talking about those non-litigation attorneys who've found their niche in the world of business transactions and contracts, among a slew of other legal matters. Let's take a gander at some of these legal flavors: corporate, real estate, commercial law, employment law, intellectual property, securities, tax law, environmental law, health law, immigration, estate planning, entertainment law, banking and finance law, franchise law, consumer protection law, technology and startup law, international business, antitrust law, family business, and non-profit.

But here's the twist, folks. Trouble brews when one of these non-litigators decides to play in the big leagues of litigation. It's like a fish trying to climb a tree—it just ain't their element. When they dabble in matters beyond their expertise, you end up being the guinea pig, and trust me, that's not where you want to be.

Litigation is like a haunted house ride at the carnival, spooky enough on its own. There's absolutely no need to crank up the fright factor by letting an attorney wander into that dark and treacherous territory unprepared. It's a recipe for disaster, my friends, and it could leave you with a legal nightmare that'll haunt you forever.

So, remember this sage advice: non-litigators should stick to what they know best. Allowing a non-litigator to experiment on your dime and take an ill-advised plunge into the world of litigation is a gamble you don't want to take. When it comes to legal matters, leave the courtroom battles to the seasoned litigators trained to wield that legal sword of combat. Your peace of mind—and your wallet—will thank you.

Chapter 20

Is Your Litigator Working For
Or Against You?

$

LET'S TALK TURKEY, FOLKS. IS YOUR ATTORNEY IN IT FOR YOU, OR ARE they secretly playing both sides of the game? The truth is, it's a bit of both, and it's a bitter pill to swallow.

Back in the day, professionals took pride in their work. They found existential satisfaction in their craft, reveled in the recognition and respect they earned in their field, and relished the opportunity to deliver top-notch results. Sure, they made a decent living, but the money was more of a bonus than the main act. Those were the days when the client and the professional were on the same page, working together toward a common goal, and pride oozed from their work like sap from a maple tree.

Fast forward to today, my friends, and you'll find a different story. Many professionals, including attorneys, have lost that existential connection to their craft. It's no longer about the joy of delivering exceptional work; it's all about the almighty dollar. The profession has become a cash cow, a means to milk as many dollars from you as humanly possible.

Consider your typical successful attorney, for instance. They're not only legal experts; they're also shrewd entrepreneurs. Their top priority? Filling their pipeline with profitable business prospects. As for handling the nitty-gritty tasks that take time away from rainmaking and the pursuit of new business, they tend to delegate the work to their junior and less seasoned colleagues. Nevertheless, they frequently maintain billing at their elevated rates.

But this pattern isn't exclusive to the legal world. It's a trend you'll find across various fields of business. It's all about the bottom line, folks, and the pursuit of the almighty dollar has clouded the noble pursuit of excellence in many a profession.

So, the next time you're in the trenches with an attorney or any other professional, keep one eye open. Are they truly in it for you, or is your hard-earned cash their only muse? Remember, my friends, the ideal for anyone you hire is their resolve to pursue excellence ahead of their expectation of gain.

Chapter 21

Who's Really Doing Your Legal Work?

§

Let's sail together through the twisting waters of the legal world, a story of in-office delegating that'll leave you shaking your head.

Now, cast your mind back to the turbulent year of 2007, a time when the financial market was in utter chaos. My bank lender, well, was on pretty much a sinking ship, and thanks to the FDIC's prodding, they were forced to file a foreclosure action against my company on an $8.5 million construction loan. So, who did I turn to? My trusty attorneys, of course. But their defenses weren't exactly filling me with confidence.

So, what did I do? I took the reins, dove headfirst into the world of legal research, and stumbled upon a legal legend—Helen Davis Chaitman. She's the national guru of lender liability, bank fraud, and RICO laws. Just to give you a taste of her prowess, she represented 1,600 folks who got tangled up with none other than Bernie Madoff, the king of Ponzi schemes. This lady knows her stuff. She's even the one who coined the term "lender liability" and wrote the definitive textbook for attorneys on the subject. I got my hands on her magnum opus, and I'll tell you, I devoured every word from cover to cover.

As I'm putting together a detailed record of my case's history in a fancy Excel spreadsheet, it hits me. Why go it alone when I could bring in a nationally acclaimed litigator? So, I pick up the phone, set up a meeting with her prestigious office, and we dive into the nitty-gritty of my case.

And, to my sheer delight, she's on board. I'm over the moon. I retain her and during our chats, she impresses me like no other.

But then the bombshell drops. A draft of the pleading arrives on my desk, just one day before it's due for filing. To call it a mess would be an understatement. And here's the zinger—I realized that most of the work was handed over to an associate attorney who, let's just say, wasn't winning any awards for legal drafting. This associate seemed more interested in spinning a melodramatic tale about how the big bad bank and the FDIC had wronged the little guy, rather than building us a rock-solid legal defense. It read like a novel, but in legal terms, it was pure trash.

So, I make the call to the guru, trying to break it to her as gently as possible. We need an adjournment, I say, to rewrite and salvage the pleading. And you know what she tells me? She says it's impossible. She claims that asking for an adjournment would tick off the judge, and our case would be toast. I'm not one to give up, so I argue my case respectfully. But here's the showstopper—she's a fifty-year legal veteran, a heavyweight in the field, and she shuts me down flat with a firm "no."

Now you see, the words "no" and "impossible" are like a red flag to a bull for me. Hearing those words from a service provider, even one at the very top of the legal game, is enough to make my blood boil. So, right then and there, I make a bold move. I show her the door. I then formalize it—sent her a simple email stating termination, a request that her firm withdraw from the case, and a request for a confirmation email of receipt of the message—and that decision and simple action buys me a couple of months to bring in another attorney and submit a pleading that's light-years better.

The lesson here, my friends, is simple and twofold: Ensure you know precisely who is drafting your legal documents before the work commences, and steadfastly reject the notion of accepting "no" for an answer, even if it originates from a world-renowned expert. Where determination exists, so does a path, and that's a lesson that holds immeasurable value.

Chapter 22

Lesson Learned:
Take Charge of Your Legal Representation

§

I N THE WORLD OF LAW, APPERANCES CAN OFTEN BE DECEIVING. WHEN you hire a high-profile attorney, you expect top-notch, personalized service. However, experience has taught me that even the biggest names may delegate your work to less experienced associates. Don't fall into the trap of assuming your case is getting the attention it deserves.

The lesson here is simple yet crucial: take an active role in your legal representation. Whether you're a seasoned client or new to the legal landscape, always be vigilant. Don't hesitate to scrutinize the work being done on your case and demand excellence. Remember, it's your rights, your money, and your future on the line. When you see something amiss, address it promptly. If necessary, be prepared to make a tough call, even if it means parting ways with a renowned attorney.

Your legal battles are far too important to be entrusted solely to others. Be the captain of your own ship, and ensure your legal team works tirelessly to secure the outcome you deserve.

Chapter 23

Legal Outsourcing Exposed:
How Litigators Job Out Legal Work

§

Picture this scenario: You've hired a top-notch attorney who's charging you a hefty $1,000 per hour. He's supposed to represent you in court for a total of three hours, adding up to a $3,000 fee. However, on the day of the court appearance, he doesn't show up himself. Instead, he hires a per-diem service that sends a substitute attorney to make an appearance in his stead for a flat fee of $150. In essence, your litigator pockets $2,850 for not making the court appearance. It's a sweet deal for him, but it leaves your wallet significantly lighter.

Now let's shift our focus to another facet of your case. Your attorney has a pleading to draft and file, but he's a bustling rainmaker, constantly on the move, meeting clients, and drumming up new business. He simply lacks the time or the inclination, or maybe even the expertise, to tackle the task himself. So, he delegates the job by having his secretary post the task on a website that connects professionals, including attorneys, with gig work opportunities.

These gig platforms attract a diverse array of legal talent, and the quality of their work isn't inherently problematic. However, issues arise when your case requires multiple pleadings over time with different individuals preparing them. This results in a patchwork of document approaches rather than preceding documents crafted by someone who's been consistently involved in your case and fully understands the facts as they've developed. This can ultimately leave you ill-prepared for effective representation.

What's more, your attorney might be outsourcing the job at a rate significantly lower than what he's charging you. For instance, he could be paying a subcontractor $75 an hour while billing you a staggering $1,000 per hour. It's not hard to see why this practice is so tempting for law firms.

Gig platforms are just one avenue attorneys use to find lower cost talent for delegating work. Another source is American expat attorneys living abroad, whom they can hire at a fraction of the cost. I once received a plan of reorganization from an attorney, which she purportedly drafted.

However, she had simply forwarded the work of an expat attorney located ten time zones away that she hired for the task. How did I find out? She forgot to remove his name from the previous email chain when she forwarded me the document. Her rates to me were sky-high, while she likely paid her expat subcontractor around $50 an hour.

Stay-at-home moms seeking to earn extra income are also a common source of affordable labor for delegating attorneys. While there's nothing wrong with this practice, there's an inherent injustice in paying $1,000 per hour and having the lead attorney do next to nothing while pocketing the delta of $900 per hour for work others perform.

I'm not casting aspersions on stay-at-home moms or gig-seeking attorneys as their work may be outstanding. My concern centers on fairness for the customer. Allowing a top-tier attorney to pocket an exorbitant sum while others handle the actual workload is simply unacceptable. A more equitable approach would be to actually charge a reasonable rate. If the gig worker costs $100 per hour, your law firm could charge $200 per hour instead of $1,000 per hour and spare you from paying an exorbitant markup. But, of course, in the world of legal billing, such a scenario is as likely as water flowing uphill!

Chapter 24

The Last-Minute Shuffle:
Attorney Procrastination Unveiled

§

I N THE WORLD OF LAW, THERE'S AN ALARMING PHENOMENON—attorneys waiting until the eleventh hour to get work done. It's a frustrating reality, especially when you're shelling out a considerable sum for their services. You expect timely, well-prepared work that allows ample room for review, discussion, and refinement. Yet, procrastination often leads to rushed and subpar results.

I once found myself at my wit's end with a sluggish attorney. Determined to keep him on track, I planted myself in his office for three grueling days, urging and assisting him to complete work on my case. As the night before our pleading deadline approached, fatigue overcame him, and he unintentionally obliterated the entire document. He fell asleep at the wheel, literally speaking. His hands went limp and pushed the wrong buttons on his keyboard, erasing days of work. Defeated, he left to catch some much-needed sleep.

It was 3 a.m., and with no other options, I took the reins. In a sleep-deprived haze, I reconstructed the entire document from memory, crafting a reasonably decent pleading. The next day, my attorney touched it up and filed it. This kind of last-minute scramble is far too common among attorneys and can jeopardize your case.

To be fair, not all attorneys engage in this procrastination dance. Some diligent ones produce high-quality work well ahead of deadlines, offering ample time for collaboration and refinement. That's the ideal scenario.

But for those attorneys who routinely push the boundaries of time, remember that attorney procrastination can have dire consequences for your case. Don't settle for subpar work—demand the diligence and timeliness your legal matters deserve.

Chapter 25

Your Legal Duty:
Scrutinizing Your Attorney's Work

§

IN THE OLD DAYS, MY COUNSEL WOULD TOSS DOCUMENTS MY WAY, expecting me to sign on the dotted line without a second thought. I mean, hey, that's what I hired them for, right? They're the experts, and I should be able to trust them to get everything in order. Well, think again! Here's the truth: When you hire a litigator, you're basically making them the captain of your legal ship. You're entering into a contract where they promise to whip up documents that not only tell your story accurately but also make compelling arguments. Some litigators are masters at this, crafting airtight narratives that could convince anyone, while others, well, let's just say they're a work in progress.

Now, don't get me wrong; even top-notch attorneys can have their off days. Lawyers are human, just like the rest of us. They've got personal stuff going on, stressors, and sometimes, they're just swamped with work. So, assuming your lawyer will always be firing on all cylinders is a big mistake.

That's where your role as the client becomes crucial. It's your job to go through every single document your attorney puts in front of you. Why? Because it's the only way to make sure that your case is being represented the way it should be—accurately and effectively.

Sure, some lawyers might grumble about it, but many actually appreciate your involvement. Of course, there's that 10 percent who see your engagement as a genuine chance to involve and give you the full picture, but the other ninety percent? Well, they're probably focused on your involvement converting to extra billable hours. They might set up conference calls, send you detailed email explanations, and find all sorts of ways to make sure you understand what's going on.

Even if you're not a legal eagle, you've got enough life experience to spot a document that doesn't smell right. If it reads well and it seems to make sense, it's a sign that your lawyer put some thought into it and probably nailed it.

But if you ever start doubting the work or you want a fresh perspective, here's an idea: Look for a second opinion. There are plenty of forums and networks out there where you can find affordable lawyers willing to give your documents a once-over through a video conference. Hire a gig attorney. It won't break the bank, and it could give you a clearer picture of what's going on.

Here's the bottom line: Whether you're knee-deep in litigation or tackling life's challenges, being vigilant and staying engaged often leads to the best results. Don't just put blind trust in your lawyer; roll up your sleeves and get involved!

Chapter 26

Legal Geography:
The Significance of the First Two Pages

§

Y̲O̲U̲'̲V̲E̲ ̲G̲O̲T̲ ̲Y̲O̲U̲R̲ ̲A̲T̲T̲O̲R̲N̲E̲Y̲ ̲W̲O̲R̲K̲I̲N̲G̲ ̲D̲I̲L̲I̲G̲E̲N̲T̲L̲Y̲,̲ ̲P̲O̲R̲I̲N̲G̲ ̲O̲V̲E̲R̲ those critical documents for an upcoming hearing. They meticulously upload them to the court docket, and you can't help but wonder: will the judge actually take the time to read them before the big day? Well, don't hold your breath!

We're not talking about the grandeur of Supreme Court hearings here; we're wading through the trenches of everyday legal proceedings. Judges find themselves inundated with case after case, leaving them with barely a moment to breathe. In those rare pauses between hearings or even during them, you might catch the judge daydreaming about golf, horseback riding, or sailing the high seas—anywhere but in the courtroom.

Sure, the judge will give your documents a cursory glance. Maybe the clerk, the unsung hero of the judge's caseload, will dive a bit deeper. But even the most dedicated clerk can become overwhelmed by the sheer volume of paperwork.

That's precisely why attorneys must present critical and compelling information within the first two pages of their pleading. The rest often becomes mere background noise.

Now, I may be painting a slightly exaggerated picture, but in this age of dwindling attention spans and smartphones glued to every hand, judges are notorious multitaskers. They could be juggling multiple cases, checking emails, scrolling through news updates, nodding off, engrossed in an augmented reality app, or even planning a vacation—all while your case unfolds.

To truly make an impact, your litigator needs to craft compelling headings and content within those initial pages to seize the judge's fleeting attention.

Chapter 27

Weighty Legal Filings Presented in Court

§

Renowned author Franz Kafka, trained as a lawyer, once humorously remarked:

> *A lawyer is a person who drafts a 10,000-word document and calls it a brief.*[6]

Legal documents often come in varying shapes and sizes. Some are packed with essential content, while others are weighed down by redundancy, excessive words, and unnecessary pages.

To begin with, it's essential not to overspend by paying attorneys to write superfluous material. Additionally, when submitting documents to the court, clarity is key as fluff can muddle your message.

Nevertheless, the sheer volume of a pleading, irrespective of its content, can have a profound impact. The weightiness of the document, both literally and figuratively, can create an aura of authority, prompting observers to think, "These documents are substantial, full of well-cited legal references—there must be merit to this side's argument."

While the artful skills of eloquent orators often illuminate the core issues at hand, it's worth noting that sometimes a document in the Kafkaesque style can pre-establish credibility for one party even before oral arguments commence. Every interaction within the courtroom is as much about the human element as it is about pinpoint precision on specific legal matters.

Chapter 28

Assessing Your Attorney's Abilities by Scrutinizing Their Work

§

As you gear up for a major legal battle and search for the right attorney, you've likely gone through the motions of interviewing several prospects. While some may excel in conversation and look the part, the ultimate measure of their worth is their performance in the courtroom. So, how can you truly gauge their courtroom prowess?

Today, it's easier than ever to get the lowdown. Thanks to the wonders of the Internet, you can tap into your local e-court reporting system. Start by punching in your attorney's name, and voilà, you can access a treasure trove of cases. Dive into each case, explore the documents they've filed, and scrutinize their written narratives. This provides a fantastic window into what your documents might look like if you decide to bring this attorney on board.

But we won't stop there. You can dive deep into the docket items, meticulously examining every move, motion, and objection made in various cases. By thoroughly sifting through multiple cases, you can accumulate a treasure trove of knowledge. You don't need to be a legal expert right from the start. With some reading skills and a dash of discernment, you can rapidly gain insights into your potential attorney and their legal skills.

I recently conducted a quick Google search on an attorney I had previously retained for a case that concluded some time ago. What did

I discover? A thirty-minute recording of appellate arguments from that very case. I clicked play and was truly enlightened. Not only did it reaffirm his excellence in written arguments, but his oral performance was equally impressive.

If you're unable to find online recordings of a litigator you're considering, there's another approach—the in-person test drive. Navigate the e-court system, search for this attorney's cases, and check their calendar. You can attend court proceedings to watch them in action. Feel free to "kick the tires" more than once and observe them in different hearings. If what you witness aligns with your expectations, it's as good as an old-fashioned test drive. After all, you're about to embark on a significant legal journey, and having the right attorney at the helm can make all the difference.

Chapter 29

Missing Filing Deadlines: A Costly Oversight

$

I N THE REALM OF LAW, A TIMELESS TALE UNFOLDS, ONE THAT CAN ultimately drain your pockets. The repercussions are nothing short of devastating. Missing deadlines can hang a client. Picture this: An attorney representing a client fails to meet a critical due date for responding to a pre-foreclosure action, compounding the problem by subsequently neglecting to address a motion filed against his client that followed for a default judgment. The negligence in filing a perfunctory answer and objection is as if the client's attorney mashed his finger onto the fast-forward button in the foreclosure process.

The client simply hoped to settle their lender's defaulted mortgage claim before matters escalated to this point. After all, the lender was the borrower's uncle, who got perturbed about some other family matter and started the litigation to bop his nephew over the head. The uncle would have very likely been swayed in state court to end the madness soon after he had started. After all, this was Brooklyn, where foreclosure proceedings often unfold at a snail's pace, spanning as long as a decade on a commercial foreclosure case. A modicum of professional diligence by the borrower's attorney in simply filing pleadings on time could have stretched out litigation for years and worn down the lender's resolve for a lengthy litigation escapade, predisposing him to settle this dispute.

This litigator, after missing the two due dates and accelerating the case toward a property auction, suggested a diversion into the realm of bankruptcy court, holding out the hope that the client could stave off the impending foreclosure sale. Declaring bankruptcy was then the only litigation play left for the client.

So, why did his litigator miss those initial, very crucial due dates and then promise to save the day in bankruptcy court? It's a question that may forever linger. What is certain is that this attorney's neglect to meet due dates accelerated what could have been a multi-year no-mortgage payment stalemate strategy in state court, which would have benefited his client. The strategy of judicial delay wasn't anyone's brainchild. It was simply built into the inefficient legal system. Bad for the lender, good for the borrower. It was automatic.

Instead, the client lost the automatic and advantageous strategic play, accelerated as many as ten years of a gear-grinding stalemate into four months, and got thrown into Chapter 11, which benefited guess who? His litigator, who could then bill vastly more in that arena and in a much shorter period than in state court litigating the original pre-foreclosure action.

So, whaddayou think? Was the client's litigator inadvertently negligent twice in a row by missing the filing due dates of two very simple pleadings? Or was this very well-known forty-year veteran New York City litigator a cunning criminal who gratuitously and callously hurt the interest of his client so that his law firm could generate more fees in a shorter span of time?

Chapter 30

Your Attorney Isn't a Genie:
Don't Get Enchanted

§

Let's unravel the mystique of your attorney, folks, because here's the deal: your attorney isn't a genie, and you shouldn't get enchanted by their initial charm!

Clients often start their legal journey on a high note, full of optimism about their new legal counsel. But as time rolls on, the rose-tinted glasses come off, and they start to see their attorney's quirks and foibles—both the strengths and the shortcomings. And boy, when those deficiencies rear their ugly heads, it can be frustrating as all get out.

Now here's where things take a peculiar turn. Clients often pledge to take action, vowing to either give their attorney the boot or, for some inexplicable reason, try to steer them back on course. It's like a strange dance of learned helplessness. I'm no shrink, but I've seen this movie play out before. They start off all determined, but somewhere along the way, they lose their resolve, get ensnared in the attorney's web, and find themselves right back where they started.

I'm not here to point fingers at the attorney, no matter how endearing or manipulative they might be. The responsibility for those weak knees and the propensity to stay in a dysfunctional attorney-client relationship falls squarely on the client's shoulders. After all, the attorney might be constantly missing deadlines, showering you with empty promises, and churning out subpar documents. It's like a twisted love affair, and it's high time such clients break free from this cycle of voluntary abuse.

So, remember, your attorney isn't a magical genie who can grant your legal wishes. It's your responsibility to ensure you're not ensnared in this dysfunctional dance. Demand the quality and service you deserve, and don't settle for less!

Chapter 31

Deconstructing the Attorney-Client Relationship: A Candid Discussion

§

AH, LET'S DISSECT THIS ENIGMATIC TANGO BETWEEN YOU AND YOUR legal eagle, shall we? We toss around the term "relationship," but most lawyers aren't about to serenade you under the moonlight. Nope, they're eyeing you as their personal cash cow, ready to milk you dry. It's a cold, hard truth that doesn't get much play.

Sure, that prospective attorney might try to sweep you off your feet with their slick sales pitch, but it's all smoke and mirrors to land the deal. Drama? That's not their scene.

The drama queens and kings in this saga are usually the clients themselves. They waltz in with these grandiose expectations, looking for a redeemer in their attorney. They're drowning in a swamp of legal mess, and suddenly, the attorney becomes their savior, even their personal deity.

You've seen those personal ads, right? People searching for that mythical "redeemer partner relationship." They want it all, from a best friend and soul mate to a personal chef and gardening guru.

But I'm going to level with you: attorneys aren't superheroes. They're more like service providers in a world of legal mazes. So, let's drop the drama, folks. Your lawyer isn't going to swoop in and save the day. It's time to set the right expectations.

You see, it's a business relationship you're after, not some over-the-top romance. Keep your expectations in check, and remember, you're the one steering this ship. Don't play second fiddle; maintain control.

That's the secret to managing your case and having a productive working relationship with your legal service provider.

Chapter 32

Personalities Unveiled: Nature or Nurture?

§

YOU SEE, WHEN IT COMES TO ATTORNEYS SPECIALIZING IN litigation, you're dealing with a whole different breed. These legal warriors thrive in the arena of conflict, and their personalities often reflect the battles they wage. It's a cutthroat world where they use every weapon in their arsenal, and sometimes, it's not for the faint of heart.

Picture this: a deposition room, the battleground where attorneys employ tactics that range from unpleasant in nature to downright ruthless. They can be masters of cruelty, using passive-aggressive jabs or going all-in with aggressive behavior to extract the truth or break down a witness.

They might not think twice about bending the truth, telling bald-faced lies, or launching defamatory salvos in their pleadings or oral arguments, all in an effort to convince the judge and jury.

But it doesn't stop there. In the courtroom, they'll go toe-to-toe with opposing counsel, launching vitriolic, demeaning critiques, even if they were sharing a drink just the night before. Some are even willing to toe the line of criminal behavior if it means securing a win.

Now you'll hear different takes on these attorneys. Some say they're just hired guns doing what it takes to win. Others suggest it's all about personality types, channeling their inner Carl Jung. And then there are those who believe it might be rooted in something darker, like personality disorders and pathologies straight out of the DSM-5.

But in the grand scheme of things, does it truly matter whether these behaviors arise from nature or nurture? The essential point is that even the so-called "good guys" in this world can have their idiosyncrasies. So, whether you're dealing with a hard-nosed pathological-flavored attorney or one of the more amicable ones, you have to grant them some breathing room, and you must master the art of dancing alongside them. Managing a litigator is far from a leisurely stroll in the park.

In the worst of cases, these attorneys will turn all that aggressive energy against you, especially when it comes to billing. That's when the line between legal battle and organized crime starts to blur. So, tread carefully, my friends, and learn how to dance that two-step with your counsel.

Chapter 33

Client Vigilance:
Marking Up Documents Gives You a Voice

§

Let's focus, folks. When it comes to your case, you are running the show. You've got the insider knowledge and an intimate understanding of the facts, and it's you who will suffer the consequences of any misstep. In this legal landscape, your role as the most well-versed player cannot be overstated.

Now take note: Some attorneys have this habit. They whip up legal documents and toss them into the court's ring or fire them off to opposing counsel without a second thought. It's like they're in a race against time, and they're sprinting alone. But here's a piece of advice that can save you from future headaches: put it in writing and email your attorney that you want to lay eyes on every draft of every document and approve a final version before it gets filed with the court or sent out.

Enter the world of markups. This is your tool, your weapon, your voice in the process. Use it to flag anything that doesn't make sense, offer corrections, suggest changes, ask questions, and generally make your attorney think twice. The result? A discussion that makes your attorney a little smarter and a little richer (because, let's face it, they'll charge for the extra time).

They'll send you a revised document, and it may get volleyed back and forth a few times. And so it continues until you email your final stamp of approval.

It might feel strange, this dance of a layman offering a legal eagle collaboration and direction. But remember, your attorney juggles multiple cases, delegates like a pro, and ultimately, they're a service provider, and he isn't thinking about you and your case 24/7. You? Well, you've got this one case, your baby, your heart, your soul, and nobody knows it better or cares about it more than you do. So, embrace your role and waltz through this legal journey, because your contribution is worth its weight in gold.

Chapter 34

Beware of the Attorney Mirage!

$

G ET READY, FOLKS, BECAUSE I'VE GOT A STORY THAT'LL MAKE your head spin faster than a tornado in a trailer park—it's the attorney mirage!

So, look: you've gone and hired yourself an attorney who looked like the legal version of a rock star, the whole package deal. You're thinking, "I've got a legal ace in my corner; this case is going to be a breeze." Well, hold onto your hats, because reality is about to slap you like a wet fish.

Once upon a time, I brought in an attorney who had all the right vibes. She seemed like a legal wizard, a blend of skills, knowledge, and confidence. Things were rolling along smoothly until I asked her for the first batch of drafted documents. I reviewed them like an English teacher armed with a red pen and handed them back with my markups. To my shock, she made the changes exactly as I'd marked them. Now don't get me wrong, I know a thing or two about the law, but I'm not the lead attorney here! This got me thinking, "What's the real deal here?"

Turns out, she had a little secret tucked away. She'd been outsourcing all the document drafting to an expat living on the other side of the world. She'd pass him the work, juggle my comments back and forth, and tell him to tweak the documents as per my markups. The big reveal: she couldn't compose legal documents, let alone modify them, herself. Suddenly, my documents were adrift without a true captain at the helm, and I was thrust into a role I neither expected nor wanted.

But wait, there's more! The plot thickened when I started noticing a pattern. Whether it was in our conversations or her court appearances, a common thread emerged. She was a master of filibustering and verbal persuasion, working overtime to convince me or the judge about this or that. But when it came to basic legal matters, well, it was like watching a deer caught in the headlights. In court, she couldn't present or argue legal points effectively. She didn't even try!

It was clear that the written word and referencing the law weren't her strong suits. I figured she might have a unique flavor of ADD that held her back.

Now for some irony: I brought her in to replace my initial attorney, the one the judge couldn't stand. That guy, with his tweed jacket and suede elbow patches, fancied himself a law professor. He was a real intellectual, but he was causing more harm than good. Looking back, the attorney who excelled at filibustering, limited as she was, neither significantly helped nor hurt my case during her tenure. That put her one step above the law professor who'd come before her.

So, here's the bottom line, my friends: Attorneys, well, they can be a real mixed bag. Some might have all the skills to steer your case to victory, while others could leave you navigating the ship all by yourself. And with a select few, your legal journey could turn into a voyage on the Titanic. It's a gamble, so choose your legal counsel wisely, and don't fall for the attorney mirage—that slick exterior might just be hiding a world of legal mayhem!

Chapter 35

Churning Bills: The Ultimate In "Billing Abuse"

§

I DON'T KNOW WHETHER TO LAUGH OR CRY, BUT LET'S AIM FOR A good chuckle:

> A lawyer arrives at the pearly gates, and the angel in charge says, "Normally, we don't allow lawyers in here, but you're in luck. We're running a special this month. You spend time in hell equal to the length of your life, and then you get to come back to heaven for all eternity." The lawyer thinks it over and says, "I'll take the deal." The angel nods and says, "Great, I'll mark you down for two hundred and twelve years in hell." The lawyer protests, "What? I'm only 65 years old!" St. Peter's response? "For lawyers, we go by billing hours."[7]

Ladies and gentlemen, brace yourselves for a dose of legal reality that'll make your blood boil!

We're talking about something the legal sharks out there don't want you to know—bill churning! It's a dirty trick in the world of attorneys that'll make your wallet weep and your faith in justice crumble. It's also way unethical and illegal, but it's a tough crime to catch.

Now let me break it down for you in terms even the most uninitiated can grasp. Bill churning, my friends, is when these slick lawyers pad their invoices with phantom hours like they're conjuring money out of thin air! They're milking your pocketbook with the sneaky tactics listed below.

1. Phony Hours: They're tacking on extra hours like they're playing a game of Monopoly with your cash.

2. Double Dipping: Ever heard of double billing? That's when they charge two clients for the same work, or they're billing you by the hour and on a contingency basis at the same time. Talk about greed!

3. Fancy Talk: They'll make simple tasks sound like intricate and sophisticated maneuvers to rack up those billable hours.

4. Blizzard of Meetings: Unnecessary meetings, endless emails, and more meetings—all with one goal in mind, folks: to pump up the bill!

5. Gang of Lawyers: Sometimes, they throw a whole gang of attorneys at a case when one would do the job. More lawyers, more staff, more charges!

6. Task-Splitting: Breaking down one job into a dozen mini tasks and charging for each one separately—it's like ordering a burger but getting charged separately for the bun, patty, lettuce, tomato … you get the picture.

7. Research Racket: They're charging you an arm and a leg for research on issues that they have seen many times over that are already pre-templated out from their last similar case, billing you and calling it "legal research."

8. Strategy Racket: They're charging you unthinkable sums for time and effort that may not have been expended whilst they claim they pondered your matters like Auguste Rodin's *The Thinker* statue.

9. Review Racket: They're charging you beaucoup cash presumably to look over work they did before. What a scam!

10. Super Prep: Charging for extensive preparation time before a meeting, deposition, or court appearances when it's not warranted. Yeah, they're pulling a fast one on you!

11. Expense Inflation: You wouldn't believe how creative they can get with expenses, padding or billing for stuff that never even happened.

12. Round Robin: Charging in nice round numbers to avoid scrutiny—because who would question a bill that looks so neat and tidy?

We began with a humorous touch, delved into the challenges of bill churning, and now let's conclude with a dash of humor:

> *Two men met on the street one very cold morning. One said to the other, "How cold is it?" The other man said, "I'm not sure, but it must be really cold. I saw our lawyer with his hands in his own pockets."*[8]

Chapter 36

Rumble in the Legal Jungle:
A Five-Minute Call, A Five-Figure Bill

§

HOLD ONTO YOUR WALLETS, FOLKS, BECAUSE WE'VE GOT A CLASSIC example of the attorney-client rope-a-dope,[9] and it's a knockout punch to your bank account!

So, there I am, minding my own business when my legal eagle swoops in with a seemingly innocuous phone call. Little did I know this was just the beginning of their cunning game. In mere minutes, they've lured in an associate, and they've both got me trapped on a conference call for a whole hour!

But wait, it gets better. They later sent me an email, recapping and summarizing our chat. Innocently enough, I started questioning a few things via email, not realizing I fell into their trap.

You see, that email gave them the perfect opportunity to inflate the bill further. They hit me with a detailed response that required "research, strategy, and extensive composition." And just when I thought it was all over, they waited more than thirty days to deliver the punch line—the bill.

Let me break it down for you:

The call with two legal eagles: A five-minute chat turned into a jaw-dropping $10,475 bill! Hold on, we forgot to add the premium for "bill composition." Tack on another 10 percent, and you're looking at a whopping $11,500!

Here are the billing details:

The conference call with two legal eagles:

| 6-9-19 | JMT | $1,200/hr | Discussion w/client | 1.0 hrs |
| 6-9-19 | WHJ | $950/hr | Conference call w/client | 1.0 hrs |

The email recapitulation of the call:

| 6-9-19 | WHJ | $950/hr | Compose email to client | 2.5 hrs |

I responded to their email recapitulation of the call.

They emailed back, which required the following "work":

6-9-19	WHJ	$950/hr	Legal research	2.0 hrs
6-9-19	WHJ	$950/hr	Discuss/strategize w/partner	1.0 hr
6-9-19	JMT	$1,200/hr	Discuss/strategize with assoc.	1.0 hr
6-9-19	WHJ	$950/hr	Draft email response to client	1.5 hrs

It's a tale as old as time, my friends. Your attorney calls, says it's urgent, brings in the big guns, and before you know it, you're stuck in a marathon conversation that's about as useful as a screen door on a submarine. Then they follow up with an email that didn't need to see the light of day.

But here's the lesson—you ask a few simple questions, and they respond with a legal dissertation that's longer than *War and Peace*. The result? A five-minute call that should've cost a hundred bucks turns into an $11,500 legal billing escapade!

Muhammad Ali, the master of the rope-a-dope, would be flabbergasted by the haymakers these attorneys throw day in and day out, leaving clients with astronomical bills, feeling not so bright, and in pain.[10]

Chapter 37

Time's Effect on Invoices:
Fading Memories, Lingering Bills

§

L ADIES AND GENTLEMEN, LET'S CUT THROUGH THE LEGAL FOG AND
shine a spotlight on what I like to call the "Billing Lag Whitewash."
It's an almost inadvertent maneuver that law firms use to blur the lines
and keep you in the dark about your own hard-earned money!

Imagine for a moment that your legal eagles sent you a daily bill. If you
found yourself in the "rope-a-dope" scenario we talked about earlier, you'd
be on that phone with them the next day, raising all kinds of hell, right? I
mean, who wouldn't?

Now picture this: they send you a weekly bill. Your memory is still
fresh, and you can recall every twist and turn of that legal circus. You'd
still be dialing them up, ready to unleash some fury if you spotted any
shenanigans.

But hold on, here's where the trickery comes into play. They decide to
send you a bill at least a whole month later! It's like they're dumping
all the billing entries and legal events into a giant cauldron, stirring it
up into one big, confusing billing soup. It seems innocuous, but it's a
diabolical move, my friends, because it becomes incredibly tricky to
decipher one over-the-top charge from another.

You see, when time passes, memories fade, and the specifics of that billing
extravaganza start to blur together. It's like trying to distinguish one flake
of oatmeal from another after they've been sitting in a bowl of water for a

month. That five-minute, five-figure phone call that should've cost you a Benjamin becomes just another scramble of line items in a sea of charges.

So, here's the bottom line. The billing time lag is a seemingly innocuous but rather deliberate strategy to leave you scratching your head, questioning your own recollection, and ultimately paying a hefty sum for what should have been a simple legal matter. It's time to call out this billing bamboozle and perhaps require weekly bills from your legal representation!

Chapter 38

A Legal Bill Felt Like a Big Bad Joke, But It Was Real

$

Alright, folks, it's time to get back to business. Brace yourselves as we dive into the harsh reality of an outrageous legal bill. We're about to unravel the layers of deception and shed light on a situation that felt more like an obscene joke than real life. But make no mistake, this is not a guide on how to become a criminal. The underworld has its own rules, and our mission here is to expose the shady side of legal billing.

Let me tell you a tale of a legal bill that left me dumbfounded. I once hired Loeb & Loeb LLP for a relatively simple one-month engagement. To my astonishment, when the dust settled, I was staring at a jaw-dropping bill of $438,000.

Insult to injury happened when the case was closed and I asked for a release of the last $100,000 of funds held on my behalf in their escrow account. Instead of returning my hard-earned money, this law firm had the audacity to submit a post-game closeout bill to snatch that exact sum! It was a master class in trickery and deceit.

You see, I brought Loeb & Loeb LLP on board during the tail end of a single-asset Chapter 11 case. The property had already been presold in a non-contingent sales contract, the court had given the green light to the sale, and the case was teed up to close in a month with little work left: a final plan of reorganization confirmation and a few conference call hearings.

But let me be crystal clear: this type of billing is not an anomaly; it's how law firms thrive. The bigger the firm, the more sophisticated the art of the grift becomes. It's the bread and butter of litigators and their law firms to craft and embellish bills, turning routine tasks into billable extravaganzas.

I was absolutely floored when I got that bill, and the sheer audacity of Loeb & Loeb LLP's charges left me in disbelief. The amount they were asking for was beyond reason, and I couldn't just let it slide. So, I took matters into my own hands, dialed up Schuyler Carroll, the lead attorney who had partner status, and laid it all out. I told him that their bill was off the charts, and there's no way I'd let myself be swindled. I suggested we sit down and have a reasonable conversation about the fees. Instead, his response was the epitome of entitlement. With an air of calm that was almost infuriating, he bluntly stated, "You're not in a position to negotiate."

Left with no other choice, I sought out an attorney to challenge this bill on my behalf. Attorneys are often reluctant to sue their own kind, so I had to take matters into my own hands. I represented myself, known as "pro se," and took on a formidable New York City law firm, ultimately exposing their shady practices for all to see. Stand by as we get ready to explore this case in detail in the pages ahead.

Chapter 39

Behind the Veneer: How Legal Bills Deceptively Dress Up Fake Charges

§

LET'S TALK ABOUT STYLE, MY FRIENDS, BECAUSE THE AESTHETICS OF a lawyer's bill can speak volumes about the credibility of all the fake billing that lies within. You see, the appearance of that bill matters a great deal; it's like the slick packaging that makes a mediocre product seem top-notch. Just take a crisp, new dollar bill, for instance. It may look invaluable, but in reality, it's worth mere pennies compared to its grand appearance. Style matters, and it can create a lasting impression.

Law firms are masters of this game. They employ fonts like Baskerville, Georgia, Century Schoolbook, Garamond, Times New Roman, Equity, or Verdigris to give an air of professionalism and substance. Even the names of the fonts imply gravitas. They slap on their emblem, which serves as both a visual treat and an imprimatur of virtue and grandeur. The layout of the text and the clever use of white space on the page all add up to a sense of stately officiality.

Now, if your bill is part of a bankruptcy proceeding, get ready for a real show. You might find a sprawling forty-page preface, filled with words and the attorney's grandiose justifications for their right to collect every last penny. Superfluous documents abound, all boasting about the supposed immense value they've delivered. It's all fluff, but this pomp is part of the performance. Oh, and by the way, they'll bill you for the time they spend assembling this magnum opus.

All of these theatrics create an aura of credibility, and suddenly, the actual bill becomes a mere afterthought, buried beneath a mountain of frills and fluff. The core of the bill is really a simple breakdown: a description of a task performed and the time and date that it allegedly happened. But listen here—these three elements can be sliced, diced, and scrambled in so many ways that it becomes a bewildering puzzle.

The goal of this trickery? To charge you for as many hours as possible, regardless of the actual work done or the time it genuinely took.

In the chapters ahead, we're going to dissect and decode this data, separating the real from the fluff and exposing the truth behind these inflated bills.

Chapter 40

Deciphering and Auditing the Data

§

LET'S BREAK DOWN THE ESSENTIAL COMPONENTS OF A LEGAL BILL. Every attorney working on a case either maintains a daily log of his activities or reconstructs it later, noting down what we'll call "entries," which typically include the following:

1. date

2. description of services rendered

3. hours spent

Now lawyers sometimes add a line item for constructing your bill and might give it a fancy name for some shade from a client's scrutiny. I once received a bill that was shadeless and explicit. The description of bill construction services was "working on time records for fee application, draft first and final fee, and finalize application." All out in the open with no obfuscation, the $58,840 charge for legal work included a whopping extra $13,700 for constructing the bill, totaling $72,540. I was billed a 23 percent premium for the actual work done. It felt like I was carjacked in broad daylight. The standard industry range for bill construction fees is lower, but I decided to swallow this pill. Objecting to these attorney fees would have ruffled the judge's feathers, and this mini rip-off was just a small screw in a larger machine. Sometimes, the cost of calling something out will cost you more in the end.

Now let's get back to the nitty-gritty of deciphering a bill and what parts can be verified and what can't.

- The date is usually straightforward and doesn't leave much room for ambiguity.

- The description of services rendered can be verified when it involves emails to you. However, many descriptions of services rendered are not verifiable. For example, tasks like attorneys conferring with their staff, conducting research, or reviewing documents for an upcoming hearing are nearly impossible to confirm.

- Hours attributed to specific tasks are often not verifiable. In general, you're left in the dark about the actual hours spent on most billing entries.

In summary, legal bill construction might involve the use of software programs or apps, but all of these allow for manual overrides to add billing entries that retrospectively and retroactively inflate hours. It's during this Picasso-like event of bill creation that many lawyers embellish both, simply because it's so easy to get away with.

Chapter 41

Bill-Padding Tactics: How to Get Away With Billing Twenty-Hour Days

§

ALAW FIRM WON'T TYPICALLY SEND YOU A NICE NEAT LIST OF chronological entries detailing every staff member's daily work. If they did, and you wanted to verify the total hours that the attorney indeed worked, here's a simple sniff test you might perform.

Just take those daily time entries for each attorney and add them up. Then ask yourself—does it genuinely make sense that the attorney worked those seemingly superhuman hours day after day?

I've heard of attorneys claiming to bill for as many as twenty hours per day, consistently, day in and day out. Yet, this seemingly superhuman work ethic often turns out to be a mere facade, concealing the truth behind a shrewd deception: law firms employ a clever tactic to divert your attention.

They abandon the straightforward chronological method of presenting their bill, as it's too easy to detect fraud, and instead, they create different chapters within the bill.

Let me break it down for you using the previously mentioned real-life example of the $438,000 one-month bill:

The Bill Chapter Headings

    A. 110/Case Administration

    B. B130/Asset Disposition

C. B160/Fee/Employment Applications

D. B170/Fee/Employment Objections

E. B190/Other Contested Matters

F. B310/Claims Administration and Objections

G. B320/Plan And Disclosure Statement

H. B420/Restructuring

Now if an attorney wants to pull off the stunt of billing excess hours per day, say sixteen-hour days, it's a breeze. They can conveniently allocate two hours of work on the same day in each of the eight general buckets listed above. Imagine the bill stretching to forty pages, with each chapter occupying multiple pages.

So, when you read through the bill as a client, you start with Chapter A, 110/Case Administration. Entry by entry is listed, and everything seems fairly reasonable—two hours of work per day per staff member. But as you progress to the next chapter, you've already forgotten what you read in the previous one. It's like Groundhog Day[11] as you navigate through each subsequent billing chapter, each feeling both fresh and simultaneously reminiscent of something eerily recycled and familiar.

That's the insidious nature of adding billing chapters. They masterfully conceal those excessive hours of work for each staff member, leaving you none the wiser.

Chapter 42

More Billing Staff: A Recipe for Confusion

§

WHEN YOU'RE DEALING WITH A CASE THAT INVOLVES MORE THAN one attorney, don't expect to see a nice straightforward, chronological list of each attorney's tasks and hours per day.

Instead, law firms often employ the chapter billing method, and let me tell you, the level of obfuscation just goes up a notch. With more staff members diligently working and billing away, deciphering any fraud or bill padding becomes a Herculean task.

The key takeaway here is simple: the bigger the legal bill, the more they can hide and befuddle.

The Art of Billing Confusion: Deliberate Deception

Let's roll up our sleeves and dive into an example of a singular billing entry:

5/27/20	WMH	DRAFT DISCLOSURE STATEMENT	15.1 HRS	$14,043

DRAFT AND REVISE DISCLOSURE STATEMENT (4.5); COMMUNICATE WITH CLIENT REGARDING TERMS OF PLAN AND DISCLOSURE STATEMENT (0.8); REVISIONS TO PLAN AND DISCLOSURE STATEMENT (5.5); REVIEW BANKRUPTCY COURT ORDER

REGARDING UPCOMING HEAR-
ING AND DEADLINES BEFORE
THEN (0.6); REVIEW SALE CON-
TRACT (1.3); DRAFT / REVISE
NOTICE OF HEARING (0.7); IN-
STRUCT M. JACKSON RE SERVICE
AND RELATED (0.4); STRATEGIZE
WITH S. CARROLL REGARDING
PLAN AND DISCLOSURE STATE-
MENT AND JUNE 24 HEARING
(1.1); REVIEW SCHEDULES AND
PROOFS OF CLAIM AS FILED (0.9)

In the first place, William M. Hawkins III had the audacity to declare
that he labored for 15.1 hours within a single day. What's even more
remarkable is that he did so openly and within one billing entry without
resorting to the chapter bucket distribution technique to conceal his
extraordinary marathon of a day.

Secondly, this entry is a hodgepodge of smaller entries all mashed
together, designed to confuse and muddy the waters. Let's break down
each of these mini entries in the above example to understand how easy
it is to inflate hours and conjure up work that might not even exist:

1. Draft And Revise Disclosure Statement (4.5 Hours)

The actual time expended is unverifiable, and this task was billed
repeatedly on different days by various attorneys in addition to this
particular attorney who billed four and a half hours on the date of this
entry. There's no way to verify if any meaningful work was conducted here.

2. Communicate With Client Regarding Terms Of Plan And
Disclosure Statement (0.8 Hours)

This could have been a phone call or email, and when you receive a bill more
than thirty days after the fact, who knows what actually transpired?

3. Revisions To Plan And Disclosure Statement (5.5 Hours)

Again, the actual time expended is unverifiable, and this task was billed repeatedly on different days by various attorneys in addition to this particular attorney who billed five and a half hours on the date of this entry. There's no way to verify if any meaningful work was conducted here.

4. Review Bankruptcy Court Order Regarding Upcoming Hearing And Deadlines Before Then (0.6 Hours)

"Reviewing" is often a nebulous and unverifiable billing entry. It's a handy way to inflate hours without accountability.

5. Review Sale Contract (1.3 Hours)

The actual time expended is unverifiable, and this task was billed multiple times by various staff members. There's no practical reason for spending this much time reviewing an already executed sales contract.

6. Draft/Revise Notice Of Hearing (0.7 Hours)

Drafting a scheduling notice should not be done at a $930/hour billing rate (if you are the client); it's work that can be delegated to a legal secretary at a much lower rate.

7. Instruct M. Jackson Re Service And Related (0.4 Hours)

"Instructing" a subordinate is often nebulous and unverifiable, yet it often finds its way onto bills.

8. Strategize With S. Carroll Regarding Plan And Disclosure Statement And June 24 Hearing (1.1 Hours)

"Strategizing," either alone or with staff, is frequently an unverifiable billing entry, and it's often a catch-all for inflating hours.

9. Review Schedules And Proofs Of Claim As Filed (0.9 Hours)

Once again, "reviewing" is an entry that's impossible to verify and frequently used to pad bills.

In summary, this crafty tactic of bundling many distinct entries (nine in the above example) into one billing entry deliberately causes confusion and obfuscation, and that's why law firms do it.

Furthermore, the tasks outlined in each entry are shrouded in uncertainty, making it nearly impossible to verify their legitimacy, and the hours attributed to these tasks are equally enigmatic. Many entries serve as lucrative avenues for inflating attorney cash flow but remain ambiguous both in description, quantity, and verifiability.

To put this into perspective, on a bill totaling a staggering $438,000 for just one month, I uncovered the law firm's audacious attempt to bill over seventy-five hours for vague activities such as "review, strategy, and research."

This was in the context of a straightforward single-asset case nearing its conclusion, with no apparent justification for such excessive billing or celestial strategizing contemplation. These attorneys were effectively charging $1,000 an hour to stargaze on my dime, and insult to injury, they did it without expending a minute.

So, fasten your seat belts, because we're about to launch into providing you with another powerful tool to decode and unravel all legal bills to root out the corruption.

Chapter 43

Clutch Moves: Billing Matter Buckets and One-Page Summaries

§

A SPRAWLING FORTY-PAGE BILL LISTING DATES, DESCRIPTIONS OF services rendered, and time expended is mind-numbing to review and is a daunting beast to decipher. The labyrinthine chapter system, the jumbled multiple time entries—all are designed to befuddle and bewilder. But what if we could reshuffle this deck of information and distill it down into a single, easily digestible one-page document?

Now, that's the winning ticket! I'll share the secrets I employed when faced with an outrageous forty-page $438,000 bill for a month's worth of legal work.

Here's the trick: Let's create a "bucket list" to get the job done.

Step 1: Review the entire bill meticulously, page by page, and extract and compile a list of "billable matters." Billable matters are each of the actual separate matters that were conducted for your case. Billable matters are exactly what they sound like: specific work tasks that you can glean from your bill. These will become your buckets. For instance, here's a list I derived from one scandalous month of billing:

1. Retention of Attorney

2. Retention of Special Counsel

3. Retention of Debtor's Principal's Counsel

4. Review of Mortgagee Plan

5. Objection to Mortgagee Plan

6. Motion Against Credit Bidding

7. Objection to Motion to Estimate

8. Objection to Motion for Trustee

9. Responsible Officer

10. Plan and DS (Disclosure Statement)

11. Vague "Strategy, Consider, Review"

12. Legal Research

13. Prehearing; Plan & Sales Amendment

14. Hearing; Plan & Sales Amendment

15. Confirmation Order

16. Schedule of Claims

17. Closing Disbursements/Reserve

18. Monthly Operating Report

19. General Administration

20. Claim Purchase

21. Settle Mortgagee Claim

22. Sales Closing

23. Fee Discussion

24. Misc.

Step 2: Convert the entire attorney's bill into an Excel sheet and break down every entry into its subparts, similar to what we did previously, turning one entry into nine distinct entries. Do that for the entire bill.

Step 3: Now painstakingly allocate each line item entry into the correct billable matter bucket. It's a meticulous process but well worth it.

At the end, you'll have information to assemble two very powerful tables:

Table One: This provides a summary of who worked on each billable matter and how many hours were billed for each. It will have the list of billable events on the left and the named legal staff across the top, followed by their hourly rates. The far right will display the subtotal of hours for each billable matter. This matrix is your dynamite for dismantling any scandalous billing.

Table Two: The lodestar analysis is often regarded as the gold standard[12] for evaluating whether the hours spent on each billable matter were reasonable. Here you'll take Table One and add a few columns that compare the subtotal of hours spent on each billable matter with an adjacent column reporting the reasonable amount of hours that should have been expended for this matter. And voilà!

This matrix provides a quick and effective means to determine whether the hours allocated per billable matter were indeed reasonable, exposing any potential irregularities or instances of overbilling.

I armed myself with these meticulously prepared matrices alongside my legal pleadings and compelling oral arguments to challenge Loeb & Loeb LLP's $438,000 bill.

The judge commended the meticulous analyses, deeming them precisely the right tools to evaluate the situation and in accord with U.S. Trustee guidelines. The judge acknowledged the excessive and outrageous billing practices, subsequently slicing off a substantial $100,000 from the bill.

While I considered it a step in the right direction and not as substantial a reduction as I had hoped for, opposing counsel Loeb & Loeb LLP, representing themselves, appeared utterly winded, as if the judge's verdict had delivered a powerful blow to their diaphragms. Law firms frequently get away with their billing sorcery without challenge.

As the hearing drew to a close, a rather peculiar camaraderie emerged, with a commiserating exchange of consolations between the judge and opposing counsel. This was the final curtain call concluding the entire Chapter 11 proceedings. The case was closed.

However, the epilogue here is when I later sought the release and refund of my remaining $100,000 sitting in Loeb & Loeb LLP's escrow account, they attempted to take another bite of the apple and gobble my money! They filed a motion in court to reopen my closed Chapter 11 case and then conjured up another shrewd bill, citing post-confirmation work necessary for closing matters out. Most thieves don't feel as entitled as some litigators do.

Remember, the primary objective of a law firm isn't necessarily to ensure client satisfaction; it's often a relentless pursuit of billing, billing, and more billing!

Chapter 44

The One-Page Matrix Reveals More!

§

B RACE YOURSELVES FOR YET ANOTHER EYE-OPENER, MY FRIENDS, because I'm about to reveal a hidden gem that will empower you to decipher the enigma of your attorney's billing practices. It's called the One-Page Summary Matrix, and by rearranging that data, we're going to unearth another nugget of unfiltered truth!

So, let's explore. Your attorney hands you a bill divided into ten chapters and tosses in an average of two hours of billing time per day of his alleged expended time for each topic. That's potentially twenty hours of alleged work in a single day by a single staff member, and guess what? You won't even notice it because those two-hour entries are scattered like breadcrumbs throughout the bill, tucked away on random pages.

But here's where it gets interesting. The beauty of slicing, dicing, and reshuffling that bill into the One-Page Summary Matrix is that you'll have prepared data ready to sort out by attorney name with just a few keystrokes.

You can create a running chronological bill for each legal eagle who billed for their time. In plain English, you'll be able to see how many hours a particular attorney billed you on Monday, Tuesday, Wednesday, and so on, all neatly lined up in chronological order.

This sorting will give you a "smell test" to determine if your attorney is stuffing those hours like a Thanksgiving turkey.

Now let's dive into some real-world numbers. Below you'll see a snapshot extracted from a chronological tally of daily hours deciphered from Loeb & Loeb LLP's timesheets, and it's quite a mother lode:

William Hawkins III

- 5/26/20: 12.2 hours

- 5/27/20: 15.1 hours

- 6/16/20: 19.1 hours

- 6/17/20: 11.3 hours

- 6/18/20: 10.1 hours

- 6/22/20: 12.4 hours

- 6/23/20: 16.2 hours

- 6/24/20: 11.9 hours

Now it's entirely possible that in a high-stakes, do-or-die case with looming deadlines, an attorney might go all-in, put everything else aside, and pull an all-nighter to meet the deadline. But, folks, the day after day hours you see above were spent on what I'd call a rather ordinary case. I'm willing to bet my last dollar that this attorney didn't drop everything else and focus solely on this case. No. Instead, it looks like he retrospectively inflated those hours when constructing his bill.

I mean, seriously, a middle-aged, out-of-shape guy working nineteen grueling hours in a single day for a single client with a whopping billing rate of $930 per hour? That adds up to an eye-popping $18,000 in a day! I'd say he's quite the "marathon biller," even though he looks to have about as much stamina as an old, worn-out battery. It's high time we examine these billing shenanigans closely, my friends, and apply the brakes to these exorbitant legal bills!

Chapter 45

Prevention Is More Powerful than Recourse

§

GET READY FOR A DOSE OF REALITY, MY FRIENDS, BECAUSE I'M about to share some wisdom on the challenging task of clawing back money for legal fees after they've already been billed or paid.

Now on paper, it may seem like you have some recourse to recoup excessive legal costs, but in practice, it's a whole different story. Let's break it down.

You find yourself waist-deep in litigation, and your bills are through the roof, so firing your attorney might cross your mind, but doing so could have negative repercussions for your case. So, most likely, you won't be parting ways with your legal counsel.

Now, what about suing your attorney later for those hefty fees? Well, after already navigating the litigation meat grinder and coming out shredded, you're probably not eager to dive into another legal battle. And even if you are, good luck finding another attorney willing to sue a fellow member of the legal tribe. Plus, more attorney fees, even if the next attorney is honest, can be yet another hefty burden. And to add insult to injury, what's stopping the next attorney from inflating their bills too?

I could go on and on about why getting into a dispute and more litigation might drive you to the brink of madness and empty your pockets.

Here's the real point I want to drive home: Forget the notion of recourse and clawing back. Instead, let's focus on prevention—a much more powerful and effective tool in your arsenal. If you are in the midst of a case while reading this book, tighten your attorney's belt the best you can.

Truth be told, prevention of a liability is preferred rather than taking on the liability and redressing an issue later.

Let me lay it out for you straight. Preventing liability up front in *all spheres* is way better than trying to clean up the mess later. I've dissected the issue of bill churning, dived into how to audit this circus, and dropped some wisdom on keeping your bills in check. But no, I won't hand you a kindergarten-style step-by-step guide for a couple of reasons.

Firstly, trying to leash your lawyer's potential payday from day one with a bunch of controls in your retainer? Forget it. It's like pulling the plug on the game before it even kicks off. Picture this: a litigator's hourly rate—it's their holy grail, their self-worth medallion. Trying to haggle over it is like challenging their very existence. Let that one slide, but aim to win the war. Agreeing to the hourly rate is like sealing the deal on a first date.

And don't even think about wrangling bill churning with specific clauses. You could add rules upon rules to the retainer, but it's like trying to control a tornado with a feather. It just won't work. Putting detailed controls in a retainer agreement before the attorney-client romance even begins is like dropping a marriage contract on the second date. Total buzz kill.

Secondly, bill churning is a crime. Trying to outsmart it with written controls in your retainer is playing the same cat-and-mouse game criminals play with legislators—a never-ending dance of action and reaction:

Action: Criminal Does the Deed

- A crafty criminal spots a gap or flaw in existing laws, pulls off the caper known as bill churning.

Reaction: Legislators Rush to the Scene

- Lawmakers, in response to the caper, whip up new laws or tweak existing ones to plug the gap, like clients desirous of an actionable list to lasso their litigators.

Adjustment: Criminal Tweaks Tactics

- The criminal, being the shifty character they are, tweaks their tactics to sidestep the new laws and clauses, finding fresh loopholes or tricks.

Result: Caper Lives On

- Despite lawmakers' and clients' heroic efforts, the cycle repeats. Crime prevails as criminals get creative with the weaknesses in the legal framework.

So, while bill churning is a dirty game, it's not exactly jail time material. It falls into the murky waters of relationship exploitation.

You won't fortify your castle against exploitation by slapping on a bunch of clauses. Maybe slip a seemingly harmless clause into your retainer, like penciling in an option to request weekly billing breakdowns for each staffer on your case. Innocent on the surface, but it's got some bite.

To protect your stash and keep your law firm on a leash, get past the awkward first few encounters, lock them in, and then take the reins. You've got the upper hand now knowing the tricks of the trade. Now it's your turn to call the shots and guard your loot.

Chapter 46

Carnival Wisdom for Legal Matters: Controlling Costs and Your Case

§

THREE DECADES AGO, I FOUND MYSELF AT THE HELM OF THE construction division within a family office, Westland Real Estate Group, under the mentorship of the remarkable Alan Alevy. Raised in humble beginnings in a Los Angeles housing project, Alan's journey began with weekend shifts at a carnival as a teenager, which ultimately led to his ownership and management of various carnivals.

He even scaled the heights of becoming the operator of the California State Fair, co-founded Circus Circus Casino in Las Vegas, and ultimately succeeded big time in the real estate world. Alan Alevy is a boss in more ways than one, a legend, and a lifelong friend.

Now here's a piece of wisdom from Alan that I'd like to impart to you, especially concerning how you can efficiently manage your case while keeping a close eye on those legal fees. In his sage-like manner, Alan shared a valuable gem of insight:

> Nik, you see, the whole world is gonna steal from you. There are no two ways about it. You see, I used to run a carnival way back, and Johnny ran my Ferris wheel. I'd watch him as folks paid, got on the ride, and got off. I figured out that he pocketed 25 cents per ride cycle. That was okay with me. I wasn't concerned that he was stealing, as everyone is a thief; I just needed to know how much, to know if I could live with it.

Alan's words carry a profound lesson: In this world of conflict and litigation, there are those who may seek to take more than they should, including legal fees. It's not about eliminating the presence of those with questionable intentions, but rather about managing the extent of it. Whether in the carnival business or during the circus of legal proceedings, knowing and limiting the magnitude of the grift is a key component in managing your litigation.

Chapter 47

The Good, the Bad, and the Ugly

§

L ET'S DELVE INTO A TOPIC THAT'S NOT ALL BAD AND UGLY, BECAUSE amidst the murky world of litigation, there's some good to talk about. In fact, this chapter is dedicated to shedding light on the brighter side of legal representation. So, what's the scoop on the "good" attorneys?

Well, these legal eagles are somewhat of a rare breed. They often operate as lone wolves, perhaps with a trusty legal secretary or paralegal by their side. They might have impressive credentials from big firms or they might not, but one thing's for sure—they're top-notch performers. You might even find them tucked away in a modest office under the train tracks in the rough part of town.

Great attorneys possess the full package: they're fierce advocates for your cause, they bill with honesty, they aim to resolve your case swiftly, they seek to minimize your pain, and they bring a touch of innovation to the table. They're like unicorns in the swamp of shady legal creatures, and finding them requires knowing where to look.

First and foremost, you're dealing with a personality that's fiercely independent and won't bend to anyone's will, not even that of the legal establishment. They take immense pride in their craft and embody true professionalism. These attorneys are a rare breed indeed.

In fact, you won't often find two of these individuals teaming up because they both cherish their independence and are each challenging the system in their own way, even while working within it.

When a law firm grows to include two or more attorneys, it inherently becomes a bigger part of the legal establishment. It begins to operate more like a business, where increasing revenues is a primary focus.

And, as outlined in this book, law firms, unfortunately, have a tendency to sink to their lowest common denominator of selfish behavior—essentially finding as many ways as possible to bilk the client and increase revenue. The larger the firm, the more ingrained this behavior becomes, particularly when it comes to billing practice sophistries.

But let's get back to these legal superstars. I've had the privilege of working alongside some of the best in the business, but they don't make the news. These are individuals who make time for you and your cause. They are old-fashioned professionals who have pride. They've honed their skills, working diligently and sincerely for their clients. So, remember this when you're on the hunt for a litigator—seek out the ones who shine as beacons of excellence in this often murky landscape.

Chapter 48

Good Litigators Revealed

$

LET ME PAINT A PICTURE OF THE "GOOD" LITIGATORS IN ACTION, MY friends. These are the real-life examples that remind us that excellence in the legal world does exist.

Allow me to take you back a decade when I penned a review for one such legal powerhouse, David Smith:

> David Smith compares to most lawyers (that I have hired through my business career) like a Navy Seal compares to a foot soldier. Both are in the same field, but David is many cuts above the crop in his profession. David Smith invested his brilliant and tenacious mental faculties and internalized the history and facts of my circumstances,[13] essentially owning and living my entire case every step of the way, dedicating himself to it like a sacred mission.

> David Smith can be trusted to sow and reap the best results possible if he decides to take on your case. David Smith's mission to win is paramount. He strategized every step of my case far in advance and re-strategized again and again as the case evolved. No part of my case was handled at the last minute.

> David handled my case like a Navy Seal operation, where an entire replica of the site may be built much in advance of the actual mission as a tool to practice and contemplate the variables that follow during the actual mission or parts thereof. David Smith is a consummate professional and deserves the accolade of being

considered a lawyer's lawyer. He brought me great results, and I am thankful for his representation.

But let's not stop there.

Introducing Joseph Haspel, another remarkable attorney with whom I've had the privilege to work. Haspel is not your conventional litigator; his legal prowess operates on a different wavelength. Working as a solo practitioner from the two-century-old basement of his home nestled on a horse ranch hill, Haspel stands out as an anti-establishment maverick. He carefully selects the cases he takes on, charging reasonably and opting not to bill every minute, demonstrating a commitment that goes beyond monetary concerns. His primary motivation lies in a genuine concern for his clients' best interests.

Unlike many in his field, Haspel is not beholden to external pressures. He is discerning in choosing cases, steering clear of questionable side deals and maintaining a focused dedication to his clients. Unafraid to convey uncomfortable truths, he remains resolute in safeguarding his clients' interests and avoids cultivating overly friendly relationships with opposition counsel at the expense of those he represents. His independence may make him seem like an untamed bronco, occasionally appearing cantankerous in his interactions. Yet, give the stallion the freedom to gallop, and he'll expertly navigate your legal journey.

Beneath Haspel's independent exterior lies a wealth of knowledge and goodwill. His approach is professorial, and he possesses the legal acumen of a Supreme Court litigator, all while maneuvering within a system he openly acknowledges for its corruption and inequity. If a title were to be bestowed upon him, Haspel would be the equivalent of an "off-the-grid attorney."

Attorneys of the caliber of David Smith and Joseph Haspel are indeed rare. Encountering such representation is a stroke of fortune. Nevertheless, the lessons from this book resound—never blindly entrust your case to an attorney; instead, collaborate with a skilled one in the management of your problem and its solution.

Chapter 49

Tangential Benefits
of Working with a Great Litigator

$

L ET ME REGALE YOU WITH THE TALE OF DAVID SMITH, THE LEGAL powerhouse I joined forces with on a high-stakes case that spanned three solid years. This man didn't just handle legal matters; he bestowed life lessons that left me in awe.

As the captain of our legal ship, David expected nothing less than my full commitment. He wanted me in the trenches, reviewing every pleading, and he sought my unwavering loyalty. It felt as though I'd been drafted into a rigorous legal boot camp.

Now picture this: David could unleash a torrent of words like a drill sergeant in the heat of battle. There were moments, especially before crucial hearings, when he'd threaten to walk away.

I often felt like I was up a creek without a paddle, and I'd find myself pleading with him to stay. At times, I questioned if there was a hint of sadism or if he possessed some secret technique to break me down and mold me into a more attentive and diligent client.

David's preparation reached its pinnacle when he readied me for a grueling three-day deposition with one of the most renowned trial lawyers in NYC, David Scharf of Morrison Cohen LLP. While I had watched some "how to answer questions during a deposition" videos, they were a joke in comparison to David Smith's rigorous training regimen.

He'd fire mock questions at me, and if I hesitated, he'd erupt like a volcano:

"You're a liar!

A true straight shooter wouldn't even flinch!

But not you!

You're staring at me like a deer caught in the headlights!

Pathetic!

You're attempting to outsmart everyone, calculating the 'correct' answer in your head!

You're not clever enough to lie!"

David's intensity would sometimes lead him to utter things unfit for publication, and in many ways, it pushed me to my limits. These sessions were emotional marathons, often leaving me emotionally shattered and in tears.

Occasionally, at the pinnacle of his roaring emotions and admonishment, he'd excuse himself briefly, claiming he needed to make a call, but in retrospect, it was more about self de-escalation from his apoplectic state and regaining his calm composure before returning to then delve even deeper into the heart of the matter. He'd probe, pummel, dissect, and examine if I'd crumble, push back, or offer a fresh perspective.

I wasn't entirely sure if this was all for my benefit. David excoriated and eviscerated me. However, as painful, degrading, and unpleasant as this preparation was, it also felt like there was a higher purpose to the torment, like some clandestine CIA or Mossad-style psychological boot camp. David was on a mission, and I had willingly enlisted.

One crucial lesson I gleaned from this experience was that my typical style of answering questions leaned toward defensiveness. I rarely answered from the gut; instead, I'd ponder and weigh the implications before responding. More often than not, I'd deflect, steering clear of a direct response in an attempt to control the narrative. While this approach may serve well in some areas of life, it's a disaster in others, especially during a deposition or in personal matters.

In the end, David Smith achieved something truly remarkable during the course of our litigation journey. He dismantled some of my internal barriers and transformed me into a more emotionally expressive and credible individual. So, how's that for the indelible mark of a great litigator?

Chapter 50

A Judge Like No Other:
The Tale of Judge David Schmidt

§

LET ME PAINT YOU A PICTURE OF A REMARKABLE ENCOUNTER, FOLKS. It was a day when I found myself inside the courtroom of none other than Judge David Schmidt, a Supreme Court Justice in Kings County, New York. This man was truly one of a kind in the world of judges.

Now, here's the backdrop: I was tangled up in a real estate development deal that had gone sour. My partner had decided to breach our agreement before we even laid the first brick. You know the drill—disputes, lawyers, and things were heating up.

But let me tell you, Judge Schmidt was no ordinary judge. He had this unique ability to mediate rather than rule from the bench. He walked into the courtroom not as a stern figure with a gavel but as a master of diffusing tension. He wasn't just there to mediate between the opposing counsel; he was a referee for both me and my partner and sidelined our lawyers to a time out. It was like watching a seasoned pro at work.

Judge Schmidt ushered us out into the hallway, and there, he talked to me like an old friend. He did the same down the hall with the other side. He treated us as equals, not just as litigants. No pontificating or power tripping—it was a breath of fresh air.

After some heartfelt discussions, he called us back into his chambers. And what did he propose? He didn't slam the gavel or lay down orders. No, sir. Instead, he penciled out broad parameters of a settlement agreement with a pen and paper. He then strongly suggested that we, along with our attorneys, head over to a nearby restaurant or bar, knock back a drink or two, and hammer out a final settlement agreement. We were to return to his chambers in two hours.

Now it wasn't all sunshine and rainbows. We went a few rounds, and my former partner pulled a disappearing act before finally agreeing to sign the settlement agreement. But here's the thing about Judge Schmidt: he was unconventional, he had empathy, and he wasn't on a power trip.

Once he became a judge, he had an intriguing approach. Schmidt was known for his preference for working in shirtsleeves at a table set up near the attorneys, foregoing his formal spot on the bench as well as his judicial robes. He even kept his father's concentration camp uniform in a glass case in his chambers as a poignant reminder. He moved in and out of his chambers with humility, dedicated to doing his best for all parties and trying to end their dispute.

His passion was crystal clear—settling cases. With a track record of over 15,000 settlements[14] in various civil cases, he was less of a traditional judge and more of a wise mediator. He had a knack for guiding people toward resolution and had no qualms about doing things his way.

In a world filled with judges who often exhibited pathological and tyrannical behavior, Judge Schmidt stood out as a shining example of practicality, empathy, and a deliverer of solutions. He was, without a doubt, a true judicial legend.

Chapter 51

Liar, Liar, Pants on Fire: Everyone Is a Pinocchio

§

O N AVERAGE, WE ALL WEAVE A WEB OF DECEIT ABOUT FOUR TIMES A day, while our ears are subjected to anywhere from ten to a whopping two hundred lies daily.[15] But how in the world does that happen? Well, let's dive into the world of human memory and the tangled threads of truth.

You see, our memories aren't pristine recordings of past events; they're more like imaginative reconstructions influenced by a medley of factors—perception, emotions, and the relentless march of time. This reconstruction process often leads to inaccuracies, distortions, and even the creation of entirely false memories. So, when people share information, it might unintentionally veer off the path of perfect accuracy. I like to call these "first-degree lies."

Now let's venture into the realm of litigation. You've got a burning desire to win, right? Well, that's where the mind's reconstruction talents truly shine. Remember O.J. Simpson and his vehement claims of innocence? Say something often enough, and you might start believing it yourself. It's almost a subconscious process. In the world of litigation, there's your truth, the opposing side's truth, and then the real truth. I call the litigant's truths "second-degree lies."

But now let's talk about the lies that attorneys spin. They've got quite the repertoire. They might fib to their clients, bend the truth before judges, and sprinkle falsehoods like confetti throughout court documents, all without breaking a sweat. Now if your attorney is spinning lies and slinging hyperbolic arrows at the other side and you benefit, let's not kid ourselves; it's a celebration. But if the opposition counsel is more adept at the game and is a spin master and hyperbolic javelin champ, well, then it's a disaster.

Opposition counsel often craft tall tales for their clients, mix in a bit of your involvement in these stories, and concoct things you've never experienced or uttered. They tell one lie after another in pleadings and oral arguments, and more often than not, it all goes unchallenged by the court. I reserve a special name for this—"third-degree bold-face" lying.

The mudslinging, spin, and outright lies that target you are an accepted practice that can utterly shatter the viability of your case and your credibility.

The most cunning litigators won't necessarily deliver a blatant lie. Instead, they'll employ implication and hyperbole, launching lies that seem as true and inertia-free as a lightning-fast jai alai throw.

Winston Churchill, Jonathan Swift, Mark Twain, and others have been credited with expressing a sentiment similar to this quote: "A lie can travel halfway around the world before the truth even has time to put its boots on." In the world of litigation, lying is almost par for the course. Sure, everyone tells a fib now and then, but it's the litigators' untruths that sting the most.

Chapter 52

Legal Blood Sport:
When Lawyers Go for the Jugular

§

IN THE UNFORGIVING ARENA OF LITIGATION, WHERE THE STAKES
include reputations, fortunes, and futures, attorneys occasionally
engage in what I've dubbed "legal blood sport." This isn't your run-of-
the-mill courtroom drama; it's a merciless game of character assassination,
where lawyers don't just seek victory in court but also strive to obliterate
the credibility and integrity of their adversaries' clients. Prepare for a
tumultuous ride, dear readers, as we navigate the treacherous waters of
defamation and character annihilation within the legal realm.

Envision this: A courtroom showdown featuring two heavyweight
litigators in a high-stakes battle. On one side stands the plaintiff's
attorney; on the other, the defendant's. They're not merely fighting for a
favorable verdict; they're engaged in a power struggle, willing to employ
any means necessary to decimate the opposition. This often entails
launching personal attacks on the character of the opposing party's
clients, sometimes devoid of concrete evidence. It's a strategic move, and
the aftermath can be nothing short of devastating.

The earliest signs of legal blood sport emerge when lawyers begin slinging
mud. Accusations and allegations are tossed around like hand grenades,
leaving behind a battlefield strewn with the wreckage of personal
reputations. It's not solely about presenting facts and law; it's about
portraying the opposing party as morally bankrupt, dishonest, or even
outright villainous.

The art of character assassination frequently revolves around the manipulation of words. Lawyers wield language like a finely honed weapon to insinuate guilt or wrongdoing.

They employ phrases such as "allegedly," "suspicious," or "questionable conduct" to sow seeds of doubt without making direct accusations. This tactic is a crafty and cunning one, leaving the target's reputation hanging by a thread without crossing the line into blatant defamation.

But make no mistake—these legal tactics have ramifications that extend far beyond the courtroom.

Clients who find themselves on the receiving end of character assassination may endure severe emotional distress, reputational damage, and even financial ruin. The scars left by such an assault can linger indefinitely, persisting long after the final gavel has fallen.

While the legal profession boasts some checks and balances, the reality is that attorneys can lie their heads off with relatively minor repercussions.

In the high-stakes world of litigation, the line between vigorous advocacy and character assassination often blurs. Lives and reputations can be left in tatters by the unrelenting onslaught of litigator lies.

Chapter 53

Covering the Other Side's Legal Costs:
A Painful Blow

§

L EGAL BILLS CAN BE A TOUGH PILL TO SWALLOW, BUT HAVING TO
foot the bill for your opponent's legal expenses can feel like a cruel
twist of the knife. Regrettably, there are situations where you might find
yourself with no alternative but to pay and suffer the brunt of the blade.

Contemplate this drama: You're caught in the throes of a divorce, thanks
to a cheating spouse serving you with divorce papers. Or perhaps your
real estate lender has taken a dark turn, embarking on a predatory loan-
to-own scheme. Maybe it's a disgruntled employee lobbing a groundless
discrimination lawsuit your way, simply because they view your deep
pockets as an all-you-can-eat buffet. The legal costs alone can cause
migraines, but the real gut punch comes later.

Let me share a case from my own experience to illustrate this point. A
client of mine found himself entangled in a heated dispute with a lender.
This feud eventually led to a Chapter 11 bankruptcy case involving a
single-asset real estate property, which was ultimately sold at auction.
Unfortunately, my client sought my advice after this legal ordeal had
played out, and the outcome was far from favorable.

Here's the twist: My client's property had a substantial value, with a gross
sales price of $96 million, a cash net of $88 million, and a loan balance of
$69 million. On the surface, it would seem that net sales proceeds would
have more than covered unpaid interest and the remainder of creditor bills.
But there's a curveball. In addition to paying his own legal costs, my client
was also on the hook for the lender's staggering $15 million legal bill!

Contentious Chapter 11 battle costs can skyrocket due to the countless billable hours, but let's be clear: there's no magic legal work at play here. Much of it boils down to procedural matters, and the cost delta between one single-asset case and another shouldn't be this astronomical. The only magic here is the hocus-pocus of bill creation.

Now you might wonder why the lender would shell out a staggering $15 million in legal fees for a single-asset case when they could have easily hired an in-house attorney for a fraction of the cost. Something indeed smells fishy, doesn't it? Let's follow the money.

Lenders, much like all astute business people, are prudent when it comes to expenses. They're willing to pay a fair price for services rendered, perhaps a bit extra for premium service, but they won't go overboard.

If they were to pay this bill outright without any expectation of reimbursement, it would likely cost them $1 million, maybe $2 million, tops! They would never willingly hand over an extra $13 million ($15 million minus $2 million) to their attorney, no matter how chummy they might be.

It's entirely plausible and likely that a behind-the-scenes arrangement was struck well before the retainer agreement was even signed.

Let's put on our augmented reality goggles and focus: The lender engages in a hushed conversation with the law firm before finalizing the retention deal. They might say something along these lines:

> We're selecting your firm for this case, but here's the deal—we need you to be over-the-top aggressive with your billing. The borrower's property has substantial equity; we want you to maximize your charges. Employ all the billing tricks. This way, we can later argue, after the case concludes, that the sale didn't generate enough cash to cover all the outstanding interest, and after the conclusion of the Chapter 11 case, we can then sue the borrower for an additional $15 million based on his personal guarantee.
>
> We won't contest your $15 million fee application in court, but here's the catch. Between us, the first $2 million of the bill will be

recognized as your legitimate fee, while any amount exceeding that will be refunded to my firm through various means—be it as credit for future work, payments to a designated outside firm, or a rebate after the case concludes.

The wheels of the business world are well-oiled by reimbursements, kickbacks, credits, or more intricate arrangements. One thing remains constant: no business willingly leaves substantial money on the table. Even if a dollar doesn't carry the value it once did, $13 million is still a hefty amount of cash, not to be left on anyone's table.

There are several reasons why the law firm might agree to this arrangement. They understand that more opportunities for lucrative billing await them when the lender calls on them for future cases. $2 million dollars in revenue for any law firm, even in a single-asset case, is also a substantial sum. The law firm may feel at ease with refunding the excess money because it was never rightfully theirs to begin with. One thing is for sure, it's a shell game with clear winners and losers.

So, who ends up bearing the brunt of this intricate arrangement? The party entangled in the legal battle, who was already crushed by his business misfortune, and who once believed that they could liquidate their property, settle all parties involved, and move forward. Instead, the lender devoured all the proceeds from the sale and is now pursuing even more with a personal guarantee lawsuit junket.

When you're confronted with the daunting prospect of covering the opposing side's legal fees, brace yourself, not only for this unwelcome expense, but also the lurking possibility of under-the-table deals between parties and bill-churning litigators that not only divert your funds but can also expose you to even more litigation.

Chapter 54

Co-Counsel:
Legal Lobbyists for Your Litigation

§

IN THE INTRICATE WORLD OF LITIGATION, THERE EXISTS A UNIQUE breed of legal eagles who appear to have struck gold. These individuals don't dirty their hands in gritty legal combat or trudge through the arduous grunt work. Instead, they make grandiose cameo entrances into courtrooms, often with minimal preparation, and yet they command substantial fees. What exactly is their role, you might wonder?

Well, they are the ambassadors of goodwill, the influencers extraordinaire. They are co-counsel.

Peer into your primary litigator's office. He conducts the day-to-day legal work, handling the nitty-gritty aspects of the case, while co-counsel adds that final touch of allure to your legal ensemble. What makes co-counsel particularly fascinating is their knack for developing close friendships with judges. In the complex world of litigation, having a familiar face on your side, especially one that the judge knows and likes, can tip the scales in your favor. And let's not forget the whispers of backroom dealings that occasionally find their way into the limelight.

So, brace yourselves, because this is how the real world of litigation often unfolds. On one occasion, I found myself in a situation where I proposed the idea of hiring co-counsel for one of my cases. I wanted the judge to spot a friendly face in our legal entourage. My primary litigator, a partner in a boutique firm, had limited experience working with co-counsel. Still, he claimed to be open to the notion if I could suggest a compatible attorney.

My mission was clear: find co-counsel who had established friendly connections with the Brooklyn judge overseeing my case. I embarked on some Internet sleuthing, and below you'll find our correspondence, which demonstrates my litigator's initial reluctance and his subsequent willingness to consider the idea, spurred by the mention of prominent attorneys who often played the co-counsel card.

Me: I've compiled a list of potential co-counsel candidates based solely on their social and professional interactions with the judge. It seems they share common ground—Brooklyn, Italian heritage, Catholic faith, and a shared journey through the bar.

Sara Gozo—I've spotted her in photos from various events, and she held the position of president in some local legal organizations; her legal gravitas remains unclear.

Frank Seddio—This well-connected individual appears more like an advocate or politician. He recently retired as the judge of the Surrogate Court of Kings County, had a six-year stint in the New York State Assembly representing Brooklyn's 59th Assembly District, and boasts titles such as former president of the Brooklyn Democratic Party and former president of the Brooklyn Bar Association. Plus, he looks like the same age range as the judge.

Frank Carone—A relatively young and politically active individual, Carone serves as the president of the Brooklyn Bar Association and holds the position of law chairman in the Kings County Democratic Party. He also received a recent appointment from Mayor Michael Bloomberg to the New York City Taxi and Limousine Commission.

My Litigator: None of these candidates seem suitable for our needs.

Me: Understood. I'll continue my search. What are your thoughts on the possibility of hiring co-counsel who formerly served as a judge at the appellate level in Brooklyn?

My Litigator: I don't possess any relevant information on this matter. As I mentioned before, if you have a recommendation and you believe it would be beneficial, I'm open to working with them. However, I can't provide insights or opinions because I lack knowledge in this area.

Me: I've received a co-counsel recommendation. I'm acquainted with [Name] from [prominent NYC real estate litigation firm]. He spoke to his partner [Name], who specializes in litigation at the firm, and they recommend Steve Cohn. Apparently, they frequently collaborate with Steve as co-counsel in Judge [Name's] commercial real estate cases.

At first, my litigator showed some reluctance when it came to the idea of working with co-counsel. However, things took a turn when I introduced him to the names of well-known attorneys who regularly collaborated with co-counsel. It was a pivotal moment that made him more open to the concept. The key lesson here is that your attorney should not be the sole authority on what's best for your case. You can engage in discussions and seek their opinions, but remember that you're the one steering the ship. To maximize the effectiveness of your case, you must take an active role in decision-making.

I got in touch with Steve Cohn, a seasoned and personable lawyer with over five decades of experience, primarily in divorce cases. He had an extensive network, both in social and political circles, often rubbing shoulders with politicians and socialites, and even hosting annual fundraisers for Bill and Hillary Clinton. Steve had also served as special counsel to a state senator and a House minority leader, and he carried the prestigious title of former president of the Brooklyn Bar Association.

What made Steve truly valuable was his close and friendly relationship with Judge [Name], the presiding judge in my case. The judge and his clerk appeared to be much more receptive to Steve than to my primary litigator. Thanks to his rapport with the judge, Steve was able to engage in candid discussions with the court, something that had proven elusive for my lead litigator. Steve was indeed worth his weight in gold.

During one of the hearings, fate had it that I crossed paths with Frank Seddio, the former Brooklyn judge and political influencer I had initially suggested as co-counsel for my attorney. Frank was waiting outside the judge's chambers for the next hearing, and you might wonder why. Well, he was about to make a guest appearance, doing what he does best these days—collecting substantial retainers and hourly rates, all the while flashing his signature *Goodfellas* smile!

A litigant may see an advantage in hiring the judge's friend as co-counsel, but what happens when the judge, U.S. Trustee, or opposing counsel involves another buddy of the judge, such as a receiver or trustee? Will the debtor or the litigant with assets in legal limbo truly benefit from the appointment of this judge's chum? We'll examine this occurrence in the following chapter and explore the dynamics of some significant players in the legal landscape.

Chapter 55

Receivers, Trustees, and the Real Scoop on Court Power Players

§

Now let's dive deeper into the world of receivers, trustees, and responsible officers, especially when you toss business litigation into the mix. It's time to pull back the curtain and shine a spotlight on their roles in this legal drama. They each go by different titles, but they're akin to wolves donning sheep's attire, all former or concurrent lawyers, all fundamentally the same voracious creature.

Receivers come into play when one party is successful in petitioning for one or if the judge deems it necessary.

Visualize this: A lender accuses a borrower of defaulting on a commercial real estate loan. Usually, there's some fine print tucked away in those loan documents, giving the lender the power to ask the judge for a receiver—and they can do it quietly, without even notifying the borrower. No heads-up is needed because this little gem was part of the loan agreement from day one.

So, what's the receiver's gig? Imagine them as the asset's keeper and/or seller. They step in, seize control of the asset, and start calling the shots. It could be real estate, a business, or any other asset, and their mission is to ensure nothing goes haywire during the legal showdown.

But here's where things get spicy. Receivers and trustees aren't just the guardians of justice; they often have a golden opportunity to rake in some serious dough. How? Well, they bill for their time just like lawyers do. High hourly rates, and they bill for every little thing—and usually have the same bill-churning opportunity that litigators do—all while they're "protecting" your assets.

Now here's where the plot thickens. These folks are typically managers from afar, not the boots-on-the-ground type. They outsource all the actual work to a myriad of professionals and management companies. And where there's a contract to be handed out, there's an opportunity for some hush-hush extras—under the table.

A small contract might lead to a small, unofficial reward to the trustee or receiver. A big contract? Well, that could mean a hefty rebate. It's like a secret handshake club, and it happens more often than you'd think.

Some likely examples are a kickback from the property management company hired, or on a property sale, a nice kickback from the sales brokerage firm hired who got paid an exorbitant commission that was actually many times higher than market rate!

Plenty of dough on the table to pinch and pocket!

Now let's get back to the super scandalous stuff. These receivers and trustees often land these cushy gigs because they're not just experts; they're buddies with one of the attorneys or, dare I say it, the judge. They rub shoulders at local bar association events, political shindigs, retirement parties, and even family weddings. They party and even live with each other, if you know what I mean. These relationships go way beyond professional connections—they're like blood bonds.

But here's the rub—you can't just stroll in and decide to start your own receiver or trustee business. The attorney or judge who nominates you and/or the judge who ratifies you into the position needs to know you, trust your abilities, and have faith in your integrity. Yet, guess what? They trust their buddies even more.

Now we're not talking about attorneys or judges taking bribes—most are as honest as the day is long. But when a judge appoints his golf buddy or childhood friend into the receiver or trustee position, things can take a different and, yes, scandalous turn.

Payola makes the world go round, my friends. Who wouldn't want a free new car for their kid or an all-expense paid family vacation, or perhaps the ability to trade a favor and get a spouse, relative, or friend a cushy job at an involved law firm, especially if it's all hush-hush? It's not just about the money; sometimes, it's about the perks. And sometimes it might be about the money, like the gold bars in the news and under investigation that found their way into Senator Menendez's safe![16]

So, there you have it, the inside scoop. Who gets the short end of the stick in all this? The poor soul with their asset stuck in court, losing control and watching leeches and parasites emerge, charging sky-high rates and scheming to suck the lifeblood out of the asset. It's like a financial vampire party.

So, if you ever find yourself tangled up in litigation with an asset on the line, brace yourself because it's a wild ride in the world of receivers, trustees, and those who feed on your assets. And remember, you're going to need all the luck you can get.

Chapter 56

Receivers, Trustees, No Responsibility, and Yet Huge, Wild Fees

§

I T'S A STORY AS ANCIENT AS TIME ITSELF. WOLVES RAID THE HEN-house house when it's dark, yet these court-approved ravenous creatures pillage your business and assets in broad daylight. They initially get their license to come into a case from one or more of the following cast: plaintiff or debtor counsel, creditor, U.S. Trustee, or the judge.

I once found myself in court with a predatory lender who tried to wrest my building from me and was arguing for control of the liquidation process of the asset so that they could assume ownership for a fraction of the building's worth. I strategized with counsel to bring in a trustee figure that my attorney had ties to, to handle a bona fide sale. The idea was to satisfy the judge with an outsider controlling the sale, but at least the outsider would kind of be on my team.

Now let's delve into excerpts from an actual proposed trustee agreement from the aforementioned case for the sale of a $30 million residential building. The trustee was titled "Windup Officer (WUO)."

Description of Services

(a) Officer. In connection with this engagement, Geron shall be duly named the Company's Windup Officer (the "WUO") by the Company, to serve as _____. Geron shall be authorized to utilize up to one attorney and up to two para-professional individuals who work in his firm (the "Additional Personnel," and with Geron, the "Engagement Personnel") to assist him with his duties under this engagement, as set forth more fully herein.

Comments: A trustee who is a seasoned attorney should have had a straightforward task—make a few calls to commercial real estate brokers, request property sale proposals, and spend fifteen minutes on this. After that, he'd simply review and sign a sales brokerage agreement, deal with some paperwork, send the sales contract to the debtor's attorney for court approval, and maybe attend a hearing or two. It's basic, minimal work, simple enough, and yet, as we'll soon discover, he had the audacity to propose a staggering hourly rate of $750 per hour.

And if that wasn't outrageous enough, this paragraph also allowed him to bring in another attorney at the same exorbitant hourly rate, even if that attorney was his own employee and was actually paid $50 or $100 per hour. To add insult to injury, he could hire two paraprofessionals at an equally absurd hourly rate of $500 each, pay them $50/hour, and pocket the delta.

This is a prime example of how legal fees can quickly spiral out of control, leaving you to foot the bill for every interaction, whether substantial or trivial, or simply churned and inflated. It's a financial recklessness that's hard to fathom.

(d) Though the Engagement Personnel are employees of Reitler Kailas &
Rosenblatt LLC ("RKR"), it is expressly understood that this engagement is
not a legal engagement of RKR, does not involve RKR directly, and none of
the Engagement Personnel will be providing any legal services or advice to the
Company, its creditors, its owners, and other parties in interest, under the Plan.
Geron's duties under this Agreement shall be solely as a fiduciary, in the same
form and function as when a trustee is appointed or elected to serve as a trustee
in Chapter 7 or 11 bankruptcy cases. Unless otherwise retained by a separate
agreement, RKR shall not serve any role in this engagement and shall owe no
legal duty to the Company, any other creditors of the Company, the Company's
owners, or any other party-in-interest in the Company's bankruptcy case.

Comments: Here we have a lawyer associated with a law firm, but don't be mistaken—his role isn't to dispense legal advice. No, he would be hired as a supposed fiduciary of the debtor. However, the stark reality is that a trustee's self-interest usually trumps the interest of other parties. He has a natural loyalty to whoever greases the wheels to get him involved in the case and to his very human nature-inspired quest to make as much money as possible; that's where his true allegiance lies.

(f) With respect to the Company, RKR shall have no liability to the Company, its creditors, its owners, or any other party in interest for any acts or omissions of the Engagement Personnel related to the performance or non-performance of services consistent with the requirements of the engagement and this Agreement.

Comments: This arrangement is indeed a cushy deal for the Windup Officer and his company, as they bear zero liability for any of their actions. It's like a dream gig where you get to call the shots without any accountability.

4. Limitation of Duties. Neither Geron nor the Engagement Personnel make any representations or guarantees that, inter alia, (i) any liquidation alternative presented to the Company will be more successful than all other possible proposals or strategic alternatives, (ii) liquidation is the best course of action for the Company, or (iii) any liquidation decision taken by Geron will be unanimously accepted by all creditors, although Geron will endeavor to build consensus on all material decisions with the Company and creditors. Further, Geron and the Engagement Personnel do not assume any responsibility for the Company's decision to pursue, or not pursue, any strategy, or to effect, or not to effect any transaction. The Engagement Personnel shall be responsible for the implementation only of the affirmative actions proposed by Geron, approved (or not objected to, with prior notice) by the Court, and implemented by Geron.

Comments: These are nothing more than disclaimers that skillfully avoid any trustee responsibility when it comes to making sound business decisions. It's as if the trustee could drive your asset off a cliff and still evade accountability. Now let's dive into the meat of the matter—his proposed compensation.

5. Compensation. (a) The Engagement Personnel shall be paid their hourly fees from the Company's funds, by payment to RKR (but without privity to RKR), as follows: (i) Geron, at the rate of $750/hour for his services under this agreement, and any other Engagement Personnel their respective standard hourly rates.

Comments: This is essentially an invitation for the trustee to engage in bill-padding with a crew of four: Geron charging an astronomical $750 per hour, the second attorney matching that rate, and two paralegals raking in $500 per hour each. It's a financial feast at your expense.

(iii) Upon execution of this Agreement, the Company shall pay Geron a $25,000 retainer, to be used in payment of hourly charges on a monthly basis.

Comments: Your company is hemorrhaging and in a financial nosedive, and yet this additional buzzard hovers, ready to swoop down and feast on your dwindling resources, demanding a $25,000 payment up front before even lifting a finger on your case.

(b) In addition, the WUO shall also be paid an incentive fee (the "Incentive Fee") of 2% of the Gross Proceeds generated from the liquidation of the Company's assets following the effective date of this agreement.

Comments: Paying a guy a princely $750 per hour just to oversee the sale of an asset is an outrageously high expense. But the madness doesn't stop there. His three other employees are billing at inflated hourly rates, and the total bill is skyrocketing like wildfire. And to add insult to injury, why in the world would you also shell out a jaw-dropping $600,000 as a bonus to the manager when you're already forking over a sky-high 6 percent sales commission of $1.8 million to the sales broker?

In regular business, one meticulously scours for the best deals, pinching pennies and conserving resources. However, in the courtroom, you and your assets become easy prey. Every participant, from your attorney to the trustee, opposition counsel, and their client, grabs their share of the pie, leaving you vulnerable, lying on your back with your belly exposed to the ruthless dismemberment of your assets and equity. These players are more reminiscent of the infamous Jack the Ripper than the embodiment of Lady Justice.

Furthermore, in this intricate legal tango, the agreement generously hands out extra indemnities to the Windup Officer, almost like offering a golden opportunity to pull off a heist, complete with a "get out of jail free" card tucked away. As we wade through the labyrinth of bankruptcy court, supposedly crafted to be a lifeline for struggling business owners and stakeholders, a nagging question arises:

Why does the entire legal machinery—judges, attorneys, and U.S. Trustees alike—seemingly give a nod to the wholesale dismantling of an owner's business or assets and allow and encourage these high hourly rates, wild incentive fees, and above-market commissions? The answer, glaringly obvious, revolves around the relentless pursuit of cold, hard cash—a pursuit that invites contemplation on whether those funds conveniently find their way into the eager pockets of the players involved.

Chapter 57

Not Every Litigator Jumps at Your Case: Legal Marketplace Realities

§

IN OUR EARLIER CONVERSATION ON THE VALUE OF CO-COUNSEL, I recounted a story where I sought advice from a friend who also happens to be a partner at a highly regarded law firm in the heart of New York City. He, as a matter of course, employed co-counsel regularly, viewing it as just another valuable tool in the legal toolbox.

What left a lasting impression on me was the sharp contrast between the wholehearted embrace of this tool by his firm and the unwarranted resistance displayed by my then-litigator, who seemed hesitant to embrace this tried-and-true widget.

This leaves us with a burning question: Why did I opt for the relative rookie when I had a seasoned pro within my reach?

To clarify, I did consult with my experienced friend when my legal journey began in this particular case. He genuinely wanted to represent me, seeing that the matter fell squarely within his firm's specialty. However, he had to regretfully decline. You see, his firm's exclusive clientele comprised heavyweight lenders—big banks, hedge funds, insurance giants—and they had an ironclad rule against representing borrowers. To them, it spelled a potential conflict of interest that could upset their lucrative business that catered to lenders who, mind you, had a bottomless pit of cash to cover their legal expenses. Clearly, these lenders made for the more appealing clients.

Now let's drill down a bit deeper into this scenario. Imagine a law firm that knows the business inside out and plays fairly when it comes to billing. They predominantly represent lenders, a sector that generates a wealth of litigation work. These lenders are the ideal repeat customers, demanding a consistent work product from their attorneys and firms, and they have the knack for negotiating relatively reasonable prices.

On the other side of the coin, you have borrowers. They might require the same legal expertise during litigation, but they don't bask in the same warm embrace of consistent representation as the heavyweight lenders do. Each lender churns out an abundance of litigation work, which bestows upon them significant clout and unwavering reliability in the legal services marketplace.

Borrowers, however, aren't blessed with the same leverage. Their legal needs often emerge sporadically, usually when they're navigating choppy financial waters.

This example is far from an anomaly; it's merely a snapshot of the realities in the legal services marketplace. Your position in the business landscape can profoundly influence your access to legal resources, even when dealing with the same legal issue or specialty.

The larger firms, equipped with fine-tuned litigation machinery, can be formidable adversaries. If you fall into the category of clients cherished by these legal giants, you'll find an array of representation options at your fingertips.

Nonetheless, if your circumstances place you in the realm that usually opposes these legal juggernauts, you'll need to work harder to identify appropriate representation but have the opportunity to find solace in the smaller boutique firms or independent operators who may be equipped with the essential experience and qualifications to aptly manage your case.

Don't let the realization of limited legal representation options overwhelm you. In fact, we discussed some of my most enlightening experiences with these nimble sole-operator firms. Remember, irrespective of a law firm's size, you remain the linchpin of your legal team!

Chapter 58

Establishment Power Play:
Gravitas in the Courtroom

§

IN THE REALM OF LEGAL BATTLES, CATCHING THE WIND OF THE establishment's favor can be the ace up your sleeve. As we dug deep into the concept of co-counsel in a previous chapter, we discovered the sheer value of not just having a judge who's acquainted with your litigator but one who shares a hearty rapport. Sometimes, these favorable vibes can work like magic, turning the tide to your benefit without breaking a sweat.

But there's another layer to securing a courtroom win, and it's all about how deep your establishment roots go. The more deeply entrenched you are in the establishment, the better your odds of securing favorable outcomes in court. Let's dive in and paint a picture using a classic battle: lender versus borrower.

In this bout, the establishment heavyweight is the lender. These are the big players: Wall Street firms, hedge funds, credit unions, or banks woven into the very fabric of the business world. They deal with hefty loan portfolios and have multiple branches, carrying an inherent gravitas that borrowers can only dream of matching. Borrowers, in contrast, are transient customers, coming and going, while lenders sit firmly in the establishment's unshakable stronghold.

Now let's talk legal representation. As we explored in the previous chapter, the law firm that caters to establishment businesses cements its reputation as an establishment-style legal heavyweight, while smaller firms may come across as quaint or out of their depth.

So, when it's time to face the judge, who packs more establishment punch? Undoubtedly, it's the bigger, more entrenched law firm that stands out, dwarfing the smaller players.

And who shares a more personal connection with the judge? Opting for a smaller law firm might mean your attorney barely knows the judge, let alone shares a buddy-buddy rapport. But with a larger, more established firm and a seasoned attorney, the judge is likely to be on a first-name basis with your attorney, having crossed paths in various cases over time.

The judge specializes in specific case types, just like the attorneys from this firm, and cases of this kind routinely find their way to the judge's docket. This creates plenty of interactions between the big firm litigator and the judge, possibly including shared stories and even time spent in social circles, making them quite the chums.

Is there an establishment-infused judicial response to lender-borrower disputes? Well, when someone borrows money, we all know the deal: it needs to be paid back. This is where the establishment firmly plants its flag. The law enforces it, and there's an inherent expectation of a smooth repayment.

Yet, complications can arise due to the lender's conduct, disrupting that smooth ride. Even the hint that the establishment entity messed up can raise eyebrows. How could a major institution drop the ball, right?

Enter lender liability, a body of law amalgamated from assorted liability theories based on contract, tort, and other common law and statutes. The common element that unifies these theories is that they are asserted against lenders, typically large financial institutions. But most judges find it tricky to apply lender liability precedents, primarily because the court tends to take an establishment stance on most matters. Who wants to complicate things, anyway?

A clearer example is seen in cases of legal malpractice. Litigators and attorneys, in all their forms, make mistakes more often than you can shake a stick at. However, they're often reluctant to challenge one of their own in court. And when they do take a non-establishment stand against another attorney by filing a lawsuit, the courts often lean toward finding the accused attorney fully competent, no matter the damage they may have caused.

The more establishment elements you have on your side, the clearer the path to your case's outcome. Opting for a larger law firm floods your strategy with establishment vigor and advantages. But as we discussed earlier, be prepared for some sky-high bills, unless, of course, you're part of the establishment yourself, armed with the deep pockets and enduring relationships needed to negotiate this intriguing landscape.

Chapter 59

Transactional Attorneys: Your Checkpoint to Litigation

§

TRANSACTIONAL ATTORNEYS ARE A UNIQUE BREED, SERVING AS THE gatekeepers to your next legal journey. They can either pave the way for a seamless transaction or create an on-ramp to litigation trouble—or fall somewhere in between.

Let me tell you about Bernie Shafran, a real estate transactional attorney who's not just a legend but also a dear friend. He's a master in negotiating deals, keeping his clients out of trouble through well-crafted documents, and his unrivaled demeanor during transactions ensures the deal is consummated. Bernie is the guy who can smooth over an unexpected storm, and his clients can rely on him without hesitation.

I've witnessed him stride into numerous high-stakes commercial real estate closings in a single day, and let me tell you, he commands the room, instilling confidence in all parties involved. When you select a transactional attorney, remember, it's not merely about finding someone who drafts good documents.

Ladies and gentlemen, here's the essence of it all: Hiring a competent transactional attorney with a blend of legal knowledge, deal savvy, and people skills can be your lifeline. This isn't just any advice; it's your ace in the hole when it comes to avoiding the treacherous waters of litigation.

You've got a skilled attorney who doesn't just know the law but also understands the nuances of the deal and has a knack for handling people. That's the winning trifecta for a top-notch transactional attorney. They're not merely about putting ink on paper; they're about crafting documents that serve as a sturdy shield against potential legal quagmires. This attorney acts as the guardian of your interests in the realm of agreements and contracts, serving as your frontline defense against litigation.

Never underestimate the importance of a well-rounded transactional attorney. They should be more than just drafters of solid agreements; they need to navigate the complexities of your deals and interact with people using finesse. This combination serves as your hidden backstop, protecting you from the perils of stumbling toward litigation.

Chapter 60

The Electronic Court System:
Your Tool for Staying in the Know

§

T HE RISE OF ELECTRONIC COURT SYSTEMS AND DIGITAL TECHNOLOGY has catapulted us into a new era of efficiency in legal case management. It's not just an upgrade; it's a game changer. Picture this: effortless document filing, timely notifications for hearings and trials, smooth tracking of crucial dates, and an organized archive of case documents at your fingertips.

But let's rewind to the not-so-distant past, where everything revolved around manual labor—paper documents, handwritten calendar entries, and a whole lot of grunt work. Case management felt like trying to juggle an array of unrelated objects, often leaving clients in the dark about their own cases. Attorneys, more often than not, doled out information in dribs and drabs, not because they were gatekeepers but because the cumbersomeness of case management made it impractical to share every nitty-gritty detail.

Clients had no choice but to lean heavily on their attorneys to navigate the convoluted maze of documents, deadlines, and court appearances. Sadly, this often led to clients being inadvertently sidelined.

But then enter the electronic court system, a true revolution in the world of case management. Attorneys now wield the power to log in and access every single document associated with a case—whether it's their own filings, documents from opposing counsel, court records, or a detailed history of past and upcoming events. This system also sends timely notifications for new document filings and impending court proceedings.

Now brace yourself for the real equalizer: the electronic court system isn't some exclusive club for attorneys—it's open to you too!

All you need to do is ask your attorney to set you up or just take the reins yourself. By subscribing, you're sidestepping any inclination your litigator may have to keep you in the dark. Whether it's a conscious effort on their part to keep you at arm's length or just an old habit, you now have the power to stay informed about every aspect of your case's history and its notification.

You deserve access to every document filed, a comprehensive record of past and future court appearances, and the convenience of court-issued e-notifications for upcoming events. These are indispensable tools for staying on top of your case.

Being privy to due dates, especially those concerning your attorney's filing responses and hearing dates, is absolutely crucial. For instance, if you're served with a lawsuit, simply log in. You'll find the filing date, the lawsuit itself, proof of service documents, and you can effortlessly calculate the deadline for your attorney's required response. Suddenly, you're not just a passenger; you're in the driver's seat.

Now you can actively collaborate with your attorney, engaging in open discussions about the case. You can inquire about their response plan, the time required for drafting, and express your desire for a review and revision period before filings. In essence, you're setting performance milestones just by asking a few seemingly innocuous questions.

You might even help prevent a number of potential problems, like litigator procrastination or your attorney even missing filing an answer altogether. Your simple inquiries essentially lead to your litigator providing and hopefully living up to a schedule.

This dynamic transforms your attorney-client relationship into a true partnership where you both work together toward a common goal.

Embracing the electronic court system empowers you to seize control of your case, all while providing your attorney with an extra tool for efficient case management. It's a win-win solution that benefits everyone involved.

Chapter 61

From Chaos to Clarity:
How Transcripts Illuminate Murky Memories

§

STEP INTO THE COURTROOM—A CACOPHONY OF VOICES COLLIDING, attorneys fervently presenting their cases, judges interjecting with wisdom or a hint of scolding, litigants finding moments to speak, and even the court clerk chiming in. With six voices orchestrating what can feel like chaos, it's no surprise that questions linger after even the most orderly hearings. Who said what precisely? When are the upcoming dates and times? That crucial point you grasped during the hearing—has it slipped away, jeopardizing your case?

Courtrooms—at times—transform into arenas of fireworks, laden with jargon, cryptic references, mumbling, or moments of confusion, leaving you yearning for a rewind button or a post-game analysis. As you play Monday morning quarterback with your litigator, there's no way to replay that hearing productively, and time travel remains elusive. But fear not, there's a solution, and it's even better than time travel—it's having a live recording or transcript of the hearing.

Courts usually collaborate with approved transcription companies who can procure the digital recording, transcribe it, and email you the transcript with an index of keywords spoken during the hearing, complete with page numbers for easy reference. And then lights! Camera! Action! Those cuttings left on the floor just might contain essential case information and clues that could significantly bolster your position.

In this meticulously choreographed script, all the hearing's players are listed, akin to characters in a play. You can see who said what and precisely what they said. With expedited same-day services, albeit at a higher cost, as well as three-day and one-week turnaround options, it's a remarkably cost-effective tool to enhance your case management and understanding. You can review the transcript, share it with your litigator, and discuss any pertinent thoughts or questions you may have.

But in this riveting drama, diving into transcripts isn't just a stroll down memory lane—it's your backstage pass to the gritty truth. Transcripts make you the fact-checker, unmasking discrepancies in the judge's and attorneys' scripts. It's like having a director's cut of the legal drama, laying bare every statement, argument, and decision. This isn't your run-of-the-mill fact-checking; it's a legal reality check, ensuring the system stays honest.

And when it comes to assessing your legal team's strategy, these transcripts are your script supervisor, flagging any unexpected plot twists or hasty edits. But that's not all. They're your magnifying glass for spotting mistakes and calling out inaccuracies mid-performance. Think of them as your legal highlight reel—every misstep caught on tape. Now when the plot takes an unexpected turn and you're facing an unfavorable outcome, just one line in the transcript could provide the basis for an encore, a golden ticket for an appeal. Uncover the courtroom bloopers and watch inconsistencies in the legal script work in your favor.

And when you're in the director's chair, navigating the twists and turns, those transcripts become your secret weapon. Want to set the record straight with your attorney? It's your playbook for enhanced communication.

But beware the blame game! If your attorney tries to pin a lousy outcome on the judge or opposing counsel, those transcripts become your courtroom arsenal. No more passing the buck—wave those transcripts like a legal sword of truth. Hold your litigator accountable because in this blockbuster legal saga, you're the star.

And as you gear up for future hearings, those transcripts are your backstage rehearsal footage. Know the lines, understand the past performances, and strut into court like a seasoned actor. It's the peace of mind you've been waiting for—an empowering script for your complex legal journey. So, grab those transcripts, cue the dramatic soundtrack, and let the legal show go on!

Chapter 62

Empower Yourself:
Researching Your Own Legal Battles

§

W HEN YOU FIRST LAY EYES ON A LEGAL BRIEF, IT'S LIKE DIVING
headfirst into the deep end of the legal pool. It's filled with
references to precedent court cases, legal jargon, and interpretations that
seem to exist in their own universe.

But wait, don't tune out just yet. Even if you're not a legal expert, there's a
lot you can do to navigate these treacherous waters.

Sometimes, all it takes is a keen eye to spot what's different between your
case and the ones cited in the brief. It's not unheard of for your attorney,
or whoever they delegated this task to, to pick cases that are only loosely
related to your situation. Clients often want to trust that their attorney
did the best job possible, but it's not only beneficial to double-check their
work in this area today, it's crucial.

U.S. District Judge P. Kevin Castel in Manhattan recently dropped
the hammer on two New York lawyers who dared to submit a legal
brief sporting six imaginary case citations conjured up by an artificial
intelligence chatbot, ChatGPT.

But not to worry, the legal maestros swear they had an alibi, no bad
intentions: "We made a good faith mistake in failing to believe that a
piece of technology could be making up cases out of whole cloth," the
firm's statement said.[17]

Now my fellow warriors of justice, in addition to keeping an eagle eye on
the potential shoddiness of your counsel's case selection (or whoever they

pawn the work off to), you must also ensure their techno-dependence doesn't accidentally turn the courtroom into a psychedelic circus of hallucinations. Because if it does, the judge might give your counsel the side-eye and ask, "What exactly is he smoking?" Or, brace yourself, your case might just crash and burn faster than a lead balloon. Stay vigilant, my legal compatriots!

You can start by copying and pasting those cited cases into your favorite search engine. You'll be amazed at the wealth of articles discussing the implications of these cases in plain English. Many law firms put out articles about common business litigation issues, serving as a blend of scholarly analysis and promotional material.

But that's just the tip of the iceberg. You can subscribe to online case law databases and dive deeper into reading the full cases cited in your brief to see how closely they align with your situation.

So far, I've talked about proofing and double-checking the legal references your attorney cited, but is that all you can do? Not by a long shot!

If you believe there's a law out there that could tip the scales in your favor, just type your sentiment into a search engine. You'd be surprised at what pops up. I once had a fee application objection in a Chapter 11 case, and the opposing attorney wanted me to pay $50,000 for his work in defending his exorbitant fee application. It seemed outrageous. But with a bit of online digging, I found legal arguments that shot down his case like a rocket.

In another instance, after converting a Brooklyn chocolate factory warehouse to forty-five loft-style condominiums and selling out, I put an end to fifteen years of trailing litigation with its condo board. How? By supplying my attorney with a case that I came across during a round of research. He presented it to opposing counsel, who was itching for a trial, and we settled a multi-million dollar claim for $100,000 within a week.

I'm suggesting another approach—trust your instincts as a layman. If you believe there's an angle worth exploring, start Googling and searching with keywords related to your gut feeling. You might find articles discussing, say, equitable estoppel or promissory estoppel, defenses your attorney never mentioned. Suddenly, you're speaking their language, and they might just say, "I didn't think of that, but it could work."

So, don't be afraid to roll up your sleeves and dive into what may seem like heavyweight legal work. You might not find a knockout punch, but you can certainly help your litigator better prepare for battle. Be bold, and remember, knowledge is power in the legal arena.

Chapter 63

Promises Or Lies: Do They Really Differ In the World of Litigation?

§

IN OUR PREVIOUS DISCUSSION, WE DELVED INTO THE REALM OF litigators spinning tales to entice you into signing that retainer agreement, promising the moon and stars with their expert legal prowess. But what happens when you've already inked the deal, embarked on the legal journey, and realized that your litigator has been peddling empty promises, if not outright lies, about your case?

Allow me to recount a chapter from my own experience. One of my companies was knee-deep in Chapter 11, and my attorney, with all the confidence in the world, assured me that he could mount a defense to suspend the required $150,000 monthly interest payments to a lender-creditor.

He confidently mentioned a court motion that would make it happen and even charged me handsomely for his research efforts, sending me a case called FAMILY PHARMACY, INC., ET AL., Debtors. Case No. 18-60521, as precedent.

This litigator was the epitome of authority. With forty years of seasoned experience in the concrete jungle of New York City, he possessed a gravitas that made you think twice about questioning him. In such moments, we often find ourselves wondering if we're qualified to question a so-called expert. After all, he had presented me with this case, and surely it must align with his confident legal opinion.

Yet, as I simply played the kid's game of "Spot the Difference" and compared it to my own situation, I discovered glaring differences. I penned him an email, my skepticism palpable:

I skimmed it and it has little to do with my case...

...it's a case about the accumulation of post-petition default rate interest when a borrower was current on his payments until after the petition, and the lender never sent notice declaring a default either... so the court saw that as a waiver... and then the lender never properly accelerated...

So I see no latitude to extrapolate much from this case...

It was clear: the attorney's promise of interest payment suspension was emptier than a desert mirage. In fact, it had all the makings of a well-crafted lie. And it wasn't just limited to this instance; throughout his employ on the case, this litigator made a series of grandiose assurances:

- You'll be able to draw a salary from the building's cash flow during Chapter 11.

- Your management company is entitled to a management fee for overseeing the building.

- You can pay a loan origination fee from the building's cash flow to refinance.

These promises, while theoretically possible, would never get delivered as they were not inherent procedural rights but rather "asks" subject to the creditor's approval, and since the creditor was known to be contentious, they would predictably never agree. My attorney spun a web of empty promises, leaving me with a bag of hot air and my case hanging in the balance.

It's a common enough occurrence that you should consider every attorney you hire as potentially being a masterful storyteller. The key to a better outcome and managed expectations lies in swift action. Your job is to research the viability of their promises throughout your case.

The moment you sense and confirm that your litigator has promised something but not delivered, consider them a liability to your case. If the liability is deemed to be great, the earlier you cut ties, the better your chances of steering your legal ship back on course.

Chapter 64

Know Your Judge: A Winning Strategy

§

IN THE GRAND THEATER OF THE COURTROOM, JUDGES HOLD THE power to shape your destiny. Behind those formidable robes, they are more than just jurists—they are individuals with their unique quirks and predispositions. Familiarizing yourself with your judge's character, their stance on cases like yours, and your litigator's legal strategy can be your secret weapon.

But beware, there's room for mishaps. Your litigator might boast a track record of handling cases similar to yours before the same judge. They may even have an inkling of the judge's tendencies and proclivities in rendering decisions.

However, if your litigator is a hands-off manager, delegating brief drafting to someone oblivious to the judge's idiosyncrasies, and then fails to scrutinize the submission before filing, he could find himself boxed into a corner during oral arguments. His ability to articulate arguments effectively in court might be hindered due to a filing lacking the essential precedents required for victory.

Conversely, your attorney might be exceptionally skilled but oblivious to the judge's thought process, temperament, or customary ruling patterns. What's the game plan in that scenario?

Overlooking the way a judge interprets cases like yours is a huge missed opportunity to advance your legal cause. The judge takes center stage in this legal drama, and it's imperative to waltz in sync with them to secure your objectives and clinch favorable rulings during your stint in court.

You, your litigator, or even a hired researcher can effortlessly access a case law repository and dive into the judge's past rulings on cases resembling yours. This investigative dive can illuminate the judge's inclinations and cast light on the potential trajectory of your case.

The results of this research can serve as a discussion starter with your litigator. They might already be privy to this information, but if not, you're now armed with invaluable insights, giving you a leg up.

- You can gain a more profound grasp of the affirmative defenses that align with the judge's preferences and past rulings.

- Your litigator knows that you're on the same page with the judge's outlook, motivating them to concentrate on a legal strategy, both in pleadings and oral arguments, that resonates with the judge's viewpoint.

In essence, when you shoot your litigator an email stating, "I've unearthed ten seemingly similar cases, and the judge's rulings were consistent each time," you're holding your attorney accountable to the cold, hard truth. This can be an eye-opener, shedding light on whether your attorney had been overly optimistic about your case's strength or perhaps less than honest with you just to secure your retainer and start the billing clock.

As your litigator churns out document drafts, you'll have a keen sense of whether the arguments presented will harmonize with the judge's inclinations. With this knowledge in your arsenal, you will hone the tool of predictability on how your judge may likely rule.

Should you have a cooperative and open working relationship with your attorney, don't hesitate to request case research regarding the judge. Alternatively, you can conduct your own research or enlist the aid of another attorney at a relatively modest cost. Then you can present the results to your litigator, attributing it to your own research to avoid any potential trust issues.

This no-nonsense strategy can exert a monumental influence on your case. Remember, legal proceedings and results are molded by the judge presiding over your matter, and understanding their psyche can be your ticket to courtroom success.

Chapter 65

Guiding Your Attorney
with the Power of Questions

§

E FFECTIVELY MANAGING AND COLLABORATING WITH PEOPLE, whether in a professional setting or at home, often requires more finesse than simply giving them orders. Even with your own children, with whom one may presume you have some authority, demanding, requiring, or commanding rarely gets you very far.

The art of asking questions, however, is a powerful tool for those who are savvy and insightful. Questions initiate a neutral interaction that invites cooperation. If your litigator doesn't appreciate questions or fails to provide satisfactory answers, it might be time to reconsider your choice of legal representation. The ability to ask and answer questions forms the bedrock of a constructive working relationship.

Let's consider a scenario where you believe it would be valuable for your attorney to research and provide you with cases similar to yours that the presiding judge has ruled on. If you were to directly instruct your attorney to do this, it might rub him the wrong way. After all, you're acknowledging your limited legal knowledge and essentially telling the expert what to do—not a recipe for harmony.

Instead, initiate a conversation by inquiring whether your attorney has prior experience with the judge in cases similar to yours. This opens the door for further dialogue. Acknowledge and validate their response and delve deeper by asking about their perspective on researching recent decisions related to your judge and comparable cases.

If they express a willingness to proceed, that's fantastic. If not, express your keen interest in the idea and inquire about how you can contribute to the research effort. This subtle approach guides your litigator toward a task that you believe will enhance your case, all while preserving a collaborative and tension-free atmosphere.

The aforementioned exchange demonstrates a brief interaction using a simple yet potent communication technique. As you journey through this book, you'll encounter various invaluable strategies for managing your case. You can apply this communication technique to discuss other strategic case management concepts.

When you're exploring ideas or strategies, ask your litigator for their thoughts, as we discussed earlier. By doing so, you express an interest in their input, which can alleviate potential resistance. If they initially oppose a particular strategy you're proposing and you are committed to the idea, reiterate your strong belief in its potential benefits for the case or your interest in pursuing it to enhance your peace of mind. Then ask once more if they would be willing to collaborate in implementing it. If they remain resistant, tell them with a sigh that you just feel it needs to be done your way to assuage your feelings. Who can reasonably object to your feelings?

The approaches of asking questions, anticipating resistance, defusing tension, and enlisting your litigator's cooperation are genuinely effective ways to navigate the world. This method, rooted in inquiry and goodwill, yields far better results than giving orders.

It might seem counterintuitive and a bit frustrating, given that you're not just shelling out a grand per hour to a service provider who may be reluctant to assist you, but you also find yourself playing the role of a psychologist, delicately navigating the relationship. However, the overarching objective is twofold: acknowledge the current reality and strive for effectiveness.

Harness the power of this approach to your advantage in your attorney-client relationship and beyond!

Chapter 66

Charlatans, Flakes, and Chokers:
Zero Tolerance

§

S O, YOU'VE DONE YOUR BEST TO SCREEN YOUR CURRENT LEGAL TEAM for any of these unsavory traits. Yet, it happens—some of these individuals manage to pull off a convincing act, getting hired under the guise of competence, only to unveil their true flaky and unreliable selves later on, often leading to dire consequences through their choke moments.

I recall an attorney I once hired; he was a gritty fighter, highly intelligent, and operated his own successful practice spanning multiple states. His initial grasp of complex cases was impressive, as he could easily digest and organize the various facets of a case, outlining defenses and all possible permutations in a coherent manner. His prowess in conversation was undeniable, but his actions told a different story.

When it came to producing quality documents and meeting deadlines, he consistently fell short. Promises to show up at meetings or even hearings were frequently broken. This pattern wasn't unique to me; he had a habit of doing this to numerous clients. Each time he messed up, he'd have a seemingly plausible explanation for why it was ultimately beneficial for the client, even if his "work-arounds" often required five times the effort compared to meeting deadlines in the first place.

This attorney had a hefty caseload, and he thrived on signing up new clients and orchestrating conversations in high-pressure situations to present himself as the savior. However, he pathologically struggled with following through, showing up when needed, or effectively delegating to his staff.

Stories of charlatans, flakes, and chokers are abundant. We encounter them in various aspects of life, both professionally and personally. We're all familiar with the old proverb: Fool me once, shame on you; fool me twice, shame on me.

In the realm of litigation, the stakes are exceptionally high. It's crucial to be as preemptive as possible when selecting your legal team. If one of these flakes manages to slip through and ends up on your team but falters just once, do not grant them a second chance. Swiftly cut ties and part ways to minimize your losses.

Navigating your case also entails addressing wounds promptly— cauterizing them to prevent further damage.

Chapter 67

The Invasive Odyssey of Discovery: Where All Secrets Are Laid Bare

§

LADIES AND GENTLEMEN, BRACE YOURSELVES FOR A JOURNEY INTO the wild world of discovery in state court litigation. It's a legal expedition that lays bare the underbelly of everyone's life for the world to scrutinize. And let me tell you, it's not a one-way street of intrusion; both the plaintiff and defendant get to feel the heat of discovery, much like the scrutiny a debtor faces in bankruptcy court with a 2004 motion and exam, which we will explore later.

1. Interrogatories: Unmasking Strategies and Secrets
First on our list are interrogatories. These are written queries flung from one litigant to the other, diving deep into the intricacies of their case. It's akin to rattling a hornet's nest of strategies, hidden agendas, and past decisions.

2. Depositions: Grillin' and Chillin' in the Hot Seat
Then there are depositions, a legal equivalent of the Spanish Inquisition. Parties, witnesses, and experts face grueling questioning under oath, every word meticulously recorded. Litigants are laid bare, their credibility sliced and diced.

3. Document Requests: The Paper Chase Begins
Litigants can demand access to relevant documents, leaving no stone unturned. Contracts, emails, letters, or any written or electronic evidence become fair game. Your paper trail is exposed, ready for dissection.

4. Requests for Admissions: Confess or Concede

Requests for admissions put litigants in a tight spot. Admit the wrong thing, and you're in hot water. It's a high-stakes game of legal cat and mouse, where every admission carries weight.

5. Physical and Mental Examinations: Probing the Physical and Mental Depths

Things get personal when litigants request physical or mental examinations by professionals. It's like a deep dive into your physical and mental state, minus the glitz of a reality show.

6. Requests for Inspection: Unlocking Pandora's Box

Litigants can demand access to and examination of physical property, premises, or objects tied to the case. No secret stays hidden, every hidden treasure is unearthed.

7. Subpoenas: Summoning the Witnesses

Subpoenas are court orders that rope in third parties. Non-parties, beware. Your secrets are fair game too. Medical records, employment records, and the words of witnesses—all exposed.

It's a no-holds-barred showdown, and both litigants are in the hot seat. They're mandated to spill the beans, and nothing is off-limits. Your strategies, your history, your reputation—all are on full display.

You're not merely posing questions; you're extracting answers, and you better deliver. Nobody's past is safe, no aspect of your life is immune to scrutiny, and no secret stays buried. This is the gritty reality of litigation, where everyone's laundry is aired, and the stakes soar sky-high.

Chapter 68

Depositions: The Invasive Legal Safari

$

PICTURE THIS, FOLKS: DEPOSITIONS, THEY'RE LIKE EMBARKING ON A legal safari, a deep expedition into the wilds of your personal life. Once you step into that room, you're caught up in the thicket of the legal jungle.

First things first, they swear you in. You're taking an oath, committing to spill the beans, and there's no wiggle room. It's like entering the truth zone, where lies don't stand a chance.

The inquisitors, those attorneys, are there, lurking like legal predators. They've got a barrage of questions lined up, and trust me, they're not holding back. The lead inquisitor has a thick script pre-prepared for him by one of his understudies, a series of questions designed to lead you down a well-camouflaged path to trip you up, sharpened bamboo sticks at the bottom of a Vietnamese jungle pit to break your fall. It's akin to a scene from a gritty noir jungle crime thriller, but this is your reality.

You're under the spotlight with a pack of hungry attorneys ready to sink their teeth into you. They'll dig into your past, your secrets, your actions— nothing is sacred. Think of it as a full-scale interrogation by a seasoned detective.

And where does this all go down? Typically in some attorney's private lair, their office. It's their territory, their turf, and you're the unsuspecting prey. This isn't your typical chitchat; it's a high-stakes showdown, and the atmosphere can be downright intense.

Every word you utter, every pause, every nervous twitch—it's all on the record. A court reporter is there, and they're rolling the cameras. It's not just a conversation; it's potential ammo for the battlefield of the courtroom.

The stakes are astronomical because that deposition transcript and video footage can make or break your case when you get to court. If you change your tune on the stand, they'll whip out that transcript and nail you to the wall. "But didn't you say this under oath?" Game over.

So, my friends, here's the deal: Depositions aren't just for friendly chitchat. They're a full-blown safari, a journey deep into your life, your history, your secrets, both business and personal, and your credibility. It's a legal battleground where words become weapons, and you're in the crosshairs. Enter this jungle with caution because, in the realm of depositions, there's no room for half-truths or dodging the tough questions. It's all or nothing, and the legal predators are watching.

Chapter 69

Legal Warfare: Legal Tactics to Systemically Decimate Businesses

§

L ITIGATION, TYPICALLY VIEWED AS A MEANS TO RESOLVE DISPUTES, often takes on a more sinister role—a quick-money grab scheme where one party initiates a lawsuit with the intent to cash in swiftly. The endgame? Either securing an early settlement or taking the case all the way to trial. But beneath this façade lies a darker side of litigation where it's wielded as a weapon to ruthlessly crush businesses, adversaries, and even clients.

Let me paint a vivid picture with the story of a client who sought my advice when the game was almost over. He was a successful owner, builder, and developer who had undertaken ten projects, each valued between $25 million and $40 million upon completion. These prime projects were either in the midst of construction or completed well-performing residential rental properties.

Then out of the blue, a private non-bank lender, a New York City hedge fund led by hungry guys, decided to play a back-alley game. They picked up the phone and began whispering like concerned colleagues to each of the developer's lenders: "Hey, we just received a funding request from [Name]. Do any of you have an outstanding loan with him? We've got some insider info that he's in financial dire straits, and his entire property portfolio could crumble like a house of cards."

This hedge fund contacted all ten lenders, instilling seeds of worry about the developer's otherwise robust assets. Regardless of the true performance of these assets, lenders by nature had to be proactive to anticipate and circumvent any non-performance of their loans. For even one missed monthly mortgage payment is often a harbinger of a default and further degradation of their loan/asset. One by one, the lenders succumbed to the hedge fund's sly tactics, and the fund proceeded to purchase, directly or through controlled straw men, $250 million worth of my client's mortgages from his former lenders at significant discounts.

The domino effect was set in motion as per the hedge fund's wicked plan. They claimed a loan default on one property, filed a pre-foreclosure lawsuit, took control of the building through a court-appointed receiver, and systematically dismantled my client's empire, one asset at a time. He found himself ill-equipped to wage a successful legal battle on ten fronts, as each property was ensnared in its unique pre-foreclosure and bankruptcy litigation quagmire.

My client was an upright individual who conducted his business with integrity, utilized his creative talents to build something of value, paid his employees, contractors, and professionals fairly, operated impeccably maintained properties, and gave back to his community through philanthropy.

However, a ruthless bunch of guys shaded by faceless business entities harnessed the power of litigation to devalue and wrest his properties away, leaving him with nothing. The hedge fund's representatives, for their part, took refuge behind the legal provisions in the loan documents, claiming they merely exercised their legal rights. After all, it's business, right? But it's the point where the law meets cannibalism, and it's brutally cutthroat.

This developer, once wealthy and charitable, was reduced to a broken, impoverished man. If he ever manages to rebuild, he'll be starting from scratch with nothing but the hard-earned doctorate in life experience he picked up along the way.

From the very moment he signed those loan documents before his first building ever stood, the odds were stacked against him. Brace yourselves as we delve into the murky territory where the law and the courts inadvertently played a pivotal role in this man's financial demise.

Chapter 70

The Brutal Business Battlefield: Litigation and Its Widespread Fallout

$

LADIES AND GENTLEMEN, LET'S STRIP AWAY THE LEGAL JARGON AND delve into the savage world of litigation and how it can unleash a barrage of chaos on businesses. It's like a legal thunderstorm with far-reaching consequences that can shake the very foundations of a company. Here are the harsh realities and a few extra punches:

1. Financial Bloodletting: Litigation doesn't just nibble away at a business's finances; it can take a big menacing bite. Legal fees, court costs, and potential settlements or judgments can bleed a company's coffers dry. It's like a financial ambush that leaves a scar.

2. Operational Quagmire: Litigation isn't a walk in the park; it's more like quicksand. It swallows valuable time and energy that should be dedicated to daily operations and strategic planning. The result? Decreased productivity and a management team left wrestling with legal alligators.

3. Reputation Demolition: Think of litigation as a wrecking ball for a company's reputation. Negative media buzz and public perception can batter trust among customers, suppliers, investors, and other stakeholders. Your pristine image? It might just crumble.

4. Competitive Chokehold: Litigation can feel like a straitjacket, limiting a business's ability to compete in the market. It introduces uncertainties that tangle business relationships, contracts, and growth opportunities. It's like trying to sprint with your shoelaces tied together.

5. Asset Depreciation: Here's a new twist: Litigation devalues a company's assets. When assets must be sold off due to legal pressures, they may fetch lower prices. It's like selling your vintage car for a fraction of its worth in a forced garage sale.

6. Regulatory Crosshairs: Litigation can put you squarely in the regulatory spotlight. Government agencies may start sniffing around, and that can spell more legal and financial woes.

7. Employee Turbulence: The courtroom saga can send shockwaves through your workforce. Employees may worry about job security and the company's stability. Morale can take a nosedive, and productivity may plummet.

8. Insurance Upheaval: The financial risks linked to litigation can shake up your insurance policies and premiums. You might find yourself forking over more money to keep your coverage intact.

9. Legal Precedent: The outcome of your legal tangle might set a precedent, rewriting the rules for your industry and how you conduct business.

10. Resource Reallocation: Money and time spent on litigation could have been invested in other crucial areas like innovation, marketing, and staff development. Instead, you're battling in the legal arena.

11. Settlements and Judgments: If the courtroom verdict falls against you, be prepared to open your wallet wide. Settlements and judgments can land on your doorstep, demanding a hefty payout.

12. Intellectual Property Wars: For companies wrestling in intellectual property disputes, litigation is often the arena where patents, trademarks, or copyrights are defended. It's a necessary battle, but one that can drain resources and time.

13. Contractual Collateral Damage: Litigation can rupture existing contracts, be it partnerships or supply agreements. Business relationships may fray at the edges.

14. Long-term Legal Obligations: Any agreements or court-ordered actions resulting from litigation may lock your company into long-term legal obligations, affecting future operations.

15. Industry and Market Quakes: Litigation involving a key player in an industry can send shockwaves through regulations and market dynamics, altering the entire sector's landscape.

16. Emotional Uproar: Don't underestimate the emotional toll. Stress and anxiety plague business owners and decision-makers, affecting their well-being.

In the savage realm of litigation, companies are thrown into the heart of the storm, facing a relentless legal tempest. The effects go far beyond the courtroom; they infiltrate every aspect of a business's life. It's a savage reality check, where strategic planning and risk management are the armor during this ferocious legal battle.

Chapter 71

Financial Warfare:
When Borrowing Takes a Savage Turn

$

IN THE CUTTHROAT WORLD OF BUSINESS, INDIVIDUALS OFTEN SEEK out lenders with impeccable reputations, well-established names, and slick marketing campaigns promising unwavering integrity. Think of those iconic Wells Fargo ads with horse-drawn wagons radiating trust and reliability. These are the lenders that people flock to, drawn in by their polished marketing. Wells Fargo, with its 160-year history and a vast network of 5,000 branches across the nation, epitomizes this image.

The expectation when choosing these lenders is that they will uphold the highest standards of legality throughout the loan term. If financial trouble arises, borrowers believe these lenders will stand by their side to navigate the turbulent waters. It's a picture painted by clever marketing.

However, the harsh reality is that these lenders often lack a true commitment to borrowers. Their name and image are more about branding than actual substance. When things get tough, they're nowhere to be found.

Once a loan is inked and funded, it's often bundled, sold, securitized, or transferred, and the original lender's connection to the borrower fades rapidly. At the slightest hint of trouble, even as minor as a single late payment, the loan may be swiftly transferred to a more aggressive entity skilled in extracting profits from distressed borrowers.

This new loan holder often has every incentive to declare the loan in default as their business model thrives on collecting default interest rates, which can skyrocket far above the original loan rate. In New York, it's often a staggering 24 percent per annum.

The borrower, who previously held warm and folksy notions about lenders like Wells Fargo and the AmericanWest, finds themselves out in the elements, hog-tied by their new lender. The new lender is circling the wagons and looking to pounce on the borrower's assets.

In many states, in the case of a home loan default, mandatory settlement conferences are held to encourage settlement and loan modifications, ensuring a fair and balanced approach to prevent lenders from exploiting distressed homeowners.

However, in the world of commercial real estate and business loans, where documents are filled with clauses intended to shield the lender, there are no such checks and balances to protect the borrower. Here, the lender can simply claim a default, file a lawsuit and an ex parte motion in court (without notifying the borrower), and, based on a buried provision in the loan documents allowing this action, the court is likely to grant the lender's request for a court-appointed receiver to take control of the business, asset, or commercial real estate during litigation. Borrowers often wonder how they unwittingly signed away so much of their power.

Commercial loan documents are often an imposing stack of papers, sometimes a foot thick. Borrowers' counsel rarely delves into the fine print due to lenders' unyielding resistance to substantial changes. Lenders operate with a "take it or leave it" attitude, and it's understandable, as they demand every protection. Borrowers, on the other hand, who are strapped for cash and desperate to access funds, often shrug off any legalese buried in the documents, rationalizing that none of it will ever apply to them.

Because these loan documents are so heavily skewed in the lender's favor, the lender can charge into court and blindside borrowers instantly.

Imagine one of those massive bicycle races with hundreds of cyclists pedaling together in formation, and one malicious bystander sabotages a single cyclist by sticking a rod in their spokes, causing a catastrophic crash of all the riders. That's the power of a commercial lender.

In the world of commercial lending, there are typically no pre-lawsuit conferences, and so the lender can unilaterally run into court, file a lawsuit, and induce the court to appoint a third-party receiver to seize and run your assets through the time of adjudication. It turns out you agreed to this nightmare. As a result, the lender feels entirely justified giving you such a wakeup call.

Now you find yourself in a massive financial crash because the truth is your business, and the many parts of its operations are more analogous to many bike riders that comprise a flock flowing in cadence. If one part of your business takes a hit, it might very well bring down your whole enterprise.

The litigation-crashing model is the modus operandi for the financial industry, and bringing borrowers to their knees is often the objective. Taking control of a borrower's assets marks the beginning of the end (for the borrower), and the initial lenders who lured borrowers in with their marketing are no longer in the picture.

The new lenders' primary concern is to deliver high returns to their investors, while the law and the court system offer little protection to borrowers, even if they are caught in a seemingly predatory web. In reality, the courts helped create this monster and exacerbated the situation because of delayed adjudication. The multi-year adjudication delay hurts the borrower or the lender, depending on whether the asset has equity or is underwater.

If the business was viable and the default was gratuitous in order to crash the company, then two years to adjudicate will often sap the remaining viability of the business, and it will disappear. If the business or asset is underwater in value, the two years to adjudicate leaves the lender with a less valuable asset and more collateral damage than was present at the original default date. The court's inefficiency and denial of due process (speedy adjudication) usually hurts everyone except the predatory lender who thrives on delays, since their claim for default interest accumulates at 24 percent with each passing day.

I once calculated the aftermath of a legal assault by a loan buyer. It was an asset rich in equity with no distress issues. The initial default notice and ex parte receiver motion initiated a legal journey that ultimately led the borrower to lose $12 million in equity, while the loan buyer, the mastermind behind this financial warfare, netted approximately $3 million.

Destroy one party's $12 million for the raiding pirate to gain $3 million. The courts are rife with such plunder, and these so-called businessmen are supported and empowered by the legal system.

Business is tough, but the courtroom can be even rougher!

Chapter 72

Flip the Script:
Seize the Game to Your Advantage

§

THAT'S RIGHT, WE'VE LAID BARE SOME OF THE SYSTEMIC INJUSTICES that could make anyone see red. And sure, it's tempting to get all hot and bothered about the supposed unfairness in the system. But remember, you're not here for an emotional thrill ride; you're here to get the job done. In litigation, that means disentangling yourself from the other side in the least agonizing way possible. As for all that injustice, well, it's just background noise on this battlefield.

This isn't about whining and pointing fingers at the zany rules, both written and unwritten, that dictate the courtroom choreography. Nope, this is about efficiency and being in control. So, let's ditch the feelings and assessments of perceived injustice and home in on the hard-earned lessons you've picked up along the way.

For instance, picture a daring litigator crashing the motion scene, dropping a fresh motion right in the middle of another hearing. It was a gutsy move, and it paid off. The judge was on board and decided that motion then and there, ignoring the rulebook that required ample notice time and the right to object in writing. Unfair? Maybe. But it's also a teachable moment. You can crash your opponent's party too. Learn the rules of the game, but don't shy away from bending them a bit to suit your needs. It might not fly in every courtroom, but with the right judge, you could garner the home court advantage.

Now, as for playing the delay game, don't see it as a denial of due process or an injustice. No way. Flip the script. You can use those delay tactics to slow down your opponent's momentum and disrupt their plans.

And here's another trump card: co-counsel. We've discussed it before.

Meeting your co-counsel separately from your litigator can be a tactical maneuver. They might have a different playbook, and after a good heart-to-heart, you can nudge them toward the strategies you think will hit the bulls-eye. And if they're willing to push the boundaries or cozy up to the judge during proceedings, well, they've got the judge's ear.

Now I'm not saying you should go all out with defamation, but if using some hyperbole, character questioning, and a bit of spin can work in your favor, why not shake the character of the other side wherever it's possible? It's all about planting those seeds of doubt in the court's mind.

The bottom line, folks, is to seize control. It's about flipping the script and running the court as best you can. Don't let the system victimize you; make the system work to your advantage. In the realm of litigation, employing the tricks of the trade and sometimes playing a little rough can pave the way to a cleaner victory.

Chapter 73

The Rollercoaster of Litigation: An Emotional Cauldron

$

LADIES AND GENTLEMEN, WHEN YOU STEP INTO THE REALM OF litigation, be prepared for an emotional whirlwind that could rival a Shakespearean drama. It's not just about presenting your case and winning arguments; it's a full-fledged emotional battle. So, let's delve into the cauldron of emotions that simmers in the world of litigation, shall we?

Stress: Ah, stress, the eternal companion of litigation. The uncertainty, financial strain, and daunting legal process often crank up that stress meter.

Anxiety: The fear of defeat, the financial hit, and the no-holds-barred contest can make anxiety your unwelcome friend throughout the process.

Anger: When you're locked in legal combat, anger can rear its head—directed at your adversaries, their legal eagles, or sometimes the very system itself.

Frustration: Ever feel like you're banging your head against a legal wall? That's the frustration that often accompanies this territory.

Sadness: In cases involving personal loss, such as family matters, sadness becomes a heavy cloak to bear.

Fear: The fear of the unknown, be it financial ruin or losing something dear, can send shivers down your spine.

Guilt: Whether it's your involvement in the dispute or its impact on others, guilt can weigh you down.

Regret: It's not uncommon to look back with regret, second-guessing past choices that led you to the courtroom.

Hope: In the legal arena, hope is your beacon in the darkest of hours, the flicker that keeps you going.

Relief: When the gavel falls in your favor or an agreement is reached, a sigh of relief often follows, like a weight lifted off your shoulders.

Confusion: The legal labyrinth can leave you utterly befuddled, questioning what's next and where to turn.

Empowerment: Winning a case or navigating it with poise can make you feel like a legal gladiator, strong and empowered.

Resentment: Oh, the bitterness that sometimes festers, whether it's toward the opposition or the very circumstances that led to this legal showdown.

Tension: High-stakes litigation can stretch your nerves as taut as piano wires.

Overwhelm: The avalanche of paperwork, court appearances, and deadlines can be overwhelming, to say the least.

Nervousness: Court dates, hearings, and legal showdowns often dial up the nervousness, no matter how experienced you are.

Vindication: Victory is elusive, but it's sweet, like a sip of fine wine, and it brings that sense of vindication, a toast to your triumph.

Desperation: In dire situations, desperation can be your unwelcome companion, urging you to grasp at straws for a glimmer of hope.

Isolation: The stress and isolation that can come with litigation can be as challenging as the legal battle itself.

Exhaustion: The courtroom battle can be utterly draining, both physically and emotionally, leaving you feeling bone-weary.

Indeed, my friends, there you have it, the emotional smorgasbord of litigation. It's not just a legal duel; it's a rollercoaster of feelings that can leave you spinning.

Nearly all of the above emotions are downers, but the two that seem like winners are not anywhere near a clear positive.

Victory, you see, is the elusive treasure buried amidst these tumultuous waves, often slipping through the grasp of both sides.

Hope becomes your lighthouse when the storms are at their fiercest, guiding you through the turbulent sea of emotions.

So, keep this in mind as you embark on this war known as the pursuit of justice. It's a battlefield of feelings, and your journey will be filled with many more lows than highs.

Chapter 74

The Strategic Paranoia:
A Crucial Weapon in Your Legal Arsenal

§

LISTEN UP, MY COMRADES, BECAUSE, IN THE REALM OF LITIGATION, A keen sense of healthy paranoia and suspicion isn't just a good idea; it's your most formidable weapon. Imagine you're playing high-stakes chess, but it's not your average game—it's a contest in the fourth dimension. You've got to plan multiple moves ahead, anticipate every twist and turn, and brace for the unexpected. Litigation, my friends, is a battleground, and you must keep your guard up at all times. This is your fight, and everyone else is but a pawn in the game.

1. The Legal War Zone
Litigation is not a genteel affair; it's an all-out war waged in the courts. In this relentless battlefield, your suspicions and calculated paranoia become your armor. They empower you to spot traps and pitfalls that others might overlook. Trusting blindly is a perilous mistake; vigilance is your shield against the storms of litigation.

2. Trust, But Verify—With a Sledgehammer
You've heard the old saying: trust, but verify. In the legal arena, trust is a precious currency that should be spent cautiously. Every claim, motive, and fact need to pass through the fiery crucible of scrutiny. Trusting without verification is akin to heading into battle with a blindfold, and we're not about to let that happen.

3. Faith, A Double-Edged Sword
Faith in humanity is admirable, but in the world of litigation, it's a

double-edged sword. Place no faith in any soul involved—not in your legal team, not in the opposition, and certainly not in the judge. Blind faith is like throwing open the gates of your castle to the enemy.

4. Murphy's Law, the Uninvited Guest

Ah, Murphy's Law—if anything can go wrong, it often will, especially in the convoluted realm of litigation. Your healthy paranoia and suspicion act as safety nets, allowing you to foresee the unforeseen and plan for every possible contingency. In this arena, you're your own first line of defense.

5. Mastering the Symphony

Think of litigation as orchestrating a symphony on four stages. It's not merely plotting individual notes; you must anticipate the harmonies and dissonances, the cascading impact of your legal maneuvers, and the court's possible responses. It's akin to conducting a symphony where each note echoes into the future, and your meticulous orchestration keeps you in tune with the evolving dynamics of the legal performance.

6. Claiming Your Rightful Place

In this legal war zone, don't consider yourself a mere pawn; see yourself as a potential king. Your battlefield may have been tumultuous and your forces may have been decimated, but even the lowly pawn can ascend to the throne and salvage the case. Your path to resolution may be arduous, but it's not impossible.

7. A Chess Grandmaster Indeed

You're not just a player; you're a chess grandmaster, thinking multiple moves ahead and preparing for any possible outcome. Even if original thinking and conclusions elude you because, after all, you're not an attorney, you can still question and filter every piece of information that comes your way. This book is your treasure trove, providing valuable tools to hold your service providers accountable.

In the world of litigation, your healthy paranoia and suspicion are your most trusted allies. They keep you vigilant, and as the old army adage goes, "Be all that you can be." Here it's not about pessimism; it's about relentless preparation. It's your fight, and you're in it to win.

Chapter 75

Measuring Success:
Stats in Sports and the Legal Arena

§

YOU SEE, MY FRIENDS, WHEN IT COMES TO SPORTS, STATISTICS RULE the arena. Be it basketball, football, soccer, baseball, or ice hockey, these numbers tell the tale of a player's performance, wins, and losses. They provide the metrics for comparison and the insights into a player's strengths and weaknesses. But let's shift gears and dive into the world of boxing—a sport that's more akin to what litigators do in the legal arena.

In boxing, statistics, often referred to as "CompuBox" stats, are the cornerstones of evaluation. Four key stats hold the secrets to a fighter's prowess:

1. Total Punches Thrown and Landed: This statistic is a punch-by-punch account of a fighter's activity and accuracy. It tells us how many punches they threw and how many found their mark. The higher the percentage of landed punches, the more effective the fighter.

2. Jabs Thrown and Landed: Jabs are the measuring sticks of a fighter's control over the distance and ring. How many jabs they throw and how many connect speak volumes about their strategy.

3. Power Punches Thrown and Landed: Hooks, uppercuts, and crosses; these are the punches that do the real damage. The number of power punches thrown and the number that land showcase a fighter's punching power and effectiveness up close.

4. Total Rounds Won: Boxing matches consist of rounds, and winning rounds is a critical step toward winning the fight. Judges assess fighters based on criteria like aggression, clean punches, defense, and ring control. The fighter who takes the majority of the rounds emerges as the victor.

Now let's pivot to litigation. It's a contest, a sport in which litigators face off in the legal arena. But here's the twist: while sports thrive on quantifiable stats, litigation tends to let the quarterbacks of the legal game off the hook. Their stats? Unquantifiable. And you know what? That's exactly how they prefer it.

So, let's embrace the power of numbers and bask in the importance of statistics in sports. In the realm of litigation, it's high time we recognize that the legal world often cloaks itself in grandiose promises and claims about competence, all wrapped in the fog of reputation and stature. Regrettably, these assertions fall far short of offering you tangible data on wins, losses, or any other metrics that would allow you to anticipate performance.

If litigators were subject to the same level of statistical scrutiny as quarterbacks or boxers, they might not even make it to the draft, let alone become contenders in the ring. It's doubtful that anyone would put any money on them.

What if we had lawyer cards, like baseball cards, complete with stats for litigators? It would be a fun way to measure legal prowess and even swap cards with fellow legal enthusiasts. Imagine collecting and trading litigator cards like they're the MVPs of the courtroom!

Chapter 76

Divorce: Litigation Mayhem

§

F OR JUST $35, A PHOTO ID, AND A LEISURELY JAUNT INTO CITY HALL,
you can snag yourself a marriage license. Now if the former lovebirds
manage to keep things amicable, smoothly deciding who gets what—
either through some good ol' self-reflection or with the guiding light of
a mediator—getting a divorce in court is as breezy as turning in your
homework and coughing up the filing fees. Easy peasy, right?

Yet in the wild, tumultuous battleground of divorce, points of contention
often rear their ugly heads. Here's a rundown of the usual suspects:

1. Child Custody and Visitation: Determining where the children will
live and the visitation rights of the noncustodial parent.

2. Child Support: Establishing financial support for the upbringing of
the children, covering expenses like education, healthcare, and daily living.

3. Alimony/Spousal Support: Determining whether one spouse will
provide financial support to the other after the divorce, and if so, the
amount and duration.

4. Division of Assets: Splitting marital property, which may include the
family home, vehicles, investments, and other assets acquired during the
marriage.

5. Division of Debts: Allocating responsibility for shared debts incurred
during the marriage.

6. Retirement Accounts: Deciding how to divide any retirement accounts or pensions accumulated during the marriage.

7. Business Interests: If one or both spouses own a business, deciding how to handle the business assets and interests.

8. Health Insurance: Determining how health insurance coverage will be maintained, especially if one spouse was covered under the other's policy.

9. Tax Considerations: Addressing the tax implications of the divorce, including issues related to filing status, dependency exemptions, and tax credits.

10. Relocation: If one parent wants to move with the children, it may become a point of contention, especially if it impacts visitation arrangements.

11. Dispute Resolution: Choosing a method for resolving disputes, whether through litigation, mediation, or collaborative divorce.

12. Pet Custody: Deciding who will retain custody of any pets and how visitation or ownership will be shared.

When a couple finds themselves entangled in the intricate web of divorce disputes, they often turn to the guiding hand of a litigator. This legal maestro steps onto the scene with reassuring words, acknowledging the tumultuous journey ahead, while clinching a substantial retainer and vowing to champion their rights. Now let's unravel the complexities and tribulations amplified by litigators and the divorce court process, dissecting each dispute item with a magnifying glass.

Child Custody and Visitation:

- Emotional toll on children due to prolonged legal battles
- Strained relationships between parents intensified by adversarial court proceedings
- Potential harm to children's well-being as court decisions become more contentious

Child Support:

- Financial strain on the paying parent, exacerbated by attorney fees

- Escalated disputes over the amount of support fueled by adversarial legal tactics

- Lingering resentment between parents due to prolonged legal battles

Alimony/Spousal Support:

- Financial strain on the paying spouse amplified by escalating legal costs

- Lengthy and contentious disputes over the amount and duration of support

- Ongoing financial dependence prolonged by adversarial litigation

Division of Assets:

- Emotional toll from prolonged legal battles over sentimental assets

- Financial strain and increased legal costs from disputes over property division

- Extended disputes over the fair division of assets due to adversarial processes

Division of Debts:

- Financial strain on the party responsible for debts heightened by legal battles

- Escalated disputes over the fair allocation of debts fueled by adversarial tactics

- Potential long-term impact on credit scores exacerbated by prolonged litigation

Retirement Accounts:

- Potential loss of retirement savings exacerbated by escalating legal fees
- Contentious disputes over the valuation and division of retirement accounts
- Impact on future financial stability prolonged by adversarial legal processes

Business Interests:

- Increased financial strain for both spouses due to rising legal costs
- Escalated disputes over the valuation and distribution of business assets
- Potential harm to the viability of the business prolonged by adversarial litigation

Health Insurance:

- Potential loss of health coverage intensified by legal battles
- Disputes over responsibility for health insurance costs exacerbated by litigation
- Impact on access to healthcare prolonged by adversarial processes

Tax Considerations:

- Potential tax implications become more complex and costly due to legal disputes
- Escalated disputes over tax-related decisions fueled by adversarial tactics
- Need for extensive financial planning prolonged by adversarial legal processes

Relocation:

- Strained relationships due to potential distance between parents exacerbated by litigation

- Escalated disputes over the impact on visitation arrangements fueled by adversarial tactics

- Emotional toll on children heightened by prolonged legal battles and changes in living environments

Dispute Resolution:

- Escalated legal costs and prolonged court proceedings

- Emotional toll from adversarial divorce processes impacting post-divorce relationships

- Potential harm to co-parenting relationships prolonged by adversarial litigation

Pet Custody:

- Emotional toll from separation from a beloved pet exacerbated by legal battles

- Escalated disputes over ownership and visitation rights fueled by adversarial tactics

- Potential harm to the well-being of the pet prolonged by adversarial legal processes

The battleground of divorce, laden with disputes, becomes the crucible of destiny, and the legal system's intervention only fans the flames of discord and agony. This entire affair is mere fodder for the courts, the medieval furnace where litigators wield their legal flint stones, turning this proxy war into a tragic and ashen epilogue of the marriage rather than a new chapter for each of the spouse's lives.

The litigants, immersed in conflict and emotionally vulnerable, sprout emotional triggers all over, visible to litigators like chicken pox on a child that they can harp on at will. Conversely, if a litigant is an anger and vengeance type, he or she is the perfect client for the attorney to conjoin with as they plan and scheme to inflict maximal litigation pain onto the opposing side.

In this legal match, involving two litigants and their respective attorneys, a minimum of four players step onto the field—akin to a squash doubles match, with two players per team. If even one player harbors natural anger or vengefulness or is easily triggered by their attorney, or if either attorney adopts the role of fiercely fighting for their client's rights (which earns more money) rather than a more conciliatory approach with the opposing counsel (earning less money), the divorce process transforms into a grueling, expensive, and painful ordeal. Even hiring a conciliatory attorney won't spare you, as they're compelled to respond to the legal jousting war initiated by the other side.

When litigants believe they're entitled to assets or custody and their attorney encourages a fight for their rights in court, the temptation to tell a little white lie surfaces. Attorneys either facilitate or instruct clients to allege child and marital abuse and misconduct—often a dubious mix of lies that further complicates matters. In an era where claims of spousal abuse abound, whether true or not, the line between reality and fiction blurs. The road to alleging spousal or even child sexual abuse, even if unfounded, becomes a short bridge, and what was initially a small white lie now looms larger.

Litigators often wield the abuse card, promoting it even when it didn't occur. Thus begins the litigious journey. As retainers are paid, documents filed, and the legal machinery activated, the reality of litigation in divorce unfolds—a process fraught with emotional turmoil, financial strain, and the unsettling prospect of navigating a legal system that often amplifies discord rather than facilitating resolution.

Navigating the divorce court system transforms what might have been a personal challenge into a harrowing odyssey, significantly impacting the litigants involved. Emotional turmoil, often intense and unrelenting, becomes magnified within the courtroom's battleground. Raw emotions, ranging from anger and sadness to fear and betrayal, create a cauldron of psychological horror, turning the legal process into an emotionally taxing ordeal.

Financial dread adds another layer, exacerbating the already tough aspects of divorce. Involving attorneys to divide assets, negotiate alimony, and determine child support can transform what was once a personal agreement into a financial nightmare. The very process of seeking a fair resolution through legal channels can lead to increased financial strain, turning the divorce into an economically draining experience.

The legal labyrinth of divorce laws and proceedings adds complexity, resembling an intricate and endless maze. Wrong turns within this system can have terrifying consequences for individuals. Legal jargon, complex paperwork, and unexpected twists in court decisions contribute to a sense of being lost in the maze, amplifying the challenges of the divorce process.

Child custody horrors emerge as the family undergoes division, with the court and attorneys becoming arenas of inherent battle. The best interests of children sometimes take a back seat to a gratuitous campaign for custody, prioritizing the legal contest over the children's well-being.

This shift in focus within the legal process adds a layer of torment for parents and children alike.

Isolation and alienation unfold as marital details are aired in court, contributing to public humiliation and social isolation. One partner may experience the horror of being alienated from friends, family, and even their own children. The very public nature of divorce court battles can have profound and lasting effects on individuals' social connections and support networks.

Lengthy litigation, feeling like an eternal nightmare, drains both emotionally and financially. The prolonged process amplifies the toll, making each step in court a potential source of stress, anxiety, and financial strain. Ghosts of the past, including past actions and unresolved conflicts, resurface in court, creating an environment where secrets, infidelity, and hidden truths may be revealed, further intensifying the emotional toll.

Unforeseen consequences loom as a constant specter in divorce court. The decisions rendered by the court may have long-lasting and haunting effects on all parties involved, introducing uncertainties and challenges that extend beyond the legal proceedings. The horror of divorce court lies not only in its predictable challenges but in the unpredictable and lasting consequences that emerge from this emotionally charged battleground.

While divorce court offers a forum for resolution and new beginnings, it often unfolds as a battleground where emotions run high and the outcome remains uncertain. It's a place where the emotional toll can be accompanied by severe financial damage.

The cost of litigation can be staggering, like a financial guillotine hanging over your head, threatening to cut away hard-earned assets. It's a realm where attorney fees, court expenses, and the division of assets can leave you economically bruised, battered, and in dire straits.

In this arena, as in life, there are both heroes and villains. The heroes are those who can find a way to navigate these stormy waters with integrity and resilience, emerging on the other side with their dignity intact. The villains? Well, they're the system itself, often riddled with inefficiencies and injustices, turning the already tumultuous journey of divorce into a more harrowing odyssey than it needs to be.

Chapter 77

The Truth About the Costs of Litigation: A Brutal Awakening

§

HOLD ONTO YOUR HATS, FOLKS, BECAUSE THE JOURNEY THROUGH the treacherous waters of litigation isn't for the faint of heart. Let me give it to you straight and summarize what we have learned so far. The costs of litigation can pile up faster than you can say "justice." Here's a raw look at what you're in for:

1. Citizen of the Judicial World: Strap in because you're about to become a full-fledged citizen of the judicial system. In this realm, you're under constant scrutiny, potentially penalized at every turn, and your rights might feel like they're hanging by a thread, subject to the whims of the judges. It's a bit like starring into a dystopian nightmare.

2. Frustration Galore: Get ready to be frustrated, my friends. You'll find yourself exasperated with every player in this drama—the judge, your litigator, their litigator, even the court clerk. They seem to hold a "citizen's privilege," while you, well, you're often treated like a second-class citizen, pouring your blood, sweat, and tears into the system.

3. Financial Invasion: Brace yourself for an invasion of your business and financial records. Discovery processes or those invasive 2004 exams in bankruptcy court will lay your financial life bare for all to see. It's like having your financial diary read aloud and entered into the public record.

4. In-Court Defamation: Prepare for in-court defamation, and if your case touches any industry or trade, get ready for your name to grace the pages of trade magazines and newsfeeds in not-so-flattering ways. It's like a public shaming, and you're at the center of it.

5. Bill-Churning Litigators: Get your wallet ready because you'll be shelling out big bucks for bill-churning litigators. In some cases, you might even be footing the bill for the other side. It's a financial rollercoaster.

6. Become a Litigation Manager: Say goodbye to your free time because you'll need to become a part-time litigation manager. Steering your case can feel like trying to drive a car from the trunk—it's out of control, and you're feeling every bump in the road.

7. On Call for Years: Whether you're a CEO, an M.D., or a small business owner, get used to being on call for years. Your attorney may summon you at a moment's notice, and you'll have to drop everything to meet court directives. It's like being on 24/7 duty.

8. Renting Out Your Mind: Your headspace will be occupied by your case, day and night. Your mind will be flooded with thoughts about your situation, and those dreams you have? They're likely not the sweetest.

9. The Gamut of Emotions: Expect to run the emotional gauntlet. You'll likely experience all or most of the eighteen negative emotions outlined earlier. Victory and hope? Well, those are rare visitors, usually making an appearance when your litigator calls to pump you up with the right hand and hand you his monthly billing request with the left.

And that's just the tip of the iceberg. There are hidden risks and costs that can blindside you. Default interest, penalties, asset devaluation, and market turbulence are just a few. You might also find yourself wrestling with receivers, trustees, and creditors eager to get their pound of flesh.

Sleep? It's a luxury you might not be able to afford. The stress of litigation can haunt your dreams, turning your nights into restless ordeals.

So, my friends, entering the world of litigation is not a decision to be made lightly. The revealed and hidden risks and costs add up swiftly, and the toll on your well-being is undeniable. It's a heavy price to pay for the pursuit of justice, which in most cases is elusive and a lot of smoke and mirrors.

In the upcoming chapters, our exploration takes a deep dive into the intricacies of bankruptcy court. Thus far, we've acquired numerous actionable techniques to rein in your litigator and effectively manage your case, and these insights are equally applicable to navigating the challenges of bankruptcy court. However, the dynamics of the venue of bankruptcy court make for an inherently less controllable atmosphere, so our journey will predominantly involve describing the lay of the land rather than pinpointing problems and suggesting specific actionable techniques.

The key takeaway is that bankruptcy court is a hostile terrain best avoided, and the goal is to make a swift exit. Furthermore, our venture into bankruptcy land will provide valuable lessons that extend beyond bankruptcy cases, offering insights that can teach and enlighten you in other facets of litigation. Ready, set, and launch into this exploration!

Part 2

Bankruptcy

Chapter 78

Bankruptcy Court Unveiled: Navigating a Harsh Frontier

§

Bankruptcy court is no leisurely stroll—it's a venture into an alternate reality, a toxic atmosphere akin to inhaling on Mars. It's a rugged, less predictable domain compared to other courts, marked by heightened adversarial dynamics, diminished control, elevated costs, and is an all-encompassing circus.

To the uninitiated, bankruptcy court may appear as a haven for debtors—a refuge where the Constitution wraps its protective arms around those facing financial shipwrecks. The founding fathers and their successors pioneered a space where financial troubles and insolvency no longer led to debtor's prison or worse. In America, debtors found sanctuary, rendering the pitchforks of creditors utterly useless. The courtroom became a haven for financial rebirth—a place tinged with patriotism and optimism for a fresh start.

Yet, this perception is largely illusory. When an asset within an entity I owned ventured into Chapter 11, the reality hit hard—bankruptcy court was nothing like the imagined sanctuary. The protective wings of the American Bald Eagle were nowhere to be found; instead, it resembled a gathering of corrupt, shadowy, and unscrupulous vultures—a grueling ordeal that tested my endurance as a businessman to its limits.

Bankruptcy litigation as a debtor was like having a financial flat tire and whilst attempting to change it, getting carjacked by multiple assailants day in and day out, as compared to other litigation, which is more of a contest, a slugfest. I was used to slugging it out in the ring, but the onslaught of carjackers when I sought a little financial respite was indeed a surreal experience.

We'll unravel the intricacies of bankruptcy court by embarking on journeys from my time in the venue and those of others I know. Some of these tales are arduous, laden with slog and strain, much like a trek through the Himalayan mountains or through a bad and dangerous neighborhood on foot and in the dead of night. Honesty demands that I reveal the true nature of the Martian landscape for you, my fellow traveler. So, buckle up as we embark on a journey through the harsh terrain of bankruptcy land.

Chapter 79

Bankruptcy Court:
Where Lawfare Takes Center Stage

§

"**L**AWFARE" IN THE CONTEXT OF LITIGATION REFERS TO THE manipulation of legal processes to achieve non-legal goals. Some say it's the weaponization of the law to achieve an unintended, immoral, and depraved end, even if technically legal. It also implies that legal actions can be weaponized or manipulated to deter a party from using their legal rights.

But in a sense, isn't the whole legal system already inherently weaponized, with plaintiffs and defendants each represented by their dueling attorneys?

If so, what sets "lawfare" apart? It's not just about pushing the boundaries; it's about crossing lines, manipulating legal procedures, and at times, even violating them to achieve shady and questionably legal objectives. While this phenomenon isn't exclusive to any particular court of law, I have a personal story from the battleground of bankruptcy court, where lawfare is the name of the game.

My first appearance in bankruptcy court as the manager of a debtor LLC fell out on the anniversary of 9/11. It was a contentious arena, where creditors were armed with aggressive litigators, the judge was a storm of anger, and there was no shelter from this whirlwind. I gained adversaries that day, adversaries who would strike at me, one by one, or sometimes in coordinated attacks, akin to a squad of snipers. The judge even cheered them on.

The environment was far less controlled than anticipated. I presumed that the court would provide protection against creditor pitchforks and that the judge would be impartial. I also expected to maintain possession and management of my business, running a single-asset real property that I had just finished building and leasing, and go about my business unencumbered while refinancing my property and then negotiating and paying off debts in an orderly fashion.

My primary creditor, a first mortgage private lender, wasn't content with a simple payback. They aimed to wrest ownership of my building from me. They used lawfare to strangle the building's operations, obstructing my use of company funds to pay for building expenses in order to maintain operations, degrading the property, and effectively forcing tenants to vacate, rendering it improbable for me to refinance. They petitioned the court to permit their chosen brokerage company and trustee to auction off and sell the building with the clear intention of "credit bidding" and essentially positioning themselves for a self-purchase at a fraction of the real estate's value.

From a moral standpoint, one could say that they were bad dudes. On the other hand, they would argue that they were merely conducting business, backed by competent lawyers, and operating within the court's established rules. Both perspectives might contain some truth, but the undeniable fact is that the judge was complicit in illicit behavior through aiding and abetting lawfare, which I'll explain.

I had a simple plan—use the shelter of bankruptcy court to catch a breather from an aggressive mortgagee private lender while I refinanced my property. Then I would pay off all outstanding bills, and any disputed claims would be resolved through a trial. However, fate had a different agenda.

The creditors, aided by their counsel, had every opportunity to disrupt my non-trial procedural moves as a debtor. While I was fortunate to have only one creditor take this approach and not more, it still made for a daunting battle, where my every procedural move was challenged and attacked with relentless motions, objections, libel, and even perjury to thwart my business of real estate management and ownership.

The U.S. Constitution provided me the right to be there and the lore of the court's graciousness toward the debtor was expected, but the judge instead held me and the debtor in disregard and instead, buoyed and advocated for the contentious mortgagee-creditor. There was no advantage to being a debtor in bankruptcy court, and it felt like a prosecution case instead of a place of resolution and shelter; if anything, the bankruptcy court gave my lender-creditor more leverage over me compared to state court.

Another sinister aspect of lawfare within the legal system is the alarming abandonment of the litigant's right to due process, a fundamental constitutional right. This issue warrants its own chapter, which I will deliver later.

I intended and endeavored to play by the rules and use them to my advantage, as anyone would in any game. However, the judge continuously both changed and eliminated the rules at whim, making the game exceptionally challenging.

Folks, this isn't a tale of spilled milk but rather a wake-up call to the harsh realities of litigation. It's a reminder that your constitutional rights are often under siege, and in the minefields of legal battles, you must continuously adapt and reevaluate every move to navigate a complex and ever-changing game.

Chapter 80

The Due Process Debacles:
A Circus of Injustice

§

IN THE LAND OF LADY JUSTICE, THE FIFTH AMENDMENT OF THE United States Constitution stands as a guardian against the unjust deprivation of life, liberty, or property. It's distilled into just eleven words, echoing a solemn promise that none shall be "deprived of life, liberty or property without due process of law."

These words mandate that all government actors, even judges, must tread carefully, adhering to certain procedures before they can snatch away a person's rights.

But what are these procedures, you ask? They're simple, really:

1. Notice

2. A fair hearing before the deprivation

In a perfect world, this should be the name of the game. However, in reality, these inherent rights are often hijacked, creating a costly and unprosecuted crime. My journey into the labyrinth of bankruptcy court, presided over by the audacious Justice [Name], opened my eyes to the bitter truth—that our constitutional embrace could be shattered with a devilish grin.

But before we plunge into the depths of these due process debacles, let's add a little humor to the mix:

> Ever wondered how many bankruptcy court judges it takes to change a light bulb?

Just one—she holds the bulb still, and the entire world revolves around her.

Example 1: Denied the Last Word

Picture this: You have the right to get the last word in a legal back-and-forth, much like a lively game of volleyball. But what if your opponent uses a sneaky move to steal that opportunity?

Let's say opposition counsel files a motion with a hearing set for May 15 at 10 a.m. Your litigator then files an objection. Opposing counsel volleys back and files a reply to your objection on May 14 in the evening. Your litigator either discovers it in his inbox the next morning or misses it altogether, leaving you no time for that final volley, a surreply. They've outplayed you, choking you out of your last chance to volley, and instead, they get to spike the ball.

Are there consequences for such a cunning move? More often than not, the answer is a frustrating "no," handicapping you in this legal game.

Example 2: A Duel of Exclusivity

Bankruptcy law offers a haven for debtors, granting them an exclusive period of 120 days with a 60-day extension period, during which only they can file and confirm a reorganization plan. I stepped into Chapter 11 ready to enjoy this exclusive right, or so I thought.

Seventy-two days in, I submitted my plan. The plan was straightforward—paying off all creditors 100 percent in full from the proceeds of a refinance of my asset. Sounds good, right? But days before the hearing, the opposing side crashed my party and struck with a motion that sought to end my exclusive period prematurely and filed their own draconian plan of reorganization, which aimed to snatch the property from my grasp with a well-orchestrated scheme.

Let's dig into the numerous due process violations:

1. My counsel filed a plan of reorganization, the hearing occurring before the requisite back-and-forth objections, replies, and sur-

replies, so I was denied the statutory right to the last written word, a final reply before the hearing.

2. My plan of reorganization was slated for a hearing date, but the day before, opposition counsel filed two motions, one to end my period of exclusivity, and the other to confirm their plan of reorganization for my company, which would wrest control of my asset from me. The judge elected to hear opposition counsel's motion to strip me of my rights of exclusivity without the requisite written volleying of back-and-forth objections, replies, and sur-replies before a hearing on that motion.

3. The judge also allowed that motion to be heard prematurely, allowing opposition counsel to crash my hearing for confirmation of my plan, all with insufficient notice.

4. The judge ruled to end my rights to an uncontested period of exclusivity for submitting and approving my plan of reorganization 48 days prematurely.

The judge stripped away my procedural sanctuary and allowed an unsettling showdown between me and the unscrupulous, predatory lender-creditor. This, despite my inherent and exclusive right to submit a plan of reorganization. She explicitly stated during hearings that she would never endorse my plan. These head-scratching deviations from the rule book left me wondering if there were closed-door alliances between her and the creditor's attorney or his client. The truth remains shrouded in mystery. Who knows what went on behind the chamber doors? Due process? Gone with the swoosh of the robe!

Example 3: The Trial That Never Was

In this courtroom battleground, where over four hundred docket events played out like an endless chess match, my quest was simply to pay off all creditors and secure a trial to resolve the claim of default interest on a loan.

I saw the writing on the wall when the judge stripped my period of exclusivity. Swiftly, I pivoted and altered my approach, deciding to expedite a sale of the property. Within mere weeks, I had secured a buyer, finalized a contract, and then faced a legal battle with the lender-creditor, who opposed the sale in court.

Ultimately, I managed to successfully sell the property, settling all outstanding debts, including the mortgage. However, I contested the claim regarding default interest and subsequently requested the court's permission for discovery with the intention of addressing this one disputed matter through a trial.

The judge's initial response was an obvious denial of my due process, a refusal to grant me a trial. The judge said during a hearing that a trial was not necessary as she would rule according to the loan documents and didn't care about my claim that I was prepared to pay off my loan before my lender went rogue and filed a pre-foreclosure action in court without notice to try and strip me of my property.

It was an alarming situation, and my special real estate counsel piped up in the hearing, exclaiming, "I do a lot of appellate work, and this case will be overturned if you deny us a trial."

The judge, recognizing her vulnerability to an appeal, eventually relented and scheduled a trial in just ten days. However, she took the time to explain the numerous ways in which she wouldn't aid in enforcing the creditor's compliance with subpoenas or depositions. It became clear that this trial would be nothing more than a charade, a stark denial of due process exclusively designed to provide cover for the judge's questionable behavior.

These are just a few glimpses into the world of stolen due process, where the rules shift like desert sands. Beware, my friends, for there are judges who hold the rule book and twist and shred them at their whim, leaving justice in the dust.

Chapter 81

Justice Delayed Is Justice Denied

§

WILLIAM GLADSTONE, A PROMINENT BRITISH STATESMAN WHO served as prime minister of the United Kingdom four separate times during the nineteenth century, coined this chapter's name.

Delays in court proceedings are a concealed and insidious breach of due process, often leading to the denial of a fair and timely adjudication. The right to due process inherently includes the right to a swift and effective legal process. Excessive delays can sabotage an individual's or business's capacity to present their case convincingly, result in the loss of vital evidence, impose unwarranted hardships, and create many liabilities, both financial and otherwise.

In the state courts, protracted delays can push a company into the abyss of the bankruptcy courts. Skilled litigators are grandmasters in the art of extending a case into what seems like an eternity. You'll notice that in court, either you or the opposition gains the upper hand by stalling proceedings, a practice the courts were designed to thwart from the outset!

For instance, a pre-foreclosure case in New York City can drag on for years, possibly even a decade, and the legal expenses can be astronomical. Meanwhile, other states operate with non-judicial foreclosures that can wrap up in a few months with relatively meager legal costs. If you're a homeowner in NYC with little equity, a protracted court case might actually work in your favor, as footing a legal bill that is less than rent is a win. But if you're the lender, it's nothing short of injustice.

And the same goes for other cases; it all hinges on the specifics and whose side you're on. Delay tactics typically benefit one party while harming another. This systemic structure practically guarantees that at least one side, if not both, will suffer from the snail-paced wheels of justice.

Judges are well-versed in the delay game and will often cooperate with attorneys to turn the courtroom into a playground for these tactics. They might do it to nudge one side or the other into making concessions or sometimes just because they have a soft spot for a particular litigator.

Now let's talk about federal courts, which are supposed to be the epitome of efficiency compared to their state counterparts. But hold your horses; it all boils down to the federal judge in charge. You see, these federal judges are appointed for life, and you might be scratching your head, wondering what keeps them on their toes when there's no one who can give them the boot.

Sure, the appellate court can theoretically overturn a ruling, but let's face it—in most cases, it's like putting a rubber stamp on the original decision. And if you want to broach the topic of potential schedule mismanagement and delays, well, you might as well forget about it. It's a conversation that often falls on deaf ears.

I've also witnessed the flip side of delays, how rushing a case can have cataclysmic consequences. During my Chapter 11 proceedings, Justice [Name] appeared like a legal juggernaut with an undeniable tilt toward the creditor/lender/mortgagee. I contemplated her recusal from my case, considering her previous affiliation with a law firm that exclusively represented lenders. However, I soon realized that pursuing recusal was impractical.

Her impending retirement date was my silver lining, and I eagerly awaited the day she'd retire, hand in her judge's robe, and ascend to partner status in one of the law firms she'd been cozy with during her time on the bench, where she'd earn a jaw-dropping $1,500 per hour.

To my delight, this meant she'd be gone before my case concluded, allowing a less contentious judge to take the reins and bring the case to a resolution.

Yet, this judge was hell-bent on expediting my case at every turn, ruling on motions prematurely, bypassing the required due process procedures, and disregarding the prescribed timeframes for notice and hearing dates. The rush to judgment was palpable.

In the world of justice, it's a complex dance where delays and hasty decisions often determine who emerges victorious. In my battle, the clock was ticking, and it was all or nothing in the race against the legal hourglass.

Chapter 82

Litigator Weak Knees:
Where Allegiance Trumps Advocacy

§

L ET'S TAKE A PEEK BEHIND THE IMPOSING DOORS OF FEDERAL COURT, where bankruptcy judges reign supreme with what could be described as dictatorial executive authority. But here's the twist: It's not just respect that your counsel has for the judge; it's downright deference. The attorneys in this legal dance often don't dare to fervently represent your case to the judges, even if it's in the best interest of their clients. Why, you ask? They fear souring their ongoing relationships with the judges as they'll invariably cross paths with them on various cases day in and day out.

So, your attorney, whom you've hired to fight in your corner, operates at half-throttle, ensuring they don't rock the boat with the judge. They tone down their representation to maintain that judge-attorney rapport, even if it means your best interests take a back seat.

Even in the bustling hub of NYC, where the caseload is overwhelming, the legal world is surprisingly small, and everyone seems to know everyone. It's not unlike a club where old buddies convene, only the ambiance here feels more like a den of serpents. That reptilian aura is almost palpable, weaving its way through the courtroom camaraderie.

While some courtrooms are devoid of shadiness, others have a sprinkle of it. However, the bankruptcy court is in a league of its own.

Chapter 83

Legal Procedures: They Might Be Legal but Could Sink Your Case

$

I ONCE ENTERTAINED THE NOTION THAT THE VAST ARRAY OF RULES and procedures in the legal world could be wielded as tools by litigants and their counsel to craft innovative and effective strategies. After all, as long as we followed the rules, why not use different combinations to our advantage?

But I was dead wrong!

Some combinations, although entirely legal and allowable, have the potential to infuriate a judge and, in turn, torpedo your case right from the start. I learned this the hard way during a single-asset Chapter 11 case. As my case came to a close and I had successfully found a buyer for my asset, the time came to settle my attorneys' fees.

Enter Wayne Greenwald of Wayne Greenwald PC, a seasoned top-tier litigator who had devised a strategy that weighed down my case like a parachute made of lead. I fired him five months into the case and hired another firm. Fast forward when all claims were long settled and I was exiting Chapter 11, I contested his fee application, where in my pro se objection filed with the court, I argued the following (verbatim from my pleading):

> WGPC's services jeopardized and damaged the entire case, the standing of the Debtor's creditors, and ultimately devalued the Debtor's sole member's equity position.

WGPC proposed a strategy:

"If a few of your creditors file an Involuntary Chapter 11, that will stop a state court receiver from taking possession of the building, and during a gap period before the bankruptcy goes on record permanently, I'll get the Bankruptcy court to allow the state court to follow through on the petition you filed there, to figure out how much you owe the Mortgagee, you will pay them, and the involuntary Chapter 11 will be dismissed."

WGPC said that he could keep getting extensions and keep the gap period open for as long as would be needed and that he did this for two years on a previous case.

The debtor went along with WGPC's counsel. The mortgagee called the involuntary petition "collusionary" in every pleading, and the court looked upon it disfavorably, and this tainted the debtor's credibility.

The debtor and its principal had nothing to hide, and there was no reason whatsoever to follow WGPC's orchestration of a fatally damaging ploy. There was absolutely nothing the debtor was poised to gain.

One might say that the debtor told WGPC that it felt uncomfortable with filing for bankruptcy, and WGPC came up with a legal strategy that satisfied that feeling.

That is analogous to someone with a malignant tumor in their chest, whom the surgeon counsels and says that he needs to do open thoracic surgery to remove the tumor, and the patient responds: "I'm afraid and uncomfortable with going under the knife," to which the doctor says, 'No problem, I'll go laparoscopically through your rectum, snake up the surgical tools, and remove the tumor, just like I've done in past surgeries."

It is a ridiculous but completely applicable analogy. The patient was not medically inclined, trusted what appeared to be a scholarly and professorial doctor, and did not seek a second opinion. Not seeking a second opinion is not too smart, but one cannot hold the patient accountable for the doctor's delusional malpractice.

The very same thing happened in this Chapter 11 case. WGPC initially presented to the uninitiated debtor as a scholarly, professorial, and well-seasoned bankruptcy attorney, and then performed legal quackery."

And so, as the gavel fell, with the judge echoing the same disdain that coursed through the entire case, well after I had fired and replaced the litigator who cooked up this failed strategy. She chose to chastise and penalize, letting her contempt for this legal strategy, and perhaps even her negative feelings toward the attorney and myself, taint her perception of the entire case.

Whether her aversion was solely due to the strategy remains a mystery. Maybe a different attorney or litigant could have presented it in a way that appeased her. Perhaps, had the case landed in front of a different judge, the outcome might have been entirely different. Who knows?

As I delved into the statistics after the case concluded, I figured out a telling truth. Involuntary Chapter 11 cases were a rare breed, representing only a minuscule fraction of Chapter 11 cases filed, mostly clustered in the bustling court districts of New York City.

It made me wonder if this particular judge had encountered similar legal strategies before, perhaps sparking a simmering resentment toward the litigants and their attorneys who employed similar procedures. Sadly, my case seemed to bear the brunt of her vitriolic outbursts.

If the judge's frequent rebukes directed at Greenwald during every hearing and her evident disdain for the debtor throughout the case were any indication, one might reasonably expect her to deny or at least reduce some of Greenwald's claimed professional fees. After all, there are numerous litmus tests in the law to pass before authorizing an attorney's fees and debtor payment.

My filed objection to Greenwald's fee application highlighted two critical benchmarks for evaluating, reducing, or stripping claimed fees from one's counsel:

1. "Reasonable compensation" as per Section 330(a) of the Bankruptcy Code, involving a comparison of the quality of services rendered and the benefit accrued to their client.

2. Section 330(a)(3)(C), which assesses the "necessity of that service" and the "benefit" derived from it.

Given Justice [Name's] consistent reprimands toward Greenwald and her overall treatment of the debtor with disdain throughout the case, one would logically expect her to acknowledge my objections, asserting that Greenwald fell short of the basic bankruptcy code gauges and thresholds of acceptable services as cited above. However, the outcome was quite the opposite; she awarded him 100 percent of his claimed bill. The proceedings concluded with congenial laughs, jokes, reminiscing, and camaraderie between the judge and Wayne Greenwald, painting a picture of a tawdry team with me standing as the odd man out.

The takeaway here is that if your litigator cooks up a legal game plan, research your judge's track record with similar cases as outlined in a previous chapter. If only I had done so, I might have swiftly torpedoed a strategy that was doomed from the very beginning. So, let my journey, filled with the sweat and tears of hard-learned lessons, serve as a beacon of wisdom. Seek wisdom and take responsibility, my friends, and may your investment in managing your case guide you toward the path of success!

Chapter 84

Courtroom Carnival: Judges, Bias, and the Bittersweet Taste of Justice

§

LET'S GET REAL HERE, FOLKS. JUDGES, PREJUDICE, TEMPERAMENT, favoritism, and raw human behavior are all part of the complex theater that unfolds within the judicial system.

Judges, often cloaked in those imposing black robes, preside from on high, projecting an air of grandeur and self-importance. They don't shy away from wielding power that stretches beyond their designated boundaries. Many a time, they'll tip their hats to indicate their leanings, taking pleasure in exerting their authority to the detriment of the opposing side. It's as if they relish the opportunity to inflict suffering, making it a rather disturbing perk of the job for those with a sadistic streak.

Now within the confines of the bankruptcy court, the U.S. Trustee, originally designated to uphold order in court proceedings, often takes on the likeness of jesters from times of yore. Their actions aren't entirely driven by their own volition but rather are in step with the intricate minuet of the courtroom. Unfortunately, they are intricately woven into the very fabric of the system, with many simply "going along to get along," while judges roam free to run the court.

Prejudice, by its very definition, implies preconceived notions. In cases of supreme importance or national-level criminal proceedings, one might hope that judges uphold their duty to be impartial. However, as much as we'd like to believe in the ideal, reality often tells a different story.

Judges, in many instances, do indeed harbor biases and subtly reveal their inclinations right from the outset.

It's not pleasant to acknowledge this, and I'm not thrilled to say it, but let's not mince words. I promised to lay it all bare and speak the unadulterated truth.

If a judge takes a disliking to you, they won't hesitate to tarnish your character, curtail your constitutional right to due process, and publicly reprimand you. This goes for your legal counsel as well. If the judge disapproves of a litigator, even if he employs strategies that are well within the legal rules, they can single out and berate the litigator for their "tactics." It's as if the judge has taken a commonplace term and turned it into a derogatory label, vilifying both the litigator and their client.

Conversely, if the attorney employing these so-called tactics points fingers and accuses the opposing counsel of using similar methods, the judge often remains unfazed, letting the accusation slide like water off a duck's back. If anything, the judge perceives the favored side as simply utilizing acceptable legal strategies and won't attribute malice or wrongdoing to it.

It's a bitter pill to swallow, but don't count on equal or fair treatment; in most cases, the judge has already picked their favorite early on.

Judges can sometimes exhibit more pathological behavior than the average litigator, having clawed their way to the top perhaps through a series of opportunistic professional favors and tactics.

I distinctly recall a case where I felt the judge's ire, even though the strategies she criticized were devised and employed by my litigators and well within the rules. Chastising them might have been unreasonable, but chastising me bordered on the absurd. When I asked her how I could be held responsible for strategies employed by my legal team, she retorted that I had hired them and provided a mandate for a vigorous defense. I was left dumbfounded. Isn't that what every attorney's mandate is all about?

Did I not inherently have the right to a robust defense? Beneath the layers of words and justifications, it was clear that the judge simply favored one side over the other.

Another puzzling aspect of the court system is the judges' tolerance for not only excessive inflammatory language in legal documents and oral arguments, but also outright lies, libel, and defamation. These transgressions appear to be accepted norms in the courtroom.

I know a fellow who ventured into the Chapter 11 territory sitting on a heap of equity, who liquidated a cool $100 million in assets. The lenders and creditors got their fair share, all loan principal paid in full, with most of the interest squared away and nothing left over. And yet, to add insult to injury, the lender is coming at him post-Chapter 11 with a lawsuit on his personal guarantee for a deficiency judgment. But here's the salt in the wound—these guys are being labeled as "grifters, welchers, pariahs, and fraudsters" in a recent pleading. It boggles the mind how litigators can sling such accusations without bearing any consequences. It's all just part and parcel of the wild, wild world of litigation.

So, what's the deal here? In the real world, outside the courtroom, such libel and defamation carry legal consequences. But within these hallowed halls, it seems judges and litigators enjoy some sort of diplomatic immunity, allowing them to unleash a verbal storm without fear of repercussions.

Chapter 85

Bankruptcy Attorney Independence and Insolence

§

IN THE PERPLEXING WORLD OF BANKRUPTCY, A PECULIAR transformation unfolds. Bankruptcy attorneys typically start out as your trusted advisors, but as your case journeys through time, a curious evolution transpires. They morph into quasi-self-employed entities, slowly veering away from acting as your counsel and protecting your interests. Under the pretext of safeguarding the debtor's best interests (remember, they represent the debtor, and you are just a member or a shareholder who will need a separate attorney), they embark on independent decisions that significantly impact your case and the future of your business.

This metamorphosis comprises four distinct stages.

Warrior

It all kicks off with the initial stage—pre-retainer meetings and consultations. Your legal team is in full warrior mode, motivated mercenaries devoted to your cause.

Co-worker

As your case unfolds, your chosen law firm assumes a different role. The warrior advocate seems to have gone AWOL, and it may feel as though they've stopped working with you. This is because, according to the system, they serve as a fiduciary to the debtor entity. Even if you're the sole member or hold a 100 percent share, the system distinguishes between your personal interests and those of the company.

Initially, you buttered their bread by cutting a check with the retainer agreement, and perhaps they coaxed you into contributing more funds with the court's blessing during the case's inception. However, from that point on, their income primarily derives from the bankruptcy estate. Their focus subtly shifts toward the equity within your assets, as that's from where the bulk of their compensation derives.

Sure, they will interact with you, but they've essentially ceased working for you in the traditional sense. Going forward, they'll certainly bill your assets, but they no longer wholeheartedly support your interests.

So, you find yourself in a realm where your interests don't always align and your legal counsel morphs into more of a co-worker. They'll keep you in the loop, and every interaction becomes a billing opportunity, but they won't have your back.

Parasite

The litigator's focus isn't solely on billing; it extends to seeking additional opportunities, including potential side deals, such as the court-appointed trustee's offerings—whether they advocate for them or simply consent. Specifically, most are on the lookout for potential kickbacks from asset sales and from any exploitable source. They possess an opportunistic awareness and acumen, much like a divining rod on a quest to extract every conceivable dollar from both you and your assets. They won't hesitate to attach a suctioning milking unit to every teat that could possibly yield them a return.

Enemy

The final stage is where your case is reaching its conclusion. It could be that your company emerges from Chapter 11 with a successful reorganization plan (unlikely), or your assets have been liquidated. This is when all the assorted service providers, including your attorney, rush to submit their bills to the court for approval. At this point, your assets will have been drained of their value, courtesy of the inefficient Chapter 11 process, which includes those cozy arrangements among attorneys, trustees, service providers, creditors, and the excessive billing from what you now know is the debtor's counsel and not yours. The debtor's counsel is gleefully cashing in while you're left picking up the pieces.

You may be battered, but you are no longer naïve. You couldn't believe that it was happening while it was happening, but now you realize that your hand-picked debtor attorney was never your attorney in the first place and became your enemy quite some time ago.

Let's call a spade a spade: the metamorphosis from trusted legal advisor to cunning adversary is the unfortunate norm in the world of bankruptcy court.

Chapter 86

Bankruptcy Attorneys:
Lawyers, Not Business Minds

$

As your attorney starts distancing themselves from their role as you and your company's guardian and embraces their newfound duty as a fiduciary to the debtor, they grow increasingly independent. This newfound independence leads them to make more procedural decisions in the case unilaterally with less, if any, client input, each decision carrying significant business implications.

Now, here's where the story takes a twist. First, it's your business we're talking about, and let's be honest, your attorney, despite their expertise in running a legal enterprise and racking up billable hours, often lacks the business acumen needed to grasp how their legal maneuvers might throw a monkey wrench into your business operations.

In this initial phase of separation, as they shift from being your hired gun to a "co-worker" and then "parasite," they often prioritize their own interests over wholeheartedly championing your case. Instead of being a staunch advocate for your business, they start focusing on maintaining relationships with various stakeholders—the judge, creditors' attorneys, and the U.S. Trustee. Your attorney gets caught in a web where their inner warrior seems to fade away, and your grip on the reins of your business loosens with each passing day.

Once a judge, other creditors, or even your attorney himself start rallying for the appointment of a trustee, you find yourself essentially booted from the driver's seat in managing your assets. The trustee, in essence, takes over the management of your assets.

Now here's the ironic twist, and it's a tough pill to swallow. These trustees are often handpicked by your attorney, who usually shares a close relationship with them, or they're selected based on the recommendations of another attorney representing a creditor—who, not so coincidentally, happens to be your attorney's buddy too.

But here's the catch—none of these folks are business-savvy. They don't have a horse in your business race, nor are they well-versed in making sound business decisions. Instead, these trustees charge exorbitant hourly rates, churn out bills that can only be described as excessive, and sometimes snag a juicy percentage of the sales price of assets as a bonus, which, as mentioned earlier, will likely be parked and divvied among various parties.

Your voice as a businessperson turns into a mere whisper on the moon—inaudible. Nobody hears you, and nobody's paying attention. Your attorney usually falls in line with whatever the trustee recommends, driven by their focus on collecting their final fees and, in all likelihood, the bonus dollars coming from a share of those parked trustee service fees and commissions.

Even if your attorney had a background as a businessman, it wouldn't change the game. Their inherent conflicts of interest predispose them, despite your instructions, to do what's best for their pocket, putting them at odds with your interests.

As a result, the decisions your counsel makes regarding your business, whether intentional or inadvertent, are often tainted by their pursuit of self-interest, billable hours, and the various fees and benefits they can receive from their friends and associates serving as trustees and other service providers.

It's a perilous transformation, and, it is systematically inherent that you eventually lose control over the very person and law firm that you initially entrusted to safeguard your company's interests. Over time, your attorney could become a force that facilitates the devouring of the business you painstakingly built and nurtured with your blood, sweat, and tears.

Chapter 87

Bankruptcy Attorney Billing: A Bonanza

$

BANKRUPTCY ATTORNEYS, DRIVEN BY THE PROSPECT OF MORE generous billing opportunities than litigators in other fields, often regard their clients, the debtor corporate entity, as an ATM to be drained rather than safeguarded. If there's even a hint of equity left in the debtor's assets, you can bet your bottom dollar that the law firm tasked with protecting those interests will be milking the coffers dry, billing with a voracious appetite.

Allow me to paint you a grim picture with a real-life example: Envision a single-asset LLC that owns a solitary building heading towards the auction block. The building fetched a handsome $16 million at auction, but when the legal dust settled, the legal bill rang in at a jaw-dropping $10 million.

These runaway bills are more common than you can shake a stick at, and yet these monstrous bills continue unabated. There is one attorney general for each of the fifty U.S. states, one for the federal government, and a few for some territories and the District of Columbia, which have their own. Yet, one can search from now until tomorrow and not find any general investigation or legislative action to rein in the litigation billing boondoggle.

Sure, discussions and debates abound about legal fees, access to justice, and the affordability of legal services in professional and academic circles, as well as in the public domain, but no one is talking about the excessive billing bonanza except the one who ends up footing the bill. He does so only in hushed tones because it's embarrassing that he got swindled to such an extent. He essentially consented to the swindle by hiring his counsel. He is doubly embarrassed. Of course, he only agreed to a high hourly rate, but he didn't anticipate the bill churning, which is largely a covert activity. So, in many ways, it's only his fault. He can't prove otherwise, and his litigator certainly stopped representing him in any practical manner once he submitted the fee application and was on his own thereafter, embarrassed, shamed, and in most cases, broke.

Sure, every attorney fee application in bankruptcy court can be objected to individually by the debtor or another creditor. Still, it rarely works out that the judge assails the litigator's fee application because, after all, they are lawyers themselves, possibly friends, certainly workmates, comrades in arms, and each has current and future interests to preserve by simply sanctioning the billing submitted to the court. The crazy taxi billing is de facto sanctioned and untouchable.

In a dream world of solutions, an attorney general somewhere might look into the RICO racketeering act, slam the brakes on the bankruptcy court in their district, and construct some dungeons and gallows in the rotunda for their overbilling peers. But in reality, attorneys recoil from the thought of testifying, snitching, investigating, or penalizing each other. So, folks, understand the lay of the land and human nature, and accept the facts. The facts will free you to strategize your end game with the tools of reality!

Chapter 88

Trustees and the Murky World
of Asset Liquidation

§

I N THE REALM OF STANDARD BUSINESS PRACTICE, WHEN IT COMES
to selling assets, the rule of thumb usually goes like this: the higher
the asset's value, the lower the percentage-based commission paid
upon the sale. But, and there's a big "but" here, this principle doesn't
apply when a trustee is involved in picking an asset sales broker and
orchestrating the sale.

Consider this: In a typical out-of-court transaction, if you were to sell
a $500,000 home, you might encounter the conventional 6 percent real
estate commission. Yet, remember, this rate isn't etched in stone; real estate
commissions are open to negotiation. So, if you were unloading a higher-
valued asset, the commission percentage paid would logically decrease.

To illustrate, I once sold a building I owned for $27 million and paid a
mere 1 percent commission. Now 1 percent may sound modest, but keep
in mind it was just one transaction, not vastly different from selling a
home, and a $270,000 commission is nothing to scoff at.

Where the plot thickens is when trustee criminology takes center stage—
the moment the trustee seals the deal with a brokerage company of their
choice and gets the court's blessing. So, what's the crime in all this?

Let me blow your mind. A client sought my advice after emerging from
bankruptcy, and one of their real estate assets had been liquidated by the
court-appointed trustee for $96 million. The net proceeds from the asset
sale amounted to $88 million. That's an astronomical $8 million shelled

out for selling a prime asset in a prime market. A substantial 8.3 percent in costs, of which 2 percent was an incentive fee for the trustee and 6 percent was the sales commission to the real estate brokerage company.

Now, I can almost see you shaking your head in disbelief, and I'm right there with you. So, let's break this down: if a $500,000 home can be sold with a 5 percent sales commission and a $27 million building can go for a 1 percent commission, wouldn't you expect that a $96 million building, a higher-class asset, in a prime and better neighborhood, should sell just as smoothly, if not more so, and for less than a 1 percent sales commission? But for the sake of argument, let's assume a 1 percent sales commission. That's still nearly a cool $1 million!

Now, don't get me wrong; it's still a far cry from the trustee's massive payout of over $8 million to his selected broker, but it's certainly a lot better than a poke in the eye with a sharp stick. Seriously, anyone in the commercial real estate business would eagerly jump at the chance for a 1 percent commission or even a half percent on a sales commission for a $96 million asset, and that's no exaggeration.

But here's where things go awry. The trustee, in crafting and agreeing to the sales commission arrangement and possibly accompanying agreements for the property sale, didn't just leave $7 million on the table (the $8 million paid out minus the $1 million that would've been a fair commission for the sale); instead, they seemingly *parked* that $7 million somewhere to be divvied up among various parties through some mysterious means.

Who are these possible parties, you wonder? Well, it's like peering into the shadows, but the facts remain. The trustee could have set up the sale for 1 percent or even less, yet they bled the equity from the asset, doling out over 8 percent of the gross sales price. Forget the sophistry of everyone acting as fiduciaries for the court and the debtor; it's become a sorry joke. For the debtor and its shareholders, it's a nightmarish tale of daylight robbery.

Chapter 89

Robbers, Gang Members, and Looting Litigators

§

I VIVIDLY RECALL A SCHOOLYARD JUMP ROPE RHYME FROM MY childhood: "Not last night but the night before, twenty-four robbers came knocking at my door."

It hails from a 1941 song by Fats Waller. Here's how it goes:

> *Last night, night before,*
> *twenty-four robbers came to my door.*
> *Opened the door and let them in,*
> *I hit 'em in the head with a bottle of gin.*
> *Just can't, understand,*
> *twenty-four robbers fighting one man.*

The song in its humor and simplicity captures many truths, two of which I'll delineate here.

First, it's reminiscent of the army of attorneys that often descends upon a client, particularly in bankruptcy court, though it can happen elsewhere too. This scenario plays out every day in court as a swarm of attorneys arrive at hearings, meetings, and even conference calls when a single attorney, perhaps even a junior one, would suffice.

If there's an opportunity to bill, these attorneys will gather like the twenty-four robbers. The more, the merrier. There's a fitting term for this kind of behavior, although it has a street gang connotation that isn't suitable for formal use.

But its dictionary definition encapsulates what these attorneys do when they swarm upon their client: *"engaging in criminal activity as carried out by a street gang upon its victim."*[18]

This phrase, although strong, accurately describes the gratuitous actions of litigators when they exploit their clients by ganging up and banging out excessive and inflated billable hours and services.

Second, the twenty-four robbers could very well be analogous to all the parties in a Chapter 11 case that find themselves knocking on the door of the debtor, like creditors, their counsel, the judge, the U.S. Trustee, an appointed trustee or receiver, the accounting firms, or any of the multitude of service providers and detractors whose number one goal is extracting from your hide rather than contributing to the well-being of your company and its assets.

Chapter 90

Bankruptcy Creditors:
A Cacophony of Pitchforks

§

CREDITORS WIELD SIGNIFICANT DISRUPTIVE POWER OVER A BUSINESS entity and its assets. They have the ability to object to the debtor's use of funds coming into their business to pay expenses and run it, essentially giving the creditors the power to bring an asset and its shareholders to their knees, subjecting operations to contentious disputes that gratuitously devalue the asset. The founding fathers would undoubtedly be shocked by such turmoil.

Each secured creditor retains one or more litigators and understands their standing in the pecking order for payment upon exiting Chapter 11. Unsecured creditors, on the other hand, often find themselves battling for survival, perched precariously at the bottom of the seniority hierarchy without any liens. Each of them secures the services of an attorney, and they often find their collective voice by forming a cacophonous creditor committee alongside other unsecured creditors.

The formation of a creditor committee is a routine occurrence, particularly in intricate Chapter 11 cases. Their primary role is to safeguard the interests of unsecured creditors and actively participate in the bankruptcy proceedings.

Key roles and responsibilities of a creditor committee in Chapter 11 may include the following:

1. Negotiating with the debtor

2. Participating in the development of the plan

3. Monitoring the debtor

4. Investigating the debtor's finances

5. Advocating for creditors' interests

6. Engaging professionals

7. Voting on the reorganization plan

In theory, you might find in textbooks that creditor committees play a vital role in ensuring fairness and transparency throughout the bankruptcy process. Their involvement aims to strike a balance among the diverse stakeholders in a Chapter 11 bankruptcy case.

In the real world, it often seems like the tail is wagging the dog because these creditor committees hold a disproportionate and overwhelming amount of influence. Just glance at that list of seven powers they possess! It's as if they have the power to scrutinize and control every aspect of your business on a daily basis, including mounting investigations to torment you and your business.

In the typical course of business, unsecured creditors have limited recourse, usually resorting to lawsuits in state court, attempting to negotiate settlements, or simply abandoning their claims. In Chapter 11, they acquire a raucously powerful voice, and more often than not, this voice comes at the expense of the debtor and their assets. In fact, if things get contentious in court, they can potentially sink the entire ship.

Creditor committees can readily wrest control of the company's management, particularly so when 1) the court lacks insight into business operations, 2) the trustee focuses solely on extracting funds from the company to pay creditor claims, and 3) the U.S. Trustee pays excessive attention to trifling details to avoid making waves during their court tenure, all while keeping an eye on potential future job opportunities at patron law firms. It's a situation where no one is truly looking out for your interests, and you're left rudderless and feeling powerless.

Not only will you end up footing the bill for everyone's attorneys' legal bills and all that churning (if your company retains any equity or emerges from Chapter 11), but this swarm of attorneys will be a relentless source of headaches during your judicial journey.

Even if unsecured creditors are low in the hierarchy for repayment and there's no equity left to pay them off, they can still disrupt your plans. For instance, if you or the secured creditors have a plan to pay off the secured creditors, unsecured creditors can thwart it by casting a "nay" vote.

They can even leverage their votes to negotiate a carve-out with the secured creditors, meaning a portion of the secured creditor's payout would go to unsecured creditors if they make a deal and cast their vote with the secured creditor's plan.

An even more cunning maneuver unfolds when, in the midst of Chapter 11, your business requires external funding to keep the cash flow going. Unsecured creditors might choose to oppose this, wielding the votes to make it happen. Their reasoning? Well, it's grounded in the fact that this outside funding would be elevated to the status of a secured creditor in Chapter 11, securing repayment precedence over their unsecured claims.

While the primary objective is to rescue your business, their shortsighted opposition, which solely revolves around how to extract payment from the debtor's hide right now, could put your business in peril and result in substantial losses.

It's a glaring reminder that, when it comes to safeguarding your interests, the court's once-promised protection, perhaps genuine in intent at its constitutional inception, has been downgraded to the point of becoming a cruel joke on the debtor. Everyone involved in the case seems to have more power, preference, and prerogative, while the debtor shoulders the entire burden of contention. Oh, the irony of justice!

Chapter 91

Intrusive 2004 Exams:
When Debtors Are Under the Microscope

§

LADIES AND GENTLEMEN, LET'S JOURNEY INTO THE WORLD OF RULE 2004 motions in the realm of bankruptcy proceedings. They turn into examinations. It's akin to the legal version of peering through someone's windows, rummaging through their closets, and exposing their deepest secrets.

In essence, it's a full-blown investigation, and it's the debtors who often find themselves squarely in the crosshairs.

So, let me shed some light on Rule 2004 examinations and why they can be downright invasive, especially for the poor soul who's already down on their luck—the debtor.

1. The Watchful Gaze of the Trustee: First up, we've got the bankruptcy trustee. This individual is entrusted to oversee the bankruptcy estate. They wield the authority to file Rule 2004 motions, and what's their mission? To lay bare the debtor's financial life, plain and simple. They're like financial detectives, delving into every nook and cranny for clues.

2. Creditors Unleashed: And if you thought that was the end of it, think again. Creditors, those to whom your company owes money, also have the green light to launch these motions. They're on an expedition to unearth every financial detail they can lay their hands on, as if prying open a treasure chest.

3. The Official Committees Join the Fray: We already mentioned how the credit committees throw down in the ring. Their curiosity leads them to want to unravel and double punch everything about the debtor's financial state and the path every penny has traveled.

4. Equity Security Holders Enter the Arena: And let's not overlook the equity security holders; they're part of the game too. Their stake is often tied to the value of the debtor's stock, and they're not about to let that slide.

Now why is this such a big deal? Why is it incredibly invasive for the beleaguered debtor? Picture this: you're already deep in the throes of financial turmoil, you've had to resort to bankruptcy, and now these folks are sifting through your life with a fine-tooth comb. Your financial history, every transaction, and every financial move you've ever made—it's all laid bare on the table.

But they're not just asking questions; they're making demands, and they're not exactly whispering sweet nothings. It's as if they're aiming to expose every financial skeleton in your closet. You're tied up, and they're dissecting your financial guts. And all of this is happening under the authority of the court. If you don't comply, you'll pay the price. No one's business accounting or practices are immune to scrutiny, so be prepared for both real and gratuitous backlash.

So, when we talk about Rule 2004 examinations remember, it's not just about gathering information; it's about turning over every stone, flipping every page, and intruding into the debtor's financial world. It's a probing, prying, and often discomforting process that can leave the debtor feeling like their financial soul has been exposed for all to see.

Chapter 92

Bankruptcy Guardian:
Essential Tasks of the U.S. Trustee

§

A U.S. TRUSTEE, ALSO KNOWN AS THE UNITED STATES TRUSTEE, IS essentially a government-appointed official by the U.S. Department of Justice tasked with supervising and managing bankruptcy cases. Their role is often seen as follows:

1. Supervising Bankruptcy Cases: U.S. Trustees are there to make sure bankruptcy cases comply with the law and regulations.

2. Appointing Trustees: In some bankruptcy situations, the U.S. Trustee can appoint trustees to manage and sell the debtor's assets, handle business dealings, and finances.

3. Creditor Committee Formation: U.S. Trustees may aid in forming committees of creditors, like unsecured creditors, who advocate for their interests in the bankruptcy process.

4. Reviewing Filings: The job of U.S. Trustees includes going through bankruptcy documents, such as financial disclosures and schedules, to check for accuracy and completeness.

5. Ensuring Compliance: U.S. Trustees see to it that debtors follow bankruptcy laws, court orders, and disclosure requirements, and they step in to prevent any abuse of the bankruptcy system. They act as watchdogs on the debtor's back since he owns the asset that all creditors are focused on. The bankruptcy system is inherently tough on debtors, and the U.S. Trustee usually adds to their burdens.

6. Fee Oversight: U.S. Trustees scrutinize and may raise objections to fees and expenses charged by debtors and their professionals, making sure they are reasonable and necessary for the bankruptcy process. Their review and objections are more symbolic than substantive. They generally won't upset the apple cart.

7. Mediation and Alternative Dispute Resolution: U.S. Trustees might offer mediation and alternative dispute resolution services in some personal bankruptcy cases. In a corporate bankruptcy, only after the involved parties agree on mediation would the U.S. Trustee then officially oversee and facilitate the mediation or dispute resolution and play a supervisory role to ensure that any mediation or dispute resolution procedures comply with bankruptcy laws and rules.

8. Educational Programs: U.S. Trustees often provide educational programs and information to help debtors and creditors understand their rights and responsibilities in bankruptcy cases.

In a nutshell, the role of a U.S. Trustee is to maintain the facade of integrity and fairness in the bankruptcy process, protect the rights of creditors, and make sure debtors follow the rules while trying to sort out their financial mess.

They earn respect from litigators, show deference to the judge, and can be influenced by attorneys representing contentious creditors. In the end, they're like court-appointed enforcers, ensuring that the debtor, the most beleaguered party in the proceedings, feels maximum pressure.

Chapter 93

U.S. Trustee Fees:
An Excessive Burden on the Depleted

§

THE U.S. TRUSTEE FEE, OFTEN REFERRED TO AS THE QUARTERLY U.S. Trustee fee, is like a relentless shadow in the world of bankruptcy cases, a fee imposed to fuel the U.S. Trustee Program and its ever-growing apparatus.

This fee is a calculation tied to the disbursements made by the debtor to creditors during the quarter. It's usually a percentage of these disbursements, and that percentage, of course, can shift over time. In theory, it appears as a reasonable service charge or perhaps a symbolic tip to the institution tasked with upholding our cherished constitutional protections.

Now let's venture into the fee schedules that have twisted and turned over the years.[19]

2008–2017:

- For disbursements between $0 to $14,999, the fee was $325.

- The fee increased as disbursements climbed, reaching $30,000 for disbursements of $30 million or more.

2018–2021:

- The fee schedule largely remained the same, with a significant change for disbursements of $1 million or more, where it became 1 percent of the quarterly disbursements or $250,000, whichever was less.

Picture this in your mind's eye: It's 2020, and I sold an asset within a Chapter 11 case for $27 million. Now had this sale occurred a mere three years earlier, the U.S. Trustee would have graciously accepted $20,000 as their tributary fee. But no, in 2020, I was greeted with a demand for $250,000. That's a jaw-dropping 1,200 percent increase in the toll for exercising my constitutional right!

This isn't merely an additional expense; it's a blow to the gut of a debtor already battered from all sides. As the case reaches its final act, after liquidation and payouts, the U.S. Trustee lines up like a vulture amongst other predators, waiting to claim their share of the spoils.

But how does the U.S. Trustee's office manage to justify such a colossal fee hike, you ask?

Well, a clever senator managed to sneak this fee reconfiguration into the Bankruptcy Judgment Act of 2017. It was quietly stipulated that if the U.S. Trustee Program's budget ever dipped below a certain line, they would unleash this new taxation game. So, now, the quarterly fee for a calendar quarter with disbursements of $1 million or more is the lesser of 1 percent of those disbursements or $250,000.

Now what's the big difference between paying $20,000 as a fee through 2017 and comparably $250,000 thereafter when we are talking about selling off a $27 million asset? With an asset sale of that magnitude, surely there is enough dough in the pie to go around. Well, if the liabilities due are high, say $26 million, then $250,000 is a huge portion of the $1 million remaining for shareholders.

Imagine a different twist to the story: A $27 million asset is sold, and $26,750,000 gets swallowed by creditors, fees, and attorneys. The crumbs left over amount to $250,000. The business shareholders have already faced the cruel reality of a $10 million loss of investment, and this is yet another bitter pill to swallow.

You'd think the shareholders might at least walk away with the final $250,000 in proceeds, a small respite after such a painful journey. But think again. The debtor exits with nothing, and the U.S. Trustee swoops down to claim the last shreds of the carcass, slapping on $250,000 in taxes when there's barely a dollar left to pinch.

It's confounding to fathom any fee imposed on a debtor, but if fairness were a consideration, it might resemble a relatively insignificant tax paid from each of the disbursements made to creditors. So, in the hypothetical above, the creditors would receive a payout of $26,750,000 minus less than 1 percent that would go to the U.S. Trustee, reaping the U.S. Trustee $250,000, the creditors $26,500,000, and the debtor could walk away from the table with $250,000 instead of walking way completely empty-handed.

Instead, the U.S. Trustee cunningly extracts funds from an already defeated debtor, who stumbles out of the courtroom with nothing to show for their arduous journey. This serves as a stark reminder of how empty the court's vow to shelter debtors truly is. Instead, it's a brutal, dog-eat-dog world, a dystopian jungle where only the strong, determined, and fortunate manage to find a foothold!

Chapter 94

Judges and Trustees:
The Not-So-Hidden Agendas

§

Let's pull back the curtain on judges and U.S. Trustees in the world of litigation and bankruptcy cases. They might appear impartial and objective, but trust me, there's more to the story than meets the eye.

First off, these folks don't wear their neutrality like a badge of honor. Nope, their decisions can be swayed by a multitude of very human factors. Take, for instance, the history they share with attorneys who've stood before them in the past. Judges tend to remember those lawyers they either adore or can't stand, and that can color their judgments.

But wait, there's more. There's a shadowy underbelly to the legal world, where judges and attorneys mix and mingle after hours. They attend parties and social gatherings and hobnob together. They might even join forces for some righteous causes that conveniently have ties to the legal profession or political affiliations. Judges get lauded, which causes attorneys and other law firms to support these causes, and judges sure remember which attorneys and law firms shower them with praise and respect, both in and out of court.

Now let's not kid ourselves. Judges and even U.S. Trustees who are attorneys in federal court, despite their public facade of impartiality, are well aware of the powerful connections they build through these daily interactions. They're counting the days until they can step down from their hallowed judicial thrones and waltz into a cushy gig, likely as a partner in one of the very law firms that argued cases before them.

I mean, think about it—a typical New York City judge pulls in a relatively modest $96 an hour. But as soon as they shed those black robes, they're looking at a sweet $1,200 an hour with their eyes half-closed. If they're feeling ambitious, they might even break the $1,800 per hour mark. As for the U.S. Trustee, maybe his prospects aren't as grand, but they're still making out like bandits.

So, behind all the solemn courtroom appearances, there's a certain inner glee among judges and even some U.S. Trustees in the midst of your legal turmoil. They're secretly rooting for one attorney over another, depending on what that lawyer might bring them in terms of respect, adulation, and future employment. It's a complex game, my friends, and it's not always as fair and square as you'd hope.

Chapter 95

Group Think: Dogpiling the Debtor

§

LADIES AND GENTLEMEN, THE COURTROOM IS A JUNGLE, reminiscent of a kid's playground, where only the strongest emerge unscathed. Litigators create quite a spectacle, making noise, clanging away, and eagerly attacking a debtor and their counsel in court papers and during hearings. They gnash their teeth, chomping at the bit, and launch assaults on cited law, opposing counsel, and the debtor with spittle flying as if with impunity. Even if their blows lack substance, the sheer contention, rancor, and public display of aggression sets the stage for onlookers to join the dogpile on the debtor.

Can't recall what a dogpile is? The dictionary defines it as "a barrage of criticism, insults, etc., directed at someone or something by many people, and a mass of people who have piled on top of one another while fighting."[20] Does anyone remember that innocent kid who got bullied, and then many once-neutral, peaceful bystanders suddenly felt animosity and license to bully the already bullied kid? Suddenly, the poor kid becomes the odd man out, fielding blows from friends who turned foes on a dime, all because one guy had a beef, threw the first punch, and set a public narrative.

What happens in the schoolyard mirrors what happens in court. Once one creditor attorney disparages the debtor, a narrative is crafted—an aura of "debtor is a bad guy." Since the debtor takes center stage in proceedings and each creditor litigator run their aggressive show to knock the debtor, it becomes a colossal dogpile.

Who is often conscripted to top off the dogpile? The U.S. Trustee hears a courtroom narrative of many creditors' attorneys ranking on and attempting to denigrate the debtor and challenge their legal prerogatives. Each creditor attorney then has the ability to lean in and email and call the U.S. Trustee to subtly influence him, and so the U.S. Trustee is repeatedly offered a leg up to rise atop the developing dogpile.

The top dog, another person with very human propensities toward being influenced, although often self-appraised as a heavenly pontificator and above the crowd, is the judge. They are not immune to the negativity and human nature flying around the courtroom.

It takes a very strong individual not to be tainted and influenced by the repetitive nature of hearing defamatory remarks, denigration, attacks, and indignation against the debtor in a contentious case. Sometimes, both the U.S. Trustee and the judge are conscripted into this mass hysteria of gratuitously beating up on and dogpiling the debtor.

Chapter 96

Celebrating a
Bankruptcy Judge Extraordinaire

§

IN THE UNPREDICTABLE REALM OF LEGAL CLASHES AND COURTROOM theatrics where our scrutiny typically targets attorneys and judges, it's only fitting to give a shout-out to one of the standout "good guys" in bankruptcy court—none other than Judge Robert Drain, who presided over the Southern District in White Plains, New York.

He retired in 2022, concluding an impressive two-decade tenure on the bench. Judge Drain emerged as a paragon of reason and fairness, devoid of the common pathology of the trade. He did not have a G-d complex.

He oversaw high-profile Chapter 11 cases involving giants like Sears Holdings Corp, Hostess Brands Inc., and Frontier Airlines, and as the sole judge in the White Plains division, he became the go-to venue for savvy companies and real estate owners who strategically filed their cases there, knowing they'd find an even-handed adjudicator.

Demonstrating an encyclopedic memory of bankruptcy law, Judge Drain wasn't just book smart; he approached the bench with humility, recognizing that, beyond the facades of companies and their gladiator litigators entering the arena, his decisions would ultimately impact the humans behind all this fog.

I reviewed a ruling for partners that comprised the debtor in a Judge Drain ruling[21] that was delivered orally and then redacted onto fifty-two pages. It was pleasantly clear that Judge Drain weighed all the arguments that the debtor's attorney argued and even offered the partners some shade—"it is possible that their naiveté is not feigned"—and granted them relief from claimed 24 percent default interest, stating, "On the other hand, in applying New York law that I previously summarized, I do not believe that this is the type of default that would serve as a basis for acceleration or enforcement of default interest," and some relief from the lender's legal fees claims, "the Debtors should have the opportunity to review those time and expense records in the light of my ruling which, again, reflected that certain of the defaults called by Lender really would not be enforceable and, therefore, might reflect on the reasonableness of fees and expenses related to attempts to enforce those defaults. Finally, such review is best taken in a clear context where there is a practical prospect of recovering such fees and expenses, whereas at this time it is unclear whether that context will ever come to pass."

So, let's raise a hearty toast to Judge Robert Drain—a sharp-witted jurist, an exemplar of even-handedness, and undoubtedly one of the genuine "good guys" in the often tumultuous world of bankruptcy court.

Chapter 97

Success in Chapter 11

§

L ET'S GET REAL ABOUT THE JOURNEY THROUGH CHAPTER 11
bankruptcy—it's like a wild rollercoaster ride, folks. Success in this
realm depends on a host of factors, from the industry's quirks and the
depth of the mess to economic whims, the prowess of your legal team,
the judge's disposition, and a dash of plain luck.

Now picture the battleground: The debtor stands in the middle, the
judge hovers high in the air, and creditors and their attorneys encircle
the debtor armed with unlimited ammunition in one hand and a claw
in the other. They fire potshots at the debtor's estate and its stakeholders,
inadvertently hitting creditors in the crossfire. The claws sporadically
lunge to extract life and substance from the debtor, jeopardizing its
vitality and hindering its escape from the pressure cooker that is
bankruptcy court. The court, instead of being a sanctuary, feels more like
a Russian roulette death circle. Oh, what a place!

Now let's contrast legal systems.

Common law operates on the principle of stare decisis, a Latin phrase
meaning "to stand by things decided." In practice, it insists that courts
and judges follow earlier decisions (case law) when dealing with similar
cases later. So, if you were caught going one mile over the speed limit,
that's illegal, and here's your fine.

Bankruptcy court, on the other hand, is a court of equity that follows law and
rules, but it is allowed to be more creative in finding a solution that is right

for the specific case at hand, and the court of equity can be less concerned about if that same ruling would work for the next case. It evolved

> ...side by side with the common law, there grew up a system of equity law much more elastic, penetrating, and far better adapted to the growing wants of the people than the inelastic and unbending common law, and which was founded upon a far higher ethical and moral plain, and more pregnant with sound reason and common sense than many rules of the common law.[22]

The original goal was to allow the court flexibility and common sense so that the debtor wouldn't get hung with the exactitude of precedent. Unfortunately, that ship of common sense sailed straight into the Bermuda Triangle.

Now here's the inside scoop: a 2019 study by the American Bankruptcy Institute spilled the beans.[23] About 42 percent of major public companies successfully navigated Chapter 11 with a reorganization plan and kept on trucking. Smaller companies, on the other hand, had a much tougher time. In fact, the overall successful emergence rate from Chapter 11 is a paltry 10 percent.

According to the odds, Russian roulette with a six-shot revolver has an 83 percent chance of survival, while Chapter 11 has a 10 percent chance to emerge alive. Which game is safer?

Part Three

Settlement

Chapter 98

Settlement: Your Exit Strategy
from the Legal Battlefield

§

IN THE VAST LANDSCAPE OF OUR NATION, DISPUTES OF ALL KINDS FIND
their way into the legal arena, often clogging the courts. These conflicts
involve everything from soured business partnerships to family disputes,
divorce battles, malpractice claims, financial wrangling, and contract
breaches. However, within the world of settlement, there's a peculiar truth:

A fair settlement is one in which both parties feel they've lost.

Let's be clear, though—settlement and litigation are two different
animals. Settlement often feels like losing, while litigation carries the
banner of "We will win!" It's like comparing apples to oranges.

Litigation is a protracted, arduous journey, often without a clear outcome
but with the promise of victory, while settlement represents a definite
destination that, true to the above quote, feels like losing. To understand
the difference better, we need to look at the pain, cost, and collateral
damage of each.

In the world of litigation, most cases conclude after a long, drawn-
out battle, leaving one side defeated and the so-called "winner" still
unsatisfied. The toll taken is financial, emotional, physiological, and
temporal. In the typical case, only about 3 percent make it to trial or final
adjudication. In the end, everyone involved feels like they've lost.

So, considering that a whopping 97 percent of cases settle before ever
reaching the courtroom, why not choose a quicker way out than targeting
going the distance? Here's the undeniable truth: Whether you navigate

the perilous terrain of litigation to claim an empty victory or opt for settlement, you're likely to feel like a loser. So, why not leave the world of conflict behind as soon as you can and prevent all that collateral damage?

The legal system and human nature share an affinity for conflict and challenges. Many find exhilaration in battle, whether it be the thrill of war, the fascination with gladiator showdowns that captivated the Roman Empire for centuries, or the adrenaline of sports like boxing, football, or squash.

However, instead of indulging in endless battles, it makes sense to calculate all the costs, both obvious and hidden, financial, temporal, and collateral, that you'll incur through litigation.

Consider the likely outcome of the fight. This is best done on day one or even in anticipation of a recognized potential conflict. Then think of that sum of costs as disposable income to make a settlement today. By doing so, you'll gain the gift of time—a chance to step away from the relentless grind of litigation.

It will certainly cost you up front, but it's an opportunity to regroup, to regain your financial footing through focused business endeavors, to enjoy restful sleep, maintain your health and sanity, and to cherish moments with your family rather than squander them in courtrooms.

Yes, settling may make you feel like a loser, but in the grand scheme of things, you're a winner. You've freed yourself from the inevitable pain and costs, preserved your health, and said goodbye to all the freeloading, mind-numbing courtroom jesters and squatters in your brain.

It's not defeat; it may feel that way when you cut the check on day one of settlement, but rest assured, you'll also cut your losses as you gain your freedom and a sense of relief that will stay with you not just in the next moment but forever. It's a strategic triumph in the complex world of Lady Justice.

Chapter 99

How Courts Play With Your Life:
Litigation Stress Syndrome

§

Litigation Stress Syndrome is as real as a heart attack and can be fatal too. It's a crude form of posttraumatic stress disorder, PTSD,[24] and was only proposed as a psychological disorder in 1989 by Paul R. Lees-Haley, PhD.[25] Doctors sued for malpractice often suffer a medically labeled variation called medical malpractice stress syndrome (MMSS).

The stigma and stress associated with a malpractice suit or any litigation often results in anxiety and depression, fatigue and emotional exhaustion, difficulty concentrating, irritability, changes in appetite and libido, apathy, anger, feelings of shame and guilt, fear of reputational fallout, insomnia, burnout, loss of confidence in decision-making, substance abuse, strain on personal and professional relationships, and even suicidal ideation.[26]

Let's explore a case study where litigation killed a man:

A fifty-seven-year-old male spine surgeon was sued for a failed anterior cervical discectomy and fusion. After five years of depositions, interrogatories, pretrial motions, and delays, the trial was finally scheduled. The history, obtained from his close colleagues and friends, revealed that anticipation of the trial "completely took over every waking moment." After prolonged sitting for five days in court during jury selection and preliminary motions, he developed mild nonspecific chest discomfort, which he attributed to stress.

Approximately thirty-six hours before the trial was to begin, he met with one of his closest friends. At that time, he was visibly distressed, anxious, apprehensive, and depressed—more than he had ever been observed to be before. He admitted to insomnia, lack of appetite, and anger at the whole experience. The accusations of professional negligence and incompetence were highly publicized in the local media. He correctly believed that his reputation as a nationally recognized premier sports medicine surgeon was under attack.

Because of pretrial stress and the required time for trial preparation, beginning a few weeks before the actual trial, he neglected his usual daily one hour or so of aerobic and resistance workout. He was on no medications, had no history of cardiac or pulmonary disease or risk factors for clotting disorders, and was in general excellent health. He did not smoke or use alcohol.

Beyond his numerous publications and professional accomplishments, he was known to be dedicated to the highest medical ethics and was firmly committed to what was in the best interest of his patients. He was known to have boundless energy, a brilliant medical mind, and skilled hands. The friend stated that throughout his career the physician always "kept it together" and was "as cool as ice" under pressure. So, his behavior and mood then were very atypical.

On the morning of the first day of trial, he walked to his car and suddenly fell to the ground and died. The autopsy revealed multiple pulmonary thromboembolisms, well organized and adherent, occluding the bilateral lower lobar pulmonary arteries, which probably caused the nonspecific chest discomfort prior to the trial. Also, there was a large non-adherent saddle embolus occluding the main pulmonary arteries that resulted in sudden death.[27] The judicial process whacked the athletic healthy doctor.

There is even a book written for doctors, *Physicians Survival Guide to Litigation Stress. Understanding, Managing, and Transcending a Malpractice Crisis*, but make no mistake about it, this syndrome, or at least some of its symptoms, will affect most folks who litigate. It's not about having a victim mentality. It's more about the physiological responses triggered by the stress inherent in litigation.

If one has other stressors or medical conditions, they are often exacerbated. Ulcers and acid reflux pop up and erupt like sprouts and volcanoes. Cognitive disruptions, such as problems with concentration and attention, are common. Irrational thoughts associated with "catastrophizing" and "awfulizing" are common, along with rumination about potentially disastrous outcomes.

Marital and family conflicts are very common consequences of litigation stress. Pre-existing strains in these relationships are magnified. As one would expect, it is not uncommon for the use of alcohol, tobacco, and caffeine to increase during this time of stress. The risk for abuse of these substances increases, along with various prescription medications, especially pain medications, anti-anxiety drugs, and sleep medication.[28]

The very process of adjudication, the legal system itself, at best inflicts harm and at worst kills and maims people. The verdict, financial losses, or lousy custody arrangements all pale in comparison to the emotional, psychological, and physical anguish wrought by the legal system's machine. In the case study explored earlier, the litigation was this doctor's death knell, literally the premature nail in his coffin.

So, folks, there you have it. Litigation is a meat grinder. It's a plague of heart attacks, strokes, and other fatal or debilitating calamities. If you are lucky, you will survive. Whether you're sitting at the plaintiff's or defendant's table, litigation takes a toll on your mental and physiological health, and let it be known that I warned you: litigation is a health risk.

Chapter 100

Mind, Body, and Soul Mastery
in the Legal Arena

§

LITIGATION IS A BATTLEFIELD WHERE YOU PAY THE PRICE DURING AND after the battle, and as the managerial leader in your litigation and settlement campaign, achieving peace of mind and body is paramount for effective management and execution. Join me on a journey to uncover daily mantras, maxims, creeds, and strategies to navigate this challenging terrain.

Weathering the Storm of Conflict
In the eye of the legal tornado, the impending loss, acrimony, and frustrations outlined in this book bear down on your soul. While a rare few may be immune, most people can't easily reframe the torrent. Amidst the dismemberment of assets, businesses, marriages, careers, or partnerships, you find yourself in the throes of battle—bullets flying, shell shocked. Relaxation seems a distant luxury.

Commander of Your Fate
In this tumultuous battlefield, there's no choice but to step up and be the commander. It demands an "about-face," shedding private citizen mindsets. Remember Nike's iconic campaign in 1988? "Just Do It" says it all, and you too can quickly acquire a mindset of determination, ambition, and resilience. You are at war, and it's either sink or swim. Let's explore mantras, maxims, creeds, and strategies to transform you into a calm commander with unwavering focus and resolve.

No Justice, No Peace
Cease gazing at your situation through the elusive prism of justice, an

often unattainable goal in legal battles. Justice won't be found in litigation or anywhere else. Instead, embrace the acknowledgment that no one wronged you intentionally.

In the throes of conflict, the victimization we feel might find some legitimacy in certain facts. However, dwelling on this wounded perspective sabotages your well-being and hinders progress in litigation or the pursuit of a settlement. It's akin to a mind stuck in a perpetual washing machine, endlessly spinning the facts of your case without resolution.

This repetitive cycle of regurgitated rot and stagnation leads to existential questions: "How could someone do this to me? Why is this happening?" The answer, though seemingly complex, can be your empowering mantra:

> [Name or Company] and its people made a disastrous choice, perhaps even an evil one, and will one day reckon with the One Above. Simultaneously and separately, the Almighty gifted me this challenge. Despite the hardship and collateral damage, it's a blessing in disguise. Soon I'll understand and find peace.

Consider this your brain and soul freshener—an elixir to disrupt the dizzying spin cycle. By uttering these words, you'll navigate the litigation and settlement journey with clarity and endurance.

Embrace the Abyss

Accept the prospect of a total loss. Envision the worst-case scenario. If you approach the conflict with a mindset that you are fighting for the retention of whatever is at stake, you will feel battle worn in no time, and the daily grind of trying to hold on for dear life will exhaust you.

I propose penciling out the worst-case scenario, detailing all potential losses if things go completely sideways, and then imagining letting go of everything and accepting that loss. It's a big ask, but follow me. Then shift your focus to what might be recouped rather than what is at stake for a loss.

You will have shifted into a more celebratory mindset because any material benefits you accrue going forward will be a gain, an acquisition, so to speak, and therefore will feel like a win. Compare this to the old mindset of holding on for dear life, which means you lost part of what you previously held onto, which is a loss even if you held onto the lion's share.

The perspective I'm suggesting is kind of like the salesman who goes into the sales arena not expecting to make the sale. It's a healthier mindset than hoping to make the sale, and in the end, he'll be more successful. He'll be calmer because the worst has already happened—he has the mindset that he didn't get the sale. Of course, he wants to make a sale, but with a better, reframed attitude, he will go into the sale area with zero nervousness and have nothing to lose, only something to gain.

Your starting position in the conflict is feeling at peace with an imagined total loss. Your level-headed pursuit of the resolution will bring you fruits, and every gain will be a celebration.

> *Mantra: I assume a total loss, walking out of here with just the shirt on my back.*

Then strive to maximize the acquisition of territory and assets in litigation and settlement.

Worry Be Gone
Worry is a futile endeavor. Just stop it. Seriously. Refuse to indulge. It's a nearly useless, feeble, and self-flagellating emotion that yields no fruits.

> *Mantra: Worry is for losers; choose strength!*

Fear No More: Rise to Victory
Being scared is utterly pointless. Envision the worst-case scenario. If and when it becomes real, confront it. Accept it now as if it has already unfolded. Be grateful that the worst-case scenario may or may not come to pass, reveling in the respite and freedom it grants.

> *Mantra: Losers fear, winners soar. Be bold!*

Grow Thicker Skin: A Battle Cry
Personal attacks in court, the ominous tone of opposing documents, and

the onslaught during discovery can unsettle even the strongest. Thicker-skinned individuals remain unruffled. If you haven't reached that point, cultivate an additional layer or two. Whether man or woman, toughen up, be robust, and become impervious to any contentious assault.

Mantra: Grow thicker skin. Defy, prevail, thrive!

As you gear up for the strategic litigation ground war, armed with the mantras provided above, cultivating a mindset of less worry, and acquiring immunity to rough words or actions with your newfound "alligator skin," let's delve into the realm of anger.

Anger

A brief burst of anger, lasting a second or two, might trigger a response that benefits your case. It's reactive, fleeting, and can be a beneficial survival instinct to wake you up. However, prolonged anger is counterproductive, revealing a loss of control. Anger becomes a deceptive drug, creating a false sense of regained control. More than two seconds of anger is a trait of immaturity. It's time to grow up. Anger is a weakness, akin to idol worship.

Creed: Anger is a delusional drug. Kick the habit and address the issue at hand with calm.

Avoid Lies and Acrimony

I don't advocate making false allegations to gratuitously smear the other side in court pleadings. First, it's not true, and second, it will likely infuriate your opponents and perhaps their counsel. If you refrain from smearing them, they may not take your litigation as personally, avoiding the swords of vendetta and retributional litigation tactics. Instead of escalating conflict, they might have been more conciliatory earlier, leading to a potential settlement.

Consider the case of an individual facing the collapse of his empire, entangled in litigation and bankruptcy. He chose to smear his lenders, escalating their determination to pursue him at any cost. Had he maintained a businesslike and truthful approach to litigation, numerous opportunities might have arisen to cut a deal and find respite from the onslaught. His use of false rhetoric and gratuitous hubris, facilitated and or supplemented by his counsel, fueled the intransigence of the opposition.

Drop acrimony and falsity. Settling a case becomes incredibly challenging when gratuitous contentiousness is the forging agent of intransigence. Avoid it from the inception of your case, leaving the door open to future settlement throughout the case's lifespan.

Creed: The truth will set you free.

You Are Not Alone In Facing Challenges
Consider the wisdom of King David, who endured trials and tribulations, expressing his experiences in the Psalms. People turn to Psalms in moments of joy and trouble, seeking comfort and guidance, and to connect with the Almighty for help and gratitude. Reflect on:

Psalm 116: I found trouble and grief, and I called out in the name of the L-rd.

Psalm 27: The L-rd is my light and my salvation; whom shall I fear? The L-rd is the stronghold of my life; from whom shall I be frightened?

These timeless words hold the power to resonate with people in various situations. As you navigate the complexities of litigation and settlement, exploring ways to deescalate your mind and soul are crucial for effective decision-making.

Therapist
Consider the potential benefits of seeking the guidance of a therapist as you focus on the essential aspects of yourself. Acknowledge that your litigation woes are not the primary concern for the therapist; rather, you seek assistance in navigating how you process challenges.

Bootcamp
Every commander, including yourself, needs to be in top physical shape. If you're new to the litigation circus, it will tax your mind, body, and soul. The moment you sign that litigation retainer, consider enrolling in a

physical boot camp. Whether joining a gym or hiring a personal trainer to come to your home or office a few times a week, the boost to your health and body will work wonders for getting in shape and reducing stress. While you may not typically budget time or money for personal trainers, consider this a legal expense. You're already investing heavily in every billable hour, and the cost of getting in shape will be a minor blip compared to the overall benefits. Your body will thank you, and your mind will command the war better as your outlook and ability to conquer are enhanced.

Run or Walk
Cover ground, and you'll experience improvements in both health and mental clarity.

Nutrition
You can spend money on nutritionists or read numerous books on diets, potentially leading to enlightenment or confusion. Alternatively, embrace the common denominator of good health practices: eat non-processed whole foods with single and recognizable ingredients like broccoli, tomatoes, mangos, and steak. Grab a multivitamin, and you're off and running.

Drugs, Alcohol, Smoking
Soldiers historically turned to drugs to enhance their combat abilities. In World War II, the American, English, German, and Japanese armies issued substances like Benzedrine, meth, and even cocaine.[29] Later, the U.S. military utilized dexamphetamine to keep soldiers awake for extended periods, aiming to "enhance courage and bravado." Captagon, a fenethylline-based performance enhancer once used widely,[30] especially in the Middle East,[31] is no longer produced in the U.S. but remains a drug of choice for fighters and terrorists.[32]

In the realm of litigation, it's a battle, but unlike wartime, you don't need drugs, alcohol, or cigarettes for either recreation or the fight. If you are a user, now is the time to reduce or quit altogether. Managing this legal battle is best done with a clear mind and all your faculties intact.

There's no need for bravado or sleepless nights; sobriety is your best ally in this war.

Sleep

We spend a significant amount of time in bed, and most of us don't sleep enough. Inadequate sleep is a major stressor on our minds and bodies. You're investing a grand per hour, and settlement is but a dream. Why not invest in the most comfortable mattress, fresh sheets, blankets, and pillows? Prioritize going to sleep at a reasonable time. You'll feel better and think more clearly, regardless of what challenges the day throws at you.

In the legal battlefield, mastering the mind, body, and soul is crucial for effective leadership. As the commander of your fate, an "about-face" is required, shedding private citizen mindsets. Much like Nike's iconic campaign, "Just Do It," so must you, which includes getting your mind, body, and soul in shape so that you transmogrify into a calm and capable leader with an unwavering focus to settle this case as soon as possible.

Chapter 101

Settlement Through Peace

§

"Be of the disciples of Aaron, loving peace and pursuing peace."[33]

THIS BIBLICAL DIRECTIVE IS THE WINNING MINDSET TO SET THE stage for the end of your litigation and the beginning of your settlement. The quotes below require no commentary, and they may inspire you to a peaceful resolution:

> Aaron [the high priest, Moses' brother], was a lover of peace and a pursuer of peace and would make peace between one person and the other.[34]

> When he would see two people quarreling, he would go to each one of them without the knowledge of his fellow and say to him, "Behold how your fellow is regretting and afflicting himself that he sinned against you; and he told me that I should come to you so that you will forgive him." And as a result of this, when they bumped into each other, they would kiss each other.[35]

Chapter 102

The Transformation from Harmony to Hostility

§

PARTIES IN A CONFLICT WERE ONCE AS CLOSE AS BIRDS OF A FEATHER, sharing amicable relations. Whether it was business partners, companies collaborating, borrowers and lenders, or even husband and wife, a rift appeared and the gulf between them widened, fueled by the influence of friends, family, in-house or external advisors, and outside forces fanning the flames of discord.

Each side then enlisted a law firm, whose primary objective was not resolution but litigation and battle. This choice drove the parties further apart. The result? Each side found themselves in a state of separation, an exile, more distanced than ever before, adopting a warlike mentality, entrenched in their adversarial positions.

They hired litigators to wage their battles in the cumbersome arena of the court system, each side flinging pleadings, motions, and pompous war cries in oral arguments onto the battlefield, occasionally engaging in gladiatorial contests before the judge.

Early settlements became unlikely, buried beneath the weight of inertia, pain, expenses, and the liabilities incurred during prolonged litigation. A war of attrition unfolded, eroding willpower. It demanded a significant investment of time, money, emotions, and disruptions to business and personal life.

As the famous writer Kurt Vonnegut often wrote in *Slaughterhouse-Five,*[36] "and so it goes." This phrase isn't about accepting life but rather about facing death. It appears in the text every time someone dies, evoking the sense that litigation can be akin to experiencing a thousand deaths.

Both litigants, once birds of a feather, are now more like warrior chickens in a back-alley cock fight. The legal system and their attorneys have affixed razor blades to your legs, and it never ends well for either party, except the law firms who collect your blood money.

Chapter 103

Business Disputes Intersect with Personal Matters

§

ALRIGHT, STRAP IN, FOLKS, BECAUSE WE'RE DIVING INTO THE WILD world where family drama and business disputes collide like a train wreck in slow motion. Picture this: It's a chaotic tango of personal relationships gone awry and business battles that make the Crips and the Bloods turf war look like a walk in the park.

Now whether it's a feud that started with a family barbecue gone sideways or a business deal that turned sour and ignited the family fireworks, it's like playing a game of "who started it" in a kindergarten sandbox. Courts get involved, throwing a Band-Aid solution on a situation that's hemorrhaging emotions and family ties. It's like putting a Band-Aid on a gunshot wound—sure, it covers the mess, but it doesn't fix what's really broken.

Take the classic family business scenario, where a father and son rivalry grips each other's throats or brothers are duking it out over who gets the bigger slice of the business pie. Add in mothers and some wives, and you've got a recipe for a Shakespearean tragedy. Family dynamics turn into a soap opera, and the court becomes the battleground for a royal rumble.

Now let's spin the wheel of family fortune and land on estate and inheritance disputes. Imagine a billionaire's legacy torn apart by siblings fighting over the family fortune like seagulls over a French fry:

> New York real estate mogul Louis Feil left his $7 billion dynasty to his four children (one son, Jeffrey, and three daughters) in equal

shares. Jeffrey ran the business and received a sizable salary, but distributed just $300,000 per year to his sisters. The three sisters sued, alleging Jeffrey was starving them out so he could buy them out at a discounted price. The family lost its glue when the parents died. A *Wall Street Journal* article noted that according to Jeffrey, when his father died, "the binding of the book came loose," and when mother Gertrude later died, "the pages fell out."[37]

The sisters each received a $1.75 billion ownership stake but were not satisfied with the yearly distribution stipend. In the realm of family problems, this was an enviable one and perhaps even solvable, had the siblings steered clear of the courts.

If the embers of family goodwill were fanned with the mindset of settlement and family reunification, whether before or soon after the litigators took control of this dispute, I'd bet the ranch there would have been less acrimony, fewer skeletons pulled from the closet, a more favorable financial deal for all involved, and perhaps even a chance to mend the torn pages of the Feil family book. Unfortunately, litigation tends to consume money and time and often solidifies greater, sometimes permanent divisions between the parties.

Now let's transition to the domain of divorce court, child custody and visitation, child support, and alimony proceedings. Employing the court's scalpel to dissect this amalgamation of business and family matters is akin to delicately attempting the separation of Siamese twins conjoined at the head, sharing a single superior vena cava. It's a process fraught with pain, significant costs, inherent risks, and immeasurable collateral damage, no matter how you slice it.

A man holds a significant portfolio of properties, an inheritance from his parents, long before he crossed paths with his wife. Together, they acquired additional properties, and she became a signatory on all bank accounts, including those linked to his pre-marital holdings. Prior to their separation, she emptied all the bank accounts.

Unable to meet monthly mortgage payments, the properties entered pre-foreclosure litigation. Seeking legal assistance, the husband enlisted a litigator. Meanwhile, a divorce, lingering on the back burner for years with no resolution in sight, demanded the attention of yet another attorney. To make matters worse, he hadn't seen his kids for three years.

This man faced the risk of losing his property portfolio with all jointly owned properties entangled in a legal quagmire. His marriage was irreparably broken, and his children were distant figures in a life marred by legal complexities. While not a high-profile media case like Johnny Depp and Amber Heard, nor as entertaining, this was a situation involving real people ensnared in a legal system that failed to pave a way out. If only he could have strategized to identify the common thread in his tribulations, a solution might have been closer than he dared to imagine.

The legal system isn't designed to double as a family counseling service, and unfortunately, family counselors are not equipped to navigate such intricate and messy situations. Fueled by run-of-the-mill emotions like anger and frustration, our protagonists found themselves blinded and trapped in a retaliatory mode within a legal system that, rather than providing resolution, seemed to escalate tensions, pushing them to ascend the step stool, metaphorically speaking, and inadvertently hang themselves.

Had one of them opted for a different route, engaging in shuttle diplomacy tactics through an intermediary to attempt a negotiated financial settlement, both parties could have salvaged some assets, finalized the divorce, and the fella might even have had a shot at reconnecting with his kids.

Inheritance disputes, family businesses, family offices, divorces, child custody battles—each contributes to the intersection of assets and the intricate web of family and personal relationships.

Here's the kicker: The default solution in these scenarios is often litigation, an adversarial process that fans the flames of pain and suffering between the parties. On the flip side, settlement attempts through shuttle diplomacy don't inflict further harm on the disputants; in fact, they might pave the way to resolution, putting an end to their litigation and perhaps fostering some semblance of family peace and closure.

Chapter 104

The Roadmap to Settlement
and Navigating Litigation

§

Litigation can sometimes be an unavoidable necessity, but it's crucial to keep settlement at the forefront of your legal journey and on your mind at every turn.

Your litigator, often trained for long-haul legal battles that stretch on for years, is focused on playing the long game, often at the expense of your time and money. It's essential to remember that law firms are in business for themselves, not exclusively for your benefit. Protracted legal work sustains their livelihood and boosts their wealth. While they may help you evaluate your case, they're unlikely to assist you in limiting your legal bills.

Why would any litigator encourage early settlement when their training and business model favor prolonged legal warfare? This is where you, or an informed third-party advisor come into play. Much like a skilled cliff climber searching for every possible foothold to ascend a steep mountain, your task is to pinpoint strategic opportunities in your case where a settlement effort can gain traction.

Engage your attorney in discussions about these emerging opportunities every time you interact with them, and inquire about how to potentially exploit them. If your litigator resists these exploratory conversations, it might be time to consider finding someone better suited to your needs.

The highest and best strategic use of litigation can be counterintuitive; it's not necessarily a direct path to resolution but rather a tool used to facilitate a settlement. While it might not be the sharpest tool in the shed, comprehending its function, as extensively explored in this book, empowers you to wield it more effectively in pursuit of your goals.

Keep in mind that litigation isn't the ultimate objective; it's more akin to an inefficient tool that may serve you as both a literal and figurative stop-gap measure, allowing you to maintain control of your livelihood and/or company assets, thwarting even a lawfare objective of the other side, and giving you time to figure out the best way to settle your case.

Chapter 105

The Path to Settlement: Bridging the Divide

§

T HE JOURNEY TO SETTLEMENT TRULY BEGINS WHEN THE FEUDING parties take the courageous step of closing the chasm that separates them, moving closer together in a bid to engage in humanizing interactions and perhaps to hear each other's voices.

In most cases, the legal system isn't designed to encourage early settlement discussions or interventions. A few exceptions exist, such as when a homeowner defaults on a mortgage, necessitating a legally mandated conversation between the lender and borrower, potentially leading to a loan modification and the discontinuation of litigation.

The idea of picking up the phone to reach out to the other side in an attempt to settle differences may seem simple, but it's far from it. Once you've entrenched yourself on one side of a battle, emerging from the trenches to engage in a calm conversation can be an arduous endeavor. Your litigator might even advise against it, citing potential risks to your case or the appearance of weakness, especially if settlement talks are on the horizon.

The challenge doesn't stop there. Even if you mustered the courage to contact the other side directly, they may refuse to take your call without consulting their attorney. And it's highly likely their attorney would advise against direct communication during litigation.

Attorneys often act as barriers to prevent open dialogue, as it might create liabilities for your case, even if in reality they're relatively minor.

The end goal of settlement would also diminish the financial windfall your paid-per-hour litigator expects from your case, so it's clear that he isn't running to help you here.

The system as it stands isn't primarily designed to foster settlement. Instead, it's tailored for litigation to play out. High emotions and both parties at odds don't make an initial approach seem feasible. And if the opposition is a ferocious lawfare gladiator that wants to eat you up, as they say in Brooklyn, "Fuhgeddaboudit."

Nevertheless, there's no chance of settlement without some form of communication between the parties. One option is to make strategic moves within the chessboard of litigation, positioning yourself for the possibility of broaching settlement offers. An alternative is to instruct your attorney to request a settlement conference through the court or by reaching out to opposing counsel.

However, there's an inherent weakness in relying on attorneys as intermediaries to broach settlement with opposing counsel. As mentioned earlier, they often lack the motivation to pursue this path transparently and may thwart your efforts.

The most effective strategy for closing the divide between parties involves reintroducing elements of the human connection that once existed. Despite the current state of being adversaries, the pain, losses, and devastation resulting from the conflict have cumulatively left their mark on both sides. And there may very well be nefarious asset-raiding intentions too, like from a predatory lender looking to consume you and your assets.

So, how can you bridge the gap and begin to understand one another, potentially leading to a settlement? Let's turn to a biblical example for inspiration.

The Book of Genesis recounts the story of Jacob sending gifts to his brother Esau in anticipation of their meeting. This gesture aimed to appease Esau following a period of conflict and estrangement. Jacob had acquired Esau's birthright and blessing, creating a deep rift between them. Fearing a hostile confrontation, Jacob sent a generous offering of livestock and valuable items to Esau as a goodwill gesture.

Their eventual encounter, as described in Genesis 33, marked a pivotal moment in their relationship. To Jacob's surprise, Esau was not hostile, and their reconciliation began. This story underscores the power of anticipation, gifts, and gestures of goodwill in approaching resolution instead of war.

The key point here is that you or an informed advisor possess the capacity to humanize the situation, narrowing the gap between both parties involved in the litigation. Even if your opposition seems determined to exact retribution or a pound of flesh, a focus on your shared humanity increases the likelihood of a quicker, cleaner divorce from the conflict and of ultimately reaching a settlement.

Chapter 106

The Significance and Ramifications of Litigation: It's All in the Players

§

WHEN WE DELVE INTO THE OUTCOMES OF LITIGATION, IT'S ALL about perspective, isn't it? It hinges on where you fit into the grand scheme of things. You see, for some, litigation is just a sign that they've made it. It's a cost of doing business that's been carefully factored into their overall expenses and projections. In their eyes, litigation is more of an irritating mosquito bite rather than a full-blown headache.

- If you're overseeing a larger operation, you've got layers of management and in-house counsel to handle these matters directly or farm them out to outside counsel. You're largely shielded from the day-to-day chaos. But hey, even in the best of scenarios, having less litigation on your company plate would undoubtedly be a financial win.

- Now if you're a secured creditor, litigation can be a real thorn in your side, and it's a stern test for your business. It all hangs in the balance of factors, such as the aggressiveness of your loan portfolio's underwriting, your ability to sell debt, current interest rates, economic conditions, and your ability to raise capital. Those are a lot of balls to juggle, right? No doubt, defaults are the kind of headaches most lenders would gladly sidestep.

- For the debt buyers out there, if the economy takes a nosedive while you're holding onto defaulted paper, those assets might sink too, even at the discounted price for which you acquired the debt. You could easily find yourself teetering on the brink of trouble with your litigation strategy to seize valuable assets hampered.

- If you're a debtor filing for Chapter 11 bankruptcy, whether you're a corporate giant or a smaller player, it's a grueling and costly ordeal. Whether you're hoping for a reorganization or looking to wrap things up with a liquidation, be prepared for a significant financial hit.

- Now let's talk about the unsecured creditors. In some scenarios, there's simply nothing left to recover from the assets after all the courtroom battles. You might end up taking a complete loss, and all those litigation expenses become nothing more than a sunk cost.

- Are you being personally named in a lawsuit? That can be an emotionally wrenching experience and an unwelcome liability.

- Are you a doctor in a malpractice lawsuit? Devastating. Not covered by your insurance? Doubly so.

- And if you're in the thick of a divorce or family court proceedings, there's hardly a hint of a smile to be found.

- Now if you're a small business, whether you're the defendant or the plaintiff, litigation will take a considerable bite out of your resources.

- And if you're stuck in a dispute with business partners, your company is often left in shambles with no viable exit strategy.

Conflict, in its very essence, is a disruptor. The outcomes depend on how both parties navigate that turmoil. Just because marriages, businesses, and financial deals crumble doesn't mean that the financial affairs of those involved are irrevocably damaged. However, the common remedy, litigation, frequently ends up being a death knell for the company, assets, and/or financial well-being of the parties entangled in conflict.

By fueling animosity, pouring vast sums of money into litigation, and dedicating years to legal battles, the collateral damage to the assets, the parties, and the businesses takes a tremendous toll, ultimately diminishing the financial value of the very objects they're battling over.

In nearly every instance, litigation tends to devalue the contested assets, leading to substantial headaches, financial losses, and squandered efforts.

In the end, litigation typically results in the parties going their separate ways. But of course, it would take at least two sides to settle a dispute, to work through the problem, and to find resolutions that allow for amicable partings. Imagine if emotions, the desire to win at all costs, and bitterness could be left out of the equation. It would be fantastic if all parties in a conflict had the capacity to approach things that way, but it would certainly be noteworthy and invaluable if at least one party saw the potential for level-headedness and the acceptance of reality.

Now what if that party understood the overall inefficiency and futility of the litigation effort? What if they considered extending an olive branch, opening a line of dialogue where both sides could sit down separately with cooler heads to assess their respective positions of viability, risks, and all litigation costs? Imagine both parties breaking down those expenses, both explicit and implicit, into a bottom-line number—what the journey of litigation will ultimately cost them. If their attorneys weren't engaged in posturing but instead played a supportive and logical role or bowed out completely, don't you think that in many cases a deal memo could be drafted and the litigation settled more quickly and efficiently than through the courts?

Just picture friendlier splits through negotiated settlements—avoiding the financial drain, the time-consuming ordeal, the strenuous effort, the exhaustive emotional expenditure and all the headaches. It's an alternative that's more than worth considering.

Chapter 107

The Legal Role Reversal: Becoming an Indentured Servant

§

IN A REMARKABLE TWIST, THE ATTORNEY-CLIENT RELATIONSHIP CAN take a surprising turn, casting you, the litigant, in the unexpected role of an unwitting indentured servant to your litigator and the court. Demanding immediate responses, constant availability, and swift cooperation, your litigator creates an atmosphere where walking on eggshells and servitude become second nature, fearing reproach for any delays. The ceaseless search for old documents and emails adds an unrelenting layer to your responsibilities.

Similar to an overwhelmed employer forced to sell or shut down a business due to feeling like an employee to their staff, you might find yourself in a comparable predicament during litigation. Jumping ship isn't an option, so you are left to navigate the challenge of being both the litigator's boss and servant—a delicate dance akin to flossing your teeth while dancing the Floss.

Picture the potential chaos if you fail to promptly address your litigator's demands; your case could unravel and blame may fall on you, regardless of your efforts. Your litigator, skilled in finding alibis and deflecting blame, relies on your unwavering support. Failure to meet this demand could lead to a swift turnaround of blame and alibis against you, jeopardizing your case. Satisfying this new employer is non-negotiable for a case to gain traction, even if it becomes a time-consuming and inefficient endeavor.

Being at your attorney's beck and call becomes an enduring commitment, and your willingness and ability to meet their demands significantly impact the success of your case. Should you be unable or unwilling to provide the necessary support, your case will inevitably suffer, regardless of the legal team's caliber. Even with a top-notch legal team in place, a client's personal challenges or lack of focus can cause more liabilities, impeding the progress and success of their case. Mastering the delicate balance of fulfilling your responsibilities while maintaining control is paramount for a successful legal journey.

If you find yourself tangled in a web of disorganization, lacking focus, or if your time is exceedingly valuable, prioritizing settlement might take precedence over almost any litigation scenario or strategy, even at a higher cost than usual. This strategic move aims to prevent the compounding of liabilities and offers the opportunity to free yourself for more productive endeavors. In the grand scheme, the investment in settlement could prove more valuable than the toll of prolonged disarray and time constraints.

Chapter 108

The Hidden Power of Settlement:
A Win-Win Solution

$

SETTLEMENT, MY FRIENDS, OFTEN FINDS ITS ROOTS ON ONE SIDE OF the battlefield. The legal system, far from being a beacon of progressive justice, often operates in the trenches of combat. So, when one side even whispers the word "settlement," it's akin to waving the white flag. Try mentioning it to your attorney, and you'll likely receive a response like, "It's not the right time, too premature."

Your fervor to end this legal quagmire is stunted like a bonsai tree at the hands of your legal gardener, your litigator, who trims and binds your olive branch desires of seeking resolution.

The urge to settle, even if the other party is still gung-ho about the fight, gains momentum only if you push for it. If your attorney or the counsel of others tries to delay or halt your settlement efforts, I've got a colossal secret for you: Both sides can benefit immensely from a settlement, if you can first displace some initial inertia. Yes, both sides can be winners.

However, for law firms that operate on an hourly billing basis, it's a different story. Settlement means you shut off the spigot and they're losing out on a steady cash flow. Your attorney in particular is motivated to maximize billable hours, so pushing for a settlement forces them to go against their own financial interests.

It may feel to them like they're not just losing your dollars but also dipping into their own pockets, as they'd already planned how much they would squeeze from your situation when they first sent you a retainer.

But remember, it's not just law firms that see revenues cease. The accountants, expert witnesses, and all the other hangers-on during the legal ordeal also see their fees come to an end. Even the court system takes a hit as it loses one more case from its backlog, resulting in fewer gears for its bureaucratic machinations.

Ultimately, settling is a chance for both sides to regain their freedom and stem the flow of collateral damage. On the other side of the conflict, no matter how contentious, there's fertile ground for settlement. Even the most predatory asset raiders among them, who seem to lack humanity, can be motivated to settle when they realize it's in their best interests. After all, even a Viking or pirate eventually grows tired of haggling in court and yearns for the thrill of upcoming adventures and fresh booty.

The holistic beauty of it all is that when each of the parties of a conflict acts in their own self-interest and considers settling for their own sake, there's a universal benefit for all involved. So, if the seed of settlement sprouts within you, nurture it.

Don't let professionals, family, advisors, or even your legal team shut you down. Always keep settlement in your thoughts and be on the lookout for opportunities to make it happen. In the end, all sides of the conflict can emerge as victors.

Chapter 109

Sinking with the Ship:
The Perils of Loving Your Business

§

FALLING IN LOVE WITH YOUR COMPANY OR ASSET CAN BE A PERILOUS affair, my friends. We're all trapped in our ways of thinking, and sometimes, it's to our detriment. This deep affection for one's asset can spell doom for its employees, stakeholders, and equity holders. Let's dissect this.

You had a vision, a dream, and you began with nothing. You nurtured it and poured your heart, soul, and creative essence into it. Sacrifices were made along the way, but you persevered.

Against all odds, you built something from the ground up, something that now thrives, whether it's a business, a property, a ship, or some other enterprise.

Then the storm clouds of conflict gathered, and your initial instinct was to hunker down, lock the hatches, and protect your assets at all costs. Why? Because a part of you is intertwined with this entity. Shielding it feels like a noble quest; after all, it's your brainchild. But is this a sound business strategy? Not necessarily, and I witness this mindset daily, even among accomplished business professionals.

Allow me to share an example from Patrick Bet-David's Miami business conference, which I attended and thoroughly enjoyed, called "The Vault." Picture this case study:

> A forty-five-year-old guy founded a software company at thirty. He's married with two kids. Fifteen friends invested $25,000 to

$50,000 each. By year three, the company generated $100 million in annual revenue with $15 million EBITDA and a 10 percent annual growth rate. A private equity firm expresses interest in investing with the intention of gaining control through board seats and, if comfortable, buying the entire company.

The founder doesn't see the need for new capital, but for further growth, he'd require it. Half of the initial investors want out, and he believes the company's value lies between $150 million and $180 million (10x-12x EBITDA). He hasn't cashed out much personally, owns two suits and his home, and feels stretched due to family commitments, board commitments, and other interests. He feels a touch of business fatigue.

Should he sell, stand still, seek investment, or continue as is?

In group discussions, the prevailing sentiment was that the company was viewed as sacrosanct, a fortress that nothing could harm. The thought of selling was unanimously met with resistance as it was seen as the founder "selling out." Most attendees were infatuated with their businesses, past or future, and seemingly forgot that numerous disruptors lurk in the business world's seas, capable of sinking a company overnight.

Remember Kodak, the film and photography empire? The digital camera arrived, smartphones followed, and *boom,* game over. Bankruptcy and liquidation ensued. Disruptors are all around, and they are like unpredictable waves in the sea. Consider these examples: legislation and regulations, technological advancements, competition, economic downturns, natural disasters, global events like pandemics, geopolitical conflicts, changes in consumer preferences, cybersecurity threats, cyberattacks, data breaches, security vulnerabilities, environmental and sustainability concerns, or disruptions in the supply chain.

Every business must factor in these variables when calculating its viability all the time. If they see a storm coming, quick thinking and adaptability can save them. But what are they saving?

If they're blindly in love with their company and believe it's immune to all market disruptors, that's double trouble, and they'll likely go down with the ship when faced with a formidable challenge.

Divorcing yourself from excessive affection for your company, asset, or enterprise is crucial. Focus on why you started it in the first place: the enhancement of your life and freedom that comes from making money. Concentrate on securing your financial interests, even if it means parting with your business, a division, or its assets for the sake of maximizing a cash payout, as the business you cherish might not be there tomorrow.

In Patrick's case study, not a single audience member recommended selling the company because they saw it as invulnerable and everlasting. I was astounded. I automatically include potential disruptors in my evaluations because I see businesses and (now formerly) financially successful people crash almost daily. Many in the audience were in love with their businesses, even a case study business, as if they were living beings rather than considering them as a means to an end.

The conflict of litigation is no different from these disruptors. It can be just as destructive to a business, asset, or individual as the list of disruptors mentioned earlier. A total loss can happen swiftly. The initial injury of a lawsuit may seem minor, but if not assessed wisely, it could cost you dearly.

Once you find yourself in or approaching a formal conflict, it's vital to explore the potential costs of this tumultuous moment. No venture or asset is invulnerable or impervious to changes in its value. Acknowledging that your company, asset, or portfolio is not infallible and is susceptible to risks is the first step. Your agility in making significant decisions, such as divesting from a division or sacrificing beloved assets, may ensure your financial survival through the gauntlet of litigation.

Chapter 110

Sacrifices and Survival:
The Power of Settling

§

SETTLEMENT, MY FRIENDS, IS AKIN TO CUTTING OUT A TUMOR OF conflict. Yes, it feels like you're removing a piece of healthy flesh along with it, and that cost can be substantial. You might part with a chunk of your hard-earned money or valuable assets, which can feel like giving away your gold. But by letting go of this gold, you can make that agonizing headache of conflict disappear. You may not come out of it entirely unscathed, but you will survive.

Think of the story of Aron Ralston, a testament to incredible survival and determination. Canyoneering alone in Utah's Blue John Canyon in 2003, a boulder trapped his right arm against the canyon wall. After days of unimaginable pain and fear, he faced the gut-wrenching decision to hack off his own arm to gain his freedom and ultimately survive.

Likewise, consider the case of Hiroshi Ouchi, a Japanese hiker who found himself trapped in the unforgiving Akaishi Mountains of Japan in 1993. With heavy snow pinning him down for two months, he realized that no rescue was forthcoming. In a desperate act of survival, he took a pocketknife and amputated his lower leg, an unimaginable sacrifice.

Litigation is no different; it's a battle you need to end proactively. You might feel like you're cutting off your right arm or giving up a pound of flesh, but in reality, it's more symbolic. Even though it may seem like you're removing a piece of your own heart, the wound left behind can heal, given time and determination. And with your freedom, you can buckle down and try earning the money you parted with.

In some inherently tough situations, like divorce, child custody, or complex business disputes, the sacrifices you make may indeed feel like tearing out your own heart. The hole left behind might never fully close.

But here's the bottom line: Settling can be painful, yet it's a proactive way to put an end to the conflict and shield yourself from potentially greater sacrifices that await if you persist in the battle. You see, the outcome won't rest in your hands; you'd be at the mercy of the relentless legal system.

It's like standing in a circle of sharp knives, and those judicial hooligans, the judges, creditor committees, trustees, and litigators, can thrust those knives into your reputation and assets, siphoning the lifeblood right out. Don't expect a glimmer of compassion from anyone. Take the reins, be proactive, and protect yourself!

Chapter 111

Settlement Strategies:
Wisdom from Two Friends

$

I N THE REALM OF BUSINESS AND LITIGATION, TWO SEEMINGLY contradictory adages have provided me with invaluable guidance, courtesy of my friends. Alan Alevy shared the first gem:

> *You don't get what you deserve, you get what you negotiate.*

This adage underscores the proactive nature of negotiation. It's all about engagement, and those who dare to try might find themselves with a deal better than they initially imagined.

On the other hand, Shlomo Karpen, a wise Brooklyn real estate developer, shared the second piece of wisdom decades ago:

> *To do good business, you don't negotiate for every dime; you've got to leave something on the table.*

The second adage emphasizes a more holistic approach to negotiation. In any negotiation, be it in business or litigation, it's essential to recognize that the other party isn't a fool. There has to be something in it for them to strike a deal. It's not about outsmarting your counterpart; the true art of negotiation lies in crafting a deal that benefits you without imposing tangible costs on the other side and conducting yourself with credibility.

Attempting to grab every last bit off the table is a surefire way to kill any potential deal. While some folks aim to maximize every deal and squeeze the other party dry, such an approach doesn't bode well for negotiated settlements. Both parties should understand that the process will be painful, and reaching a final agreement will also come with its share of sacrifices, including leaving something on the table.

Ultimately, the decision of whether the deal is worth concluding or not is in your hands. Even if you don't reach a final agreement, the very act of negotiating, even for an almost deal that gets abandoned, increases the chances of reaching some form of agreement later on. It's far better to try than never to attempt a deal in the first place.

Remember, it's about finding a balance, leaving something for everyone, and making the negotiation process a stepping stone toward the final resolution of the conflict.

Chapter 112

Settling Disputes the Smart Way:
A Guide to Shuttle Diplomacy

§

SHUTTLE DIPLOMACY IS LIKE A LIFESAVER WHEN A COUNTRY IS IN A sea of conflict. It's a slick diplomatic method where a middleman, often a mediator or diplomat, shuttles back and forth between the feuding parties. Why all this back-and-forth, you ask? It's about getting these folks to sit down and talk, start building some trust, and hopefully, hammer out a deal or an agreement.

This nifty tactic comes in handy when those face-to-face talks are just a no-go. It might be because they can't stand each other or they're not quite ready to play nice—the reasons are aplenty. That's where the mediator, a middleman, steps in, carrying messages, offers, and demands, and trying to help everyone meet in the middle.

Now let's talk about settling legal battles. Here's where it gets interesting. It's not exactly mediation—it's more like settlement brokerage. In mediation, both sides need to buy into the game and follow the mediator's final word. Sometimes that's a good idea, and sometimes not so much. But with settlement brokerage, you can start the game with just one party keen on negotiating.

And here's a heads up: Anyone can tap out of the game whenever they fancy. If both sides are sniffing around the idea of a settlement, they can give it a whirl without locking themselves into anything. No harm, no foul if talks go south.

Here's how it goes down for the third-party advisor who shuttles back and forth in the effort of litigation settlement:

Preparation

- Get the lowdown. Dive into the nitty-gritty of the legal beef—the facts, the legal mumbo-jumbo, and who's throwing punches.

- Understand what they want. Figure out what both sides are after and what they'd kill for.

Initial Meetings

- Divide and conquer. Start by cozying up to each side separately.

- Start with one party, and then figure out how to access the other party directly.

- Listen to their tales of woe and get a sense of whether they're down for some negotiation action.

Building Trust

- Show 'em you're no pushover. Prove that you're a neutral go-between, not someone playing favorites.

- Lock down the secret stuff. Assure both parties that whatever they spill will stay in the vault.

Facilitating the Chat

- Let it all hang out. Create a space where everyone feels comfy sharing their gripes and goals.

- Figure out the beef. Help them lay out what's really bugging them.

Shuttling Like a Pro

- Let's talk proposals. Time to start the shuttle service, ferrying each side's concerns, hopes, and maybe some concessions back and forth.

- Bridge those gaps. Use soothing and conciliatory words and a calm demeanor to help them meet in the middle.

Being the Solution Guy

- Suggest some solutions. Based on all the back-and-forth, throw out some ideas for compromise.

- Hands off, please. Remember, you're Switzerland—no taking sides, and definitely no forcing solutions.

Harvesting Feedback

- Grab their thoughts. Get input from both sides on what's on the table. Be ready to tweak things as you go.

Paper Trail

- Keep records. Jot down every little detail, from proposals to counterproposals, and any progress that gets made. If either side wants no notes, no problem.

- Seal the deal. Make sure both sides are on the same page before moving forward.

Memo of Understanding Time

- Help 'em spell it out. Assist in drafting a memo of understanding for the settlement agreement.

- Once they're all thumbs up, get an attorney to draw up the formal settlement agreement.

- Back and forth it goes between the parties until it's ready for a John Hancock.

Tying Up Loose Ends

- When the dust settles, celebrate the successful end of the litigation drama if the mood is right. It's a pat on the back and a fresh start.

Shuttle diplomacy in the litigation world is a test of patience, a calculated but low-risk gamble, and a good idea. An attorney at a conventional law firm isn't cut out for this role, and you can't lead the charge either. That's where a third-party advisor comes in. Generally hired by one side, they'll grease the wheels of settlement for both sides.

The goal is to end the litigation headache, get folks to find a middle ground, and write "The End" to their courtroom saga. It's all about brokering a deal and giving both sides a shot at closure. So remember, shuttle diplomacy in the litigation world is all about brokering a deal, and it might just be the lifeline you need to get out of that deep-seated dispute.

Chapter 113

The Natural Instinct to Settle

§

Y OU SEE, MY FRIENDS, THE WILLINGNESS TO SETTLE, WELL, IT'S A curious thing. It all boils down to the essential elements of a case and the individuals in the ring.

When two parties similar in background and financial standing find themselves tangled in litigation with no clear-cut legal slam dunk, they can take the path of early negotiations and resolve their dispute. But hold on, there's a twist! Depending on the dynamics of the personalities involved, they might just choose to duke it out in court until the bitter end. You see, when both sides stand on level ground and the case is a legal coin toss, the motivation to settle may or may not be there, even if settling would actually be in the best interest of both parties.

Now let's shift gears a bit. What happens when you have a two-party brawl, but the odds are stacked against one of them? Picture this: A borrower faces off against a lender. The lender, by every measure, has the upper hand in this showdown. They've got top-notch in-house or external counsel, deep pockets, and the law, and well, it's about 99.9 percent on their side. You see, defaulted loans, my friends, are just part of the lender's daily grind.

But now look at the borrower's side of the ring. They've hired lower-tier legal counsel, and they've got virtually no legal defenses. They're scraping the bottom of the financial barrel, and their asset is in a real pickle, ready to set off a chain reaction of trouble across their entire portfolio.

On the surface, the stronger party has no incentive to exit the litigation highway and settle the case. But that borrower? They'd give their right arm for a settlement lifeline. The stronger party, you see, often believes they'll walk away unscathed, or at least pretty darn close, by following the established rules of the business system, which includes a good old-fashioned legal tussle. So, in this scenario, a loan goes south, and the lender might just sell that loan off to let someone else deal with the collection headache. Or they might kick-start a pre-foreclosure dance themselves, expecting their legal eagles to see it through to the endgame: foreclosure and property sale.

The lender has no reason to mess with their legal department's well-oiled machine because, when the dust settles, that property will be theirs to foreclose upon, and they'll sell it at market rate, maximizing the returns for that distressed asset.

Now don't get me wrong, folks. This might hold true in some cases, but let's take notes—in many others, the stronger party ends up biting the bullet by sticking to the same old business-as-usual litigation routine. Let me paint a picture for you.

Once, I waded into the fray, stepping up to a lender on behalf of a client who'd defaulted on an $11 million loan for a class C multifamily property located in another neck of the woods. Things had gone south—minor vandalism, tenants skipping out on rent, and the property hurtling toward the abyss. I looked that lender square in the eye and said, "You know, that borrower's lost their grip on this property, gone belly-up. How about they hand you the keys, a 'deed in lieu,' or a friendly foreclosure in exchange for wiping the slate clean on that personal guarantee they signed when they took the loan? Why, you ask? Because that poor guy is now flat broke, and his personal guarantee for any judgment shortfall is about as useful as a screen door on a submarine." But I didn't stop there. I dangled an even more tempting carrot for a settlement, one that would work in the lender's favor rather than playing out the legal drama.

If that lender accepted the property pronto, got it insured, hired a management crew to nurse it back to health, and put it on the market, they could very well recover 90 to 100 percent of their loan amount.

But here's the twist: If they dawdled and went the litigation route, each passing day would drag that property through the mud, suffering vandalism and looting, going straight to hell. The lender would end up kissing goodbye to a whopping 90 percent of their loan value. Meanwhile, their attorneys would be laughing all the way to the bank, collecting litigation fees, following the well-trodden path of foreclosure.

So, let's run the numbers again, folks. It's an $11 million loan gone south. The lender can stick to their attorneys' typical in-the-box litigation protocol, watch the asset crumble, and eventually sell it for $2 million, leaving them with a total loss of $9 million. Or they can embrace a proactive settlement mindset, taking a hit of just $1 million on the loan, collect $10 million, and redeploying that capital to earn new income.

It's a slam-dunk decision, but once litigation fires up, standard business sense often takes a back seat. Those litigators, bless their hearts, are usually oblivious to the financial repercussions, billing away until the bitter end. And guess who's left holding the bag with the heftiest loss? That strong-positioned lender with the most skin in the game.

This, my friends, is a prime example of how the stronger party, initially hesitant to settle, can end up taking it on the chin, when, believe it or not, they could've raked in the most chips by settling right from the get-go—even if it meant breaking away from the same old script when loans go south.

Chapter 114

The Systemic Lethargy
Blocking the Path to Settlement

$

FOLKS, LET'S DISCUSS THE MAMMOTH-SIZED ROADBLOCK THAT WE'RE dealing with when it comes to settling disputes. Imagine just for a moment that a gust of fresh, new air sweeps across America, where settling disputes becomes all the rage. Who'd be cheering it on, and who'd be gnashing their teeth in opposition?

Now let me tell you, the judges—those honorable folks who sit on their high chairs in the courtroom—they'd be absolutely livid. Why, you ask? Well, it's simple. If disputes were settling left and right, their caseload would dwindle faster than a snow cone in the desert. And there's not a job out there that's quite like theirs. You see, they get to bask in the glory of being one of the almighty ones, soaking in the adulation of the masses.

They cast their will upon the little people at their beck and call with the unquestioned authority of the country's government behind them. They control the fate and fancy of all parties involved, not to mention they have a guaranteed shot at earning ten to twenty times their current salary once they retire and step into their next gig at a tony law firm. Who knows, maybe North Korea is on the hunt for a new emperor?

Now let's talk about the litigators. If disputes were settling like hotcakes, they'd be doing a sort of verbal hari-kari, literally falling on their own double-talking tongues. No more clients to bamboozle with their legal jargon, no more double-billing shenanigans, because litigation, my friends, would be as extinct as the dodo bird. Instead, you'd find transactional attorneys drafting those settlement agreements. And the litigators? Well, they'd be out of a job.

And then there are the receivers and trustees, folks who might just be sobbing in their pillows. Why, you ask? Because there would be no more astronomical incentive fees rolling into their pockets, in addition to their already generous hourly rates. They'd be writhing in pain over losing the opportunity to skim off the top of someone else's holdings.

But it doesn't stop there, my friends. The accountants, asset managers, appraisers, expert witnesses, and all the other hangers-on in the legal circus, well, they'd be downright miserable. They'd have to go out there and find another host to latch onto for their livelihood.

So, you see, it's crystal clear. Settlement, it's a sweet deal, but it's only in the best interest of the principals of the dispute and their shareholders. As for the professionals tangled up in the legal skirmish, well, they've got a vested interest in keeping that dispute train chugging along.

One could say that sometimes these players are a necessary evil toward a resolution, and I wouldn't argue with that. But the bottom line is that there's a natural and vested interest for all these players to make sure your case doesn't settle. It's a dog-eat-dog world out there, folks, and these legal sharks aren't ready to give up their piece of the pie.

Chapter 115

Settling Disputes:
Cutting Through Legal Red Tape

§

LADIES AND GENTLEMEN, LET'S TALK ABOUT SETTLING YOUR litigation and, more specifically, the fine art of direct contact between the disputing parties.

Now there are a rare few litigators out there who are willing to roll up their sleeves and get the settlement train moving. They don't mind stepping aside, letting the principals in the dispute have a go at finding common ground. Some may even facilitate the conversation. It's a breath of fresh air to work with that kind of attorney, let me tell you. But let's face it: Most lawyers take a different route, and it often leaves the clients to fend for themselves.

When you've got attorneys actively playing defense and preventing those informal chats between the disputing parties, well, it can feel like you're trudging uphill in cement shoes. Your chances of settling the matter can start to look about as bright as a cloudy day.

But don't fret, my friends, because you've got a couple of options up your sleeve.

First, you can have your trusty litigator request a court-ordered mediation. If that's on the table, grab it with both hands. Courts these days can be solicited to push for alternative dispute resolution methods. A court order, now, that's the golden ticket. It'll nudge those parties right into the ring for some mediation.

If that's not in the cards, there's always the old-school approach. You or a skilled advisor can reach out to the other principal directly. Sure, it might catch them off guard at first, but once you lay it out plain and simple that what's good for the goose is good for the gander, they might just take the bait. Remember, the benefit of settlement for one side can be a reciprocal benefit for the other, and that's the angle you want to play.

Now you might face a bit of resistance in the beginning, but you know what they say: Breaking the ice can lead to warmer conversations down the road. So go ahead, take the plunge. The path to settling those disputes may be a bit rocky, but with the right approach and a dash of persistence, you just might find yourself on the road to resolution. It's not for the faint of heart, my friends, but remember, where there's a will, there's a way.

Chapter 116

Fast-Track Resolution:
Navigating Sit-Down Settlements

§

ALRIGHT, FOLKS, LET'S DELVE INTO THE WORLD OF SIT-DOWN agreements and settlements. Picture this: Instead of playing legal ping-pong with contracts for eons, like those lawyers who seem to enjoy the back-and-forth revisions, first with their clients and then back to the opposing counsel, why not take a cue from real estate movers and shakers? They're the folks who often scoff at the idea of back-and-forth negotiations dragging on for months when they can seal the deal in a matter of hours.

Enter the sit-down contract—a grand powwow where buyers, sellers, and their legal eagles armed with laptops gather around a table to hash out a contract and its terms in one fell swoop. The beauty of it? A binding contract in record time.

The modus operandi of the real estate sit-down contract can be emulated with a sit-down meeting between the feuding parties, doing away with the slow-motion traditional back-and-forth volley of hashing out a settlement deal.

But what if trust is as scarce as a friendly game of poker? Well, in the real estate world, transactions sometimes kick off without a written contract. They order the title, wait for it to clear, and then with a price tag in mind, dive into the closing. There is no leap of faith; a contract only materializes at the moment of funding. No need to dance around potential chaos with negotiated contingencies—they've leapfrogged over all the potential drama.

So, why is this relevant to settling disputes? It's the blueprint for efficiency. Sure, the parties might despise each other, there might be some shouting, and an agreement might not pop out like a rabbit from a hat on day one. But at the core, there's engagement—messy, loud, but undeniably human. Introduce a settlement advocate into the mix, and you might just turn the dial down on the emotional fireworks, paving the way for something productive.

Here, attorneys step out of their default courtroom bickering mode and morph into agents of resolution. Imagine leading your attorney for a change, steering them toward solving your problem instead of hurtling toward the abyss of never-ending litigation costs. It's a switch-up worth considering.

Chapter 117

The Deal Memo:
Don't Let Lawyers Steer the Ship

$

L ADIES AND GENTLEMEN, LET'S SHARPEN OUR DEAL WITH A FENCING foil—the deal memo. We all know lawyers have a knack for being called "deal killers."

They've earned this reputation, and you might wonder how to keep them at bay while ensuring your deals flourish. Let's explore the strategy that can save your deals from being torpedoed.

In the realm of business and settlement negotiations, it's crucial to understand that the stakeholders are the heart and soul of the process. They engage in a delicate dance of negotiation, ironing out the intricate details and striving to find common ground.

Lawyers, the architects of legal documents, play an essential role, but their position is more akin to that of a backup dancer than a leading performer in this complex waltz.

One thing's for sure; involving your legal counsel prematurely in the negotiation process can often be like tossing a heavy paperweight into a crystal-clear pool. The ripples they create can obscure the clarity of your deal, causing it to sink rather than float.

So, what's the solution to prevent your litigation settlement deal from drowning before it even begins? That's where the deal memo enters the scene. This one-page document is a beacon of simplicity, serving as a summary of the key points, intentions, and expectations of the deal. Whether your deal is a minor agreement or a colossal business endeavor, the authors of this one-page deal memo lay the foundation for a successful deal.

It's essential for you or the stakeholders to be the authors of the initial terms and leaders in the creation of the deal memo. While lawyers can certainly assist in shaping the terms under consideration and offer their expertise, you should be the architect of the settlement as you are the one who best understands the nuanced intricacies of the negotiation.

Once the deal memo is agreed upon, it's time to formalize the deal. Consider employing a transactional attorney to draft the settlement agreement instead of your litigator. Transactional attorneys have a vested interest in bringing the deal to a swift conclusion, unlike litigation-focused attorneys who may unintentionally prolong the dispute.

The beauty of the deal memo is that it allows you to remain in control of the negotiation process and ensure lawyers don't prematurely obstruct the path to a successful settlement. Whether it's a small-scale partnership or a grand business endeavor, the simplicity of the deal memo can be the key to keeping negotiations flowing smoothly.

In summary, the deal memo is your secret weapon in the world of deal-making. It helps you keep lawyers at bay during the delicate early stages of settlement negotiation, ensuring the parties establish a strong foundation for the deal.

Remember that even the most grandiose deals often begin with a one-page agreement, sometimes even just hastily jotted scribble on the back of a napkin, and effectively forged between the essential parties to the transaction so that even the most determined "deal-killing" attorneys can't undermine the deal.

So take charge, lead the way, and use the deal memo as your compass to navigate the intricate world of deals and settlements. Your litigation settlement deserves a fair chance to flourish, and with the right approach, it certainly can.

Chapter 118

Uncovering Hidden Profits: Scrutinizing Your Litigation Portfolio

§

LADIES AND GENTLEMEN, WE'VE TRAVERSED THE TUMULTUOUS terrain of litigation, and we've come to realize that, in most cases, no one emerges from the battlefield feeling like a triumphant hero.

Litigation is a domain where all parties incur losses, both in terms of finances and collateral consequences. The ultimate aim in the legal arena is to minimize these losses and fast-track the road to settlement.

But what if you're not dealing with a lone legal skirmish? What if you find yourself at the helm of a larger entity with a portfolio of ongoing litigation battles? In our previous chapter, we dissected a straightforward case where settling early would have meant a $1 million loss compared to a post-litigation loss of $9 million. A critical business element that the litigator failed to grasp or communicate to the division head became apparent.

In business, it's a tale of profits and losses—a straightforward narrative. While we all understand the concept of profits, losses dwell in a murky realm. When your business is of considerable scale and you've factored in losses as part of your financial landscape, what do you call it when you systematically reduce those losses? Good business practice, a better bottom line, and a profit boost.

Carefully scrutinizing your portfolio of ongoing litigation cases can unveil a strategy to systematically cut losses and boost your bottom line. Picture having someone step in to assess each case, gauging the probable losses from a proactive, negotiated settlement viewpoint versus the conventional litigation path. Chances are you would realize that a substantial portion of your litigation portfolio is ripe for settlement, leading to reduced losses in each case. Cumulatively, this would translate into substantial savings.

Litigation is a costly, unsustainable, and unfortunate expense of conducting business. While it can't be entirely eradicated, larger businesses possess the unique opportunity to disrupt their own portfolio of predicaments by identifying and settling cases that make solid business sense. However, beware. This endeavor requires rolling up your sleeves and disrupting the usual course of business on the litigation journey.

This process demands business acumen, the ability to evaluate the long-term risks and costs connected to each case, and the willingness to cauterize the bleeding by opting for settlements. The systematic and periodic culling of cases from your litigation portfolio can lead to an improved financial bottom line for your business. This approach reduces the workforce handling these cases, cuts down on outside counsel legal fees, mitigates collateral damage, and alleviates the mental toll associated with prolonged conflicts.

The common practice of passing files to legal and then onto outside counsel with the expectation that these professionals will resolve them out of sight and out of mind often falls short. Instead, it provides an ideal environment for problems to fester, much like the breeding ground of a petri dish nurturing a wretched bacteria or virus. These litigation cases ferment in the darkness of the courts with financial losses expanding like a relentless virus until they break free from the lab, resulting in uncontrolled and significant costs and collateral damage.

Simply dispatching files to legal, even as an established cost of conducting business, without periodic reevaluation for settlement opportunities deprives you of the chance to enhance your financial bottom line by culling and exterminating the festering troubles of litigation.

Your legal team might not be enthusiastic about this approach and may even attempt to obstruct your path, but fear not! While litigation is their realm, your business's financial health is your domain, and so is the pursuit of greater profits!

Chapter 119

Advisory Services and Increasing Your Headspace and Clarity

§

LITIGATION IS LIKE A WILD BULL, AND OVER TIME, WE'VE HONED A variety of techniques to try and wrestle it into submission, whether through clever management or by attempting to neuter it with a well-executed settlement. The real question is how can we make that happen?

First things first, we've got to ensure that you, the chief in command, whether you're an individual, a business mogul, a division leader, or a CEO, and an active participant in the conflict, are in top form, fortified and sound enough to spearhead the drive toward a resolution. You could very well use a peace-of-mind booster.

It's a remarkable thing that even eminent medical doctors, experts in their own right, seek consultations with less esteemed colleagues for their own health evaluations. The expert doctor, while often possessing a wealth of knowledge and skills, gives the less eminent doctor the upper hand. This less prestigious doctor can provide an impartial evaluation of the situation at hand, a fresh perspective, and a clearer viewpoint unclouded by familiarity. The expert doctor may indeed have superior knowledge, but they often heed and respect the guidance of their less esteemed counterpart.

In fact, these two doctors may brainstorm together to reach a conclusion. So, the more conventional doctor ends up offering something that's often elusive to the expert doctor: a fresh perspective and an uncluttered sharing of headspace for his patient to find breath to focus on his health, problems, and solutions.

You might be excellent at calling the shots within your company or division, but sometimes expanding your mental horizons by bringing in an external advisor can provide that extra head space. You'd hear them out, yet the executive decisions would remain in your hands. You'd still be the one calling the shots but with newfound vigor in leading your battle.

The hired gun outsider who can lead the charge may or may not be in the cards for you. But much like the doctor analogy, external advice, even if acquired piece by piece from various sources, can be an asset, especially when you're navigating the treacherous waters of litigation and anticipating settlement.

If you're part of a bigger business concern, you can delegate the situation to a competent division head while an advisor supports them through the labyrinth of litigation.

However, for smaller businesses, where the luxury of a hired advisor might be out of reach, it falls on your shoulders to take the reins more directly. Gathering sound external advice, even if it's in bits and pieces during your litigation journey, can be invaluable. We've learned that the system is riddled with conflicts of interest. So, when you do seek advice, stepping outside the system can work to your advantage. If that advice comes from someone who is not motivated by racking up bills and extracting every last cent from you, its value increases, elevating its credibility index.

Even with a lead advisor, you'll still need input from other experts to keep your legal counsel in check. So, the question boils down to this: Can you ride out this conflict solo, or are you in need of assistance to lead this rodeo, and is it accessible to you?

Chapter 120

Where to Discover a Top-Notch Advisor

§

Now if you've been following my lead, you know I'm all about no-nonsense guidance. But here's the rub—finding the perfect litigation-negotiation advisor isn't as easy as strolling into a store and picking one up off the shelf. There isn't a cookie-cutter job title that encompasses all the necessary skills for navigating litigation and settlement.

The legal system is designed so that your litigator is perceived as an authority and your de facto boss. I've advocated for the idea that, in reality, they are but service providers and you are their boss. Now the challenge and conundrum are to find an advisor to help you be your litigator or law firm's boss. Unfortunately, there is no current marketplace for this essential service.

You may need to navigate this journey on your own, consulting with various players at different times to fulfill your needs as some service providers have attributes that could be partially helpful for your cause. To get by, you essentially need three separate skill sets. Let's explore some existing service provider titles and how these players may assist you during your journey.

Legal Management Skill Set with an Owner's Perspective
A temporary partner familiar with legal management and strategy would have the requisite mindset to help you take the reins. However, the job title for someone who operates as if they have skin in the game and cares about your legal endeavors is elusive. You might just need to go solo on

this part of the game and employ all the tricks and methodologies offered in this book.

Asset/Business Skill Set

A chief restructuring officer (CRO) is the title of an individual who assists you in an official role in Chapter 11, during other litigation, or a business crisis. They focus on the asset and are usually familiar with legal procedures but are not typically steeped in legal management and settlement strategy. The ideal CRO can offer you:

1. Financial Wizardry: A CRO brings a treasure trove of financial knowledge and experience to the table, guiding your company in making savvy financial moves.

2. Financial Roadmap: Your CRO can chart a comprehensive financial course for your company, detailing how it will navigate its finances during the bankruptcy process, complete with budgets, cash flow forecasts, and financial projections.

3. Cost-Cutting Maestro: Sniffing out opportunities to save on costs, renegotiating contracts, streamlining operations—your CRO has it covered.

4. Cash Flow Guru: When you're in Chapter 11, managing cash flow is like a high-stakes game. Your CRO will devise strategies to keep the cash flowing smoothly, ensuring your company has the financial muscle to fund its operations and meet its obligations.

5. Debt Whisperer: Your CRO can sit down with creditors and work out debt-restructuring deals. That could mean extending payment terms, slashing interest rates, or settling debts for less than the full amount.

6. Financial Compass: Accurate and punctual financial reporting is Chapter 11 gold. Your CRO will make sure your company checks all the reporting boxes, offering transparency to stakeholders.

7. Liaison Extraordinaire: As the point person for creditors, your CRO can address their concerns, keeping them in the loop with financial info, building trust, and making negotiations smoother.

8. Long-Term Strategist: Beyond the nitty-gritty of bankruptcy, a CRO can help you hatch a long-term financial game plan for your company's resurgence. That might involve finding new revenue sources, identifying market opportunities, or exploring potential partnerships.

9. Risk Tamer: Your CRO evaluates financial risks during Chapter 11 and crafts strategies to keep them in check so that you're not playing with fire when it comes to your company's financial stability.

10. Investor Magnet: Having a top-notch CRO on board boosts the confidence of shareholders, investors, and other stakeholders. It sends a clear signal that your company means business about its financial recovery and is backed by a seasoned pro.

11. Legal Compliance Ace: Chapter 11 brings a heap of legal and compliance obligations. Your CRO ensures your company plays by the rules, reducing the risk of legal headaches or holdups in the process.

12. Reboot Facilitator: If you're gunning for a reorganization plan, your CRO takes the lead in managing the financial side of things and gauging the plan's feasibility.

13. Cost vs. Benefit Guru: Your CRO can crunch the numbers and run cost-benefit analyses for various financial decisions, helping you make choices that maximize the benefits of Chapter 11 while keeping costs in check.

Settlement Skill Set

A formal mediator typically won't initiate shuttle diplomacy by calling the other side, but an available mediator acting as a consultant might provide invaluable ideas on how to reach out and navigate contact with the other party. It takes more guts than brains to make that initial contact. A CRO might be able to carry out your bidding. Consider someone from your immediate circle whom you haven't thought of before, direct them to reach out but provide guidance and a framework, possibly after consulting with a mediator type. They can handle the initial legwork, allowing you to step in at a later point and communicate directly.

So, what benefits does an advisor tailored for settlement bring to the table? Let's break it down.

1. Your Champion: With an advisor, you gain a staunch advocate working tirelessly on your behalf. It's not about their gain; it's about achieving your objectives.

2. Neutrality: Even when one side brings in an advisor, an air of neutrality blankets the proceedings. Advisors often focus on conveying the mutual advantages of settling, defusing tension, and establishing common ground. They carry no emotional baggage into the fight.

3. Diplomacy and Finesse: A skilled advisor brings a diplomatic finesse to the negotiations. They are the experts at navigating treacherous waters, calming egos, and keeping dialogues on the right course. Think of them as the peacemakers in the legal Wild West.

4. Creative Problem-Solving: When you're deadlocked, these experts become the MacGyvers of negotiation, crafting innovative solutions that others might overlook.

5. Speed and Efficiency: Time equals money, and a proficient advisor understands this well. They expedite the negotiation process, ensuring you don't drown in the mire of protracted and costly legal battles.

6. The Art of Listening: Every party in a conflict needs empathetic listening, clarifying their needs and transforming them into tangible demands. This is the bedrock for identifying variables that can be adjusted and proposed for a settlement.

7. The Gift of Compromise: Sometimes, the key to unlocking a settlement lies in finding that middle ground. A skilled advisor/negotiator excels at uncovering compromise solutions that satisfy both sides.

The trifecta of indispensable skill sets to complete your advisory circle has been unveiled. I genuinely trust that the insights within these pages have fortified your ability to navigate a litigation and settlement affair. Most crucially, if you stand on the brink of litigation, let me emphasize once more: If there's any room for choice, stepping into the realm of litigation is not a choice to be taken lightly.

Conclusion

§

Throughout this book, I've been drilling a fundamental concept into your consciousness: you must bear the responsibility to navigate your ship out of the stormy sea of litigation. Embracing this truth and mindset will thrust you to the fifty-yard line. Yet, if you want to shift things into high gear and enlist a top-tier advisor, you need someone who is not merely out to line their pockets; they must authentically desire to witness your triumph.

In conclusion, I extend my congratulations for embarking on this odyssey with me. It has been my privilege to be your litigation-negotiation Sherpa through the terrain of legal challenges, shedding light on the unknown and unveiling shortcuts to resolution and new beginnings. Until our paths cross again, it's been an honor, and may success accompany your every step forward.

Appendix

§

Courts Where Litigation Takes Place
Below are the different types of courts where litigation takes place, along with the types of cases they typically handle, including those that deal with business issues:

1. Supreme Court of the United States

    A.   Constitutional issues

    B.   Federal law interpretation

    C.   Landmark cases

2. Federal Court of Appeals

    A.   Appeals from federal district courts

    B.   Constitutional challenges

    C.   Patent and trademark cases

3. Federal District Court

    A.   Federal criminal cases

    B.   Civil rights violations

    C.   Bankruptcy cases (including Chapter 11 business reorganization)

    D.   Environmental disputes

4. State Supreme Court

    A. State law interpretation

    B. Appeals from lower state courts

    C. Death penalty appeals

5. State Court of Appeals

    A. Appeals from lower state courts

    B. Criminal convictions

    C. Family law disputes

6. State Circuit Court (or Superior Court)

    A. Felony criminal cases

    B. Divorce and child custody

    C. Personal injury lawsuits

    D. Business and commercial litigation

    E. Contract disputes and breach of contract claims

7. Family Court

    A. Divorce and separation

    B. Child custody and support

    C. Domestic violence restraining orders

8. Probate Court

    A. Wills and estate planning

    B. Guardianship and conservatorship

    C. Trust administration

9. Small Claims Court

    A. Minor contract disputes

B.   Landlord-tenant disputes

C.   Consumer complaints

10. Bankruptcy Court

A.   Chapter 7 liquidation

B.   Chapter 11 business reorganization

C.   Chapter 13 debt repayment plans

D.   Business bankruptcy and creditor disputes

E.   Financial distress and insolvency cases

F.   Corporate debt management and repayment plans

11. Tax Court

A.   IRS tax disputes

B.   Income tax challenges

C.   Tax penalties and audits

D.   Corporate income tax and tax deductions

12. Traffic Court

A.   Speeding and traffic violations

B.   Parking tickets

C.   DUI and reckless driving cases

13. Juvenile Court

A.   Delinquency cases

B.   Child abuse and neglect

C.   Foster care and adoption matters

14. Municipal Court

A.   Misdemeanor criminal offenses

B. Traffic citations

C. Violations of city ordinances

15. Tribal Court

A. Tribal law matters

B. Disputes among tribal members

C. Cultural heritage and land rights

16. Veterans Court

A. Veterans' benefits and claims

B. Appeals of veterans' disability decisions

C. Cases related to veterans' health care and treatment

16. Arbitration and Mediation Tribunals

A. Alternative dispute resolution forums for business disputes

B. Contractual disputes between businesses

C. Commercial arbitration and mediation proceedings

17. International Business Courts (e.g., Commercial Courts)

A. International trade disputes

B. Cross-border business and contract disputes

C. Disputes involving multinational corporations and foreign entities

18. Maritime Court

A. Admiralty and maritime law cases

B. Shipping and navigation disputes

C. Cargo damage claims

19. Court of International Trade

A. International trade and customs cases

B. Disputes related to tariffs and trade regulations

C. Import and export issues

20. Drug Court

A. Cases involving drug offenses

B. Rehabilitation and treatment programs

21. Immigration Court

A. Cases involving immigration and deportation issues

B. Asylum claims and visa disputes

Please note that the specific types of cases a court handles can vary by jurisdiction, and this list provides a general overview of the common case categories associated with each court type in the United States.

Courts Where Litigation Is Limited or Absent

In some of the specialized courts mentioned in the list, litigation in the traditional sense may be limited or even absent. Here are some examples where litigation may not be the primary focus.

1. Mental Health Court: Mental health courts typically aim to divert individuals with mental health issues away from traditional criminal court processes and toward treatment and support services. While legal issues may be addressed, the emphasis is on rehabilitation and mental health treatment rather than litigation.

2. FISA Court (Foreign Intelligence Surveillance Court): The Foreign Intelligence Surveillance Court primarily deals with national security and intelligence matters, including authorizing surveillance and data collection for counterterrorism purposes. It does not involve litigation in the conventional sense as it operates in a classified and non-adversarial setting.

3. Environmental Court: Environmental courts focus on cases related to environmental law and regulations, such as pollution and conservation disputes. While legal issues are addressed, these courts often prioritize resolving environmental challenges and promoting compliance with environmental laws rather than traditional litigation.

4. Labor Court: Labor courts handle employment-related cases, including labor disputes and wage claims. While legal disputes are involved, the goal is often to resolve workplace issues through mediation, arbitration, or negotiation rather than protracted litigation.

5. Veterans Treatment Court: Veterans treatment courts aim to provide support and treatment options to veterans with legal issues, particularly those related to substance abuse and mental health. While legal matters are addressed, the primary focus is on rehabilitation and support services for veterans.

6. Diversion Court: Diversion courts offer alternative programs for certain non-violent offenders with an emphasis on rehabilitation and community service rather than adversarial litigation.

7. Housing Court: Housing courts handle cases related to landlord-tenant disputes, including eviction proceedings and housing code violations. While these courts involve legal proceedings, the goal is often to find practical solutions for housing-related issues, such as settlement agreements or compliance with housing regulations.

8. Indian Tribal Courts: Indian tribal courts have jurisdiction over legal matters within tribal reservations and often follow tribal law and governance principles. While legal issues are addressed, the focus is on tribal governance and adherence to tribal laws.

It's important to note that the extent of litigation can vary within these specialized courts, and some cases may still involve traditional litigation processes to a certain degree. The specific goals and approaches of these courts may differ from those of general litigation courts.

Glossary

§

Unless otherwise noted, these basic legal terms are taken from the U.S. Department of Justice. (https://www.justice.gov/usao/justice-101/glossary)

A

affirmative defense - A defense in which the defendant introduces evidence, which, if found to be credible, will negate criminal liability or civil liability, even if it is proven that the defendant committed the alleged acts. The party raising the affirmative defense has the burden of proof on establishing that it applies. Raising an affirmative defense does not prevent a party from also raising other defenses. (From https://www.law.cornell.edu/wex)

allegation - Something that someone says happened.

answer - The formal written statement by a defendant responding to a civil complaint and setting forth the grounds for defense.

appeal - A request made after a trial, asking another court (usually the court of appeals) to decide whether the trial was conducted properly. To make such a request is "to appeal" or "to take an appeal." Both the plaintiff and the defendant can appeal, and the party doing so is called the appellant. Appeals can be made for a variety of reasons including improper procedure and asking the court to change its interpretation of the law.

appellate - About appeals; an appellate court has the power to review the judgment of another lower court or tribunal.

B

bankruptcy - Refers to statutes and judicial proceedings involving persons or businesses that cannot pay their debts and seek the assistance of the court in getting a fresh start. Under the protection of the bankruptcy court, debtors may discharge their debts, perhaps by paying a portion of each debt. Bankruptcy judges preside over these proceedings.

bankruptcy estate - The property of the debtor who filed bankruptcy. The estate includes all property in which the debtor has an interest, even if it is owned or held by another person – like obvious and tangible assets, or intangible things: stock options, the right to inheritances received within 6 months after the bankruptcy is filed, tax refunds for prepetition years, and intellectual property like copyrights, patents and trademarks. The exception would be certain pensions, educational trusts and the assets that the debtor will need to maintain a job and household. (From https://www.law.cornell.edu/wex)

bench trial - Trial without a jury in which a judge decides the facts. In a jury trial, the jury decides the facts. Defendants will occasionally waive the right to a jury trial and choose to have a bench trial.

brief - A written statement submitted by the lawyer for each side in a case that explains to the judge(s) why they should decide the case (or a particular part of a case) in favor of that lawyer's client.

C

case law - The use of court decisions to determine how other law (such as statutes) should apply in a given situation. For example, a trial court may use a prior decision from the Supreme Court that has similar issues.

chambers - A judge's office.

chief judge - The judge who has primary responsibility for the administration of a court. The chief judge also decides cases, and the choice of chief judges is determined by seniority.

clerk of court - An officer appointed by the court to work with the chief judge in overseeing the court's administration, especially to assist in managing the flow of cases through the court and to maintain court records.

common law - The legal system that originated in England and is now in use in the United States. It is based on court decisions rather than statutes passed by the legislature.

complaint - A written statement by the plaintiff stating the wrongs allegedly committed by the defendant.

contract - An agreement between two or more persons that creates an obligation to do or not to do a particular thing.

counsel - Legal advice; a term used to refer to lawyers in a case.

counterclaim - A claim that a defendant makes against a plaintiff. Counterclaims can often be brought within the same proceedings as the plaintiff's claims.

court - Government entity authorized to resolve legal disputes. Judges sometimes use "court" to refer to themselves in the third person, as in "the court has read the briefs."

court reporter - A person who makes a word-for-word record of what is said in court and produces a transcript of the proceedings upon request.

credit bidding - Credit bidding is a mechanism that allows a secured creditor to acquire the assets of the debtor on which it holds a lien in exchange for a full or partial cancellation of the debt, allowing it to acquire the assets without paying any actual cash for them. Credit bidding can be used as a defensive strategy by lenders to protect the value of their collateral from falling asset prices. It can also be used as a defensive loan-to-own strategy by investors to acquire distressed assets at below-market prices. (From https://content.next.westlaw.com/practical-law)

cross-examine - Questioning of a witness by the attorney for the other side.

D

damages - Money paid by defendants to successful plaintiffs in civil cases to compensate the plaintiffs for their injuries.

default judgment - A judgment rendered because of the defendant's failure to answer or appear.

defendant - In a civil suit, the person complained against; in a criminal case, the person accused of the crime.

deposition - An oral statement made before an officer authorized by law to administer oaths. Such statements are often taken to examine potential witnesses, to obtain discovery, or to be used later in trial.

direct evidence - Evidence that supports a fact without an inference.

discovery - Lawyers' examination, before trial, of facts and documents in possession of the opponents to help the lawyers prepare for trial.

docket - A log containing brief entries of court proceedings.

E

evidence - Information presented in testimony or in documents that is used to persuade the fact finder (judge or jury) to decide the case for one side or the other.

exhibit - Physical evidence or documents that are presented in a court proceeding. Common exhibits include contracts, weapons, and photographs.

F

file - To place a paper in the official custody of the clerk of court to enter into the files or records of a case. Lawyers must file a variety of documents throughout the life of a case.

I

injunction - An order of the court prohibiting (or compelling) the performance of a specific act to prevent irreparable damage or injury.

interrogatories - Written questions asked to one party by an opposing party, who must answer them in writing under oath. Interrogatories are a part of discovery in a lawsuit.

issue - (1) The disputed point in a disagreement between parties in a lawsuit. (2) To send out officially, as in to issue an order.

J

judge - Government official with authority to decide lawsuits brought before courts. Judicial officers of the Supreme Court and the highest court in each state are called justices.

judgment - The official decision of a court finally determining the respective rights and claims of the parties to a suit.

jurisdiction - (1) The legal authority of a court to hear and decide a case. Concurrent jurisdiction exists when two courts have simultaneous responsibility for the same case. Some issues can be heard in both state and federal courts. The plaintiff initially decides where to bring the suit, but in some cases, the defendant can seek to change the court. (2) The geographic area over which the court has authority to decide cases. A federal court in one state, for example, can usually only decide a case that arose from actions in that state.

juror - A person who is on the jury.

jury - Persons selected according to law and sworn to inquire into and declare a verdict on matters of fact. State court juries can be as small as six jurors in some cases. Federal juries for civil suits must have six jurors; criminal suits must have twelve.

jurisprudence - The study of law and the structure of the legal system.

L

lawsuit - A legal action started by a plaintiff against a defendant based on a complaint that the defendant failed to perform a legal duty, resulting in harm to the plaintiff.

law clerk (or staff attorney) - Assist judges with research and drafting of opinions.

litigation - A case, controversy, or lawsuit. Participants (plaintiffs and defendants) in lawsuits are called litigants.

M

motion - Attempt to have a limited issue heard by the court. Motions can be filed before, during, and after trial.

O

oath - A promise to tell the truth.

objection - A protest by an attorney, challenging a statement or question made at trial. Common objections include an attorney "leading the witness" or a witness making a statement that is hearsay. Once an objection is made, the judge must decide whether to allow the question or statement.

opinion - A judge's written explanation of a decision of the court. In an appeal, multiple opinions may be written. The court's ruling comes from a majority of judges and forms the majority opinion. A dissenting opinion disagrees with the majority because of the reasoning and/or the principles of law on which the decision is based. A concurring opinion agrees with the end result of the court but offers further comment possibly because they disagree with how the court reached its conclusion.

oral argument - An opportunity for lawyers to summarize their position before the court in an appeal and also to answer the judges' questions.

P

parties - Plaintiffs and defendants (petitioners and respondents) to lawsuits, also known as appellants and appellees in appeals, and their lawyers.

plaintiff - The person who files the complaint in a civil lawsuit.

pleadings - Written statements of the parties in a civil case of their positions. In federal courts, the principal pleadings are the complaint and the answer.

precedent - A court decision in an earlier case with facts and law similar to a dispute currently before a court. Precedent will ordinarily govern the decision of a later similar case, unless a party can show that it was wrongly decided or that it differed in some significant way. Some precedent is binding, meaning that it must be followed. Other precedents need not be followed by the court but can be considered influential.

procedure - The rules for the conduct of a lawsuit; there are rules of civil, criminal, evidence, bankruptcy, and appellate procedure.

pro se - A Latin term meaning "on one's own behalf;" in courts, it refers to persons who present their own cases without lawyers.

prosecute - To charge someone with a crime. A prosecutor tries a criminal case on behalf of the government.

public defenders - Represent defendants who can't afford an attorney in criminal matters.

R

record - A written account of all the acts and proceedings in a lawsuit.

reporter - Makes a record of court proceedings, prepares a transcript, and publishes the court's opinions or decisions.

S

service of process - The service of writs or summonses to the appropriate party.

settlement - Parties to a lawsuit resolve their difference without having a trial. Settlements often involve the payment of compensation by one party in satisfaction of the other party's claims.

statute - A law passed by a legislature.

statute of limitations - A law that sets the time within which parties must take action to enforce their rights.

stay - A temporary pause or suspension of a judicial proceeding. Stays are usually designed to terminate upon the completion of specified event (e.g., a judicial decision in a separate case or the end of a government shutdown) or after a specific period of time.

subpoena - A command to a witness to appear and give testimony.

summary judgment - A decision made on the basis of statements and evidence presented for the record without a trial. It is used when there is no dispute as to the facts of the case, and one party is entitled to judgment as a matter of law.

T

testify - Answer questions in court.

testimony - Evidence presented orally by witnesses during trials or before grand juries.

tort - A civil wrong or breach of a duty to another person as outlined by law. A very common tort is negligent operation of a motor vehicle that results in property damage and personal injury in an automobile accident.

transcript - A written, word-for-word record of what was said, either in a proceeding such as a trial or during some other conversation.

trial - A hearing that takes place when the defendant pleads "not guilty," and the parties are required to come to court to present evidence.

U

uphold - The decision of an appellate court not to reverse a lower court decision. Also called "affirm."

V

venue - The geographical location in which a case is tried.

verdict - The decision of a petit jury or a judge.

W

witness - A person called upon by either side in a lawsuit to give testimony before the court or jury.

writ - A formal written command, issued from the court, requiring the performance of a specific act.

Notes

§

1. "Number of Lawyers in the United States from 2007 to 2022 (in 1,000s)," *Statista*, www.statista.com/statistics/740222/number-of-lawyers-us/, accessed 10 Dec. 2023.

2. "FAQs: Judges in the United States," *Institute for the Advancement of the American Legal System* (IAALS), iaals.du.edu/sites/default/files/documents/publications/judge_faq.pdf, accessed 10 Dec. 2023.

3. Moore, Derick, "U.S. Population Estimated at 334,233,854 on Jan. 1, 2023," *United States Census Bureau*, 22 Dec. 2022, www.census.gov/library/stories/2022/12/happy-new-year-2023.html.

4. "Santa Claus," *Jokes.One*, https://jokes.one/joke/santa-claus-santa-claus-the-tooth-fairy-an-honest-lawyer-and-an-old-drunk-are-wa, accessed 10 Dec. 2023.

5. "Court Review," *The American Judges Association*, Dec. 2006, https://digitalcommons.unl.edu/ajacourtreview/22/.

6. "Franz Kafka," *Wikipedia*, en.wikipedia.org/wiki/Franz_Kafka, accessed 21 December 2023.

7. Martin, James R., PhD, "Lawyer Jokes," *Management and Accounting Web*, maaw.info/GadgetsandGames/LawyerJokes.htm, accessed 10 Dec. 2023.

8. Martin, "Lawyer Jokes."

9. "Rope-a-Dope," *Wikipedia*, en.wikipedia.org/wiki/Rope-a-dope, accessed 10 Dec. 2023.

10. *"Muhammed Ali,"* *Wikipedia*, en.wikipedia.org/wiki/Muhammad_Ali, accessed 10 Dec. 2023.

11. *Groundhog Day* was a 1993 Bill Murray classic movie following the concept of a time loop, where the main characters are trapped in the same day, day after day, with no recall of the preceding day.

12. Denniston, Lyle, "Analysis: The Lodestar as Gold Standard," *Scotusblog*, 21 April 2010, www.scotusblog.com/2010/04/analysis -the-lodestar-as-gold-standard/.

13. Author's Note: I co-developed the 630-foot NY Wheel in Staten Island. My then-partner cut me out of the deal and signed a partnership agreement with (entities controlled by) Lloyd Goldman, Jeffrey Feil, and Joseph Nakash. I sued the partnership and separately my then-partner. David Smith represented my interests. We first beat Paul, Weiss, Rifkind, Wharton & Garrison LLP, on their motion to dismiss my case, which lead to a quick settlement with the New York Wheel LLC. We continued litigation against my former partner, going up against Morrison Cohen LLP, and settled before trial. This case was chock-full of intrigue, private investigators and surveillance, expert witnesses, and dramatic depositions. I learned a tremendous amount from the experience and came out a winner.

14. Eller, Sandy, "Retired Orthodox Supreme Court Judge Dies At 66," *VINnews*, 16 Sept. 2018, vinnews.com/2018/09/16/brooklyn-ny -retired-orthodox-supreme-court-judge-dies-at-66/.

15. Meyer, Pamela, "How to Spot a Liar," *Ted Talks*, July 2011, www.ted .com/talks/pamela_meyer_how_to_spot_a_liar?language=en.

16. "Gold Bars, Cash-Stuffed Envelopes: New Indictment of Sen. Menendez Alleges Vast Corruption," *US News*, 22 Sept. 2023, www.usnews.com/news/politics/articles/2023-09-22/sen-menendez-wife-indicted-on-bribe-charges-as-probe-finds-100-000-in-gold-bars-prosecutors-say.

17. Bohannon, Molly, "Lawyer Used ChatGPT in Court—and Cited Fake Cases. A Judge Is Considering Sanctions," *Forbes*, 8 June 2023, www.forbes.com/sites/mollybohannon/2023/06/08/lawyer-used-chatgpt-in-court-and-cited-fake-cases-a-judge-is-considering-sanctions/?sh=21482ee27c7f.

18. "Gang bang," *Merriam-Webster.com Dictionary*, www.merriam-webster.com/dictionary/gangbang, accessed 9 Dec. 2023.

19. "Chapter 11 Quarterly Fees," *U.S. Department of Justice*, U.S. Trustee Program, www.justice.gov/ust/chapter-11-quarterly-fees, accessed 22 Dec. 2023.

20. "Dogpile," *Merriam-Webster.com Dictionary*, www.merriam-webster.com/dictionary/dogpile, accessed 22 Dec. 2023.

21. United States v. Stanhope, *U.S. Bankruptcy Court*, Southern District of New York (2021), www.nysb.uscourts.gov/sites/default/files/opinions/293124_191_opinion.pdf.

22. Kittle, Warren, "Courts of Law and Equity—Why They Exist and Why They Differ," *26 West Virginia Law Review* (1919), researchrepository.wvu.edu/wvlr/vol26/iss1/3, accessed 10 Dec. 2023.

23. American Bankruptcy Institute, https://www.abi.org/.

24. Paterick, Zachary R., et al, "Medical Malpractice Stress Syndrome: A 'Forme Fruste' of Posttraumatic Stress Disorder," *National Library of Medicine*, PubMed, Jan. 2017, pubmed.ncbi.nlm.nih.gov/29969550/.

25. "Lawsuit Stress: The Dark Side of Litigation," *Mental Healthy*, www.mentalhealthy.co.uk/anxiety/anxiety/lawsuit-stress-the-dark-side-of-litigation.html, accessed 28 Dec. 2023.

26. Maroon, Joseph C., MD., "Catastrophic Cardiovascular Complications from Medical Malpractice Stress Syndrome," *Journal of Neurosurgery*, 29 Mar. 2019, thejns.org/view/journals/j -neurosurg/130/6/article-p2081.xml.

27. Maroon, "Catastrophic Cardiovascular Complications from Medical Malpractice Stress Syndrome."

28. "Litigation Stress," *Criminal Justice*, iResearchnet.com/criminal -justice.iresearchnet.com/forensic-psychology/trial-consulting /litigation-stress/, accessed 28 Dec. 2023.

29. Andreas, Peter, "How Methamphetamine Became a Key Part of Nazi Military Strategy," *Time*, 7 Jan. 2020, time.com/5752114/nazi -military-drugs/.

30. "What Exactly Is Captagon and Why Is It Banned?" *Drugs .com*, updated 5 Apr. 2023, www.drugs.com/lifestyle/captagon -available-2961377/.

31. Holley, Peter, "The Tiny Pill Fueling Syria's War and Turning Fighters Into Super Human Soldiers," *The Washington Post*, 19 Nov. 2015, www.washingtonpost.com/news/worldviews/wp/2015/11/19 /the-tiny-pill-fueling-syrias-war-and-turning-fighters-into-super -human-soldiers/.

32. Rennolds, Nathan, "Hamas Militants Were High on 'Poor Man's Cocaine' During the October 7 Terrorist Attacks, Report Says," *Business Insider*, 28 Oct. 2023, www.businessinsider.com/hamas -militants-high-poor-mans-cocaine-oct-7-attacks-report-2023-10.

33. Prikei Avot 1:12:1.

34. Babylonian Talmud Sanhedrin 6b.

35. Bartenura on Pirkei Avot 1:12:1.

36. *Slaughterhouse-Five* was written by Kurt Vonnegut and was first published in 1969. The novel is a blend of science fiction and satire and is known for its unique narrative structure, which explores the experiences of its protagonist, Billy Pilgrim, during World War II, particularly the bombing of Dresden, as well as his experiences of time travel and alien abduction.

37. Blum, Marvin, "Five Famous Families Undermined Sibling Conflict," *Wealth Management*, 29 June 2022, www.wealthmanagement.com /high-net-worth/five-famous-families-undermined-sibling-conflict.

Index

$

361

ChatGPT, use of, 155–156
chief restructuring officers (CROs), 332–333
child abuse allegations, 198
child custody and visitation, 194, 199, 284–285
child support, 195, 284–285
chronological versus chapter method for bills, 91–92
chronologies, development of, 21–23
cigarettes, avoiding use of, 276–277
co-counsel, 127–130, 141, 143, 184
Cohn, Steve, 129–130
collaboration, procrastination impacting, 55–56
common law, 261
communications, review of prior to discovery phase, 21–22
conflicts of interest
  bankruptcy court, 236, 255–256
  quality versus money as focus of litigators, 47–48
  receivers and trustees, 136–137
  retainer agreements and, 31–32
  settlement and, 12–13, 37, 43–44
Constitution, U.S., 213
contingency fees, 41–42
corporations. *See* businesses
court-ordered mediation, 319
courtroom skill, researching before hiring attorney, 63–64
courts, types of, 339–344
co-worker stage, 231–232
creditor committees, 243–245, 247–248, 249
CROs (chief restructuring officers), 332–333

D
daily billing logs, 89–90
deadlines, missing of, 65–66
deal memos, 323–324
death from stress, 267–268
defamation, 201–202, 229. *See also* character assassination

default of commercial loans, 173–174, 180–182. *See also* bankruptcy court
defenses, chronology development and, 23
delay, 181–182, 184, 217–219
delegation of work to lower-paid staff, 33–34, 49–50
depositions, 113–115, 169, 171–172
discovery phase
  overview of, 169–170
  communications sweep prior to, 21–22
  depositions, 113–115, 169, 171–172
  personal impacts of, 201
dispute resolution, divorce and, 197
division of assets and debts in divorce, 195
divorce, 193–200, 284–285
document requests, defined, 169
documents
  brevity and clarity in, 61
  first two pages as most important, 59–60
  researching filings in previous cases to select attorney, 63–64
  review of, 57–58, 73–74
dogpiling the debtors, 257–258
double billing, 78
Drain, Robert, 259–260
drugs, avoiding use of, 276–277
due dates, missing of, 65–66, 150
due process, 213–219

E
e-court system, 63–64, 149–150, 152
emails, review prior to discovery phase, 21–22
emotions
  divorce and, 198–199
  during litigation, 185–187, 202, 267–269, 273–274
employment law cases, contingency fees and, 41
enemy stage, 232–233
equity, courts of, 261–262
equity security holders in bankruptcy court, 248

litigation. *See also* bankruptcy court;
    settlement defined, 3–4
    impacts of, 175–177, 185–187, 201–203,
        294–295
    managing stress during, 271–277
    number of cases, 15
    perspectives on, 293–294
    risk assessment for, 301–303
    scrutinizing portfolio of, 325–327
    trajectory of, 281–282
    trial, odds of reaching as small, 35, 39
    used to crush businesses, 173–174
Litigation Stress Syndrome, 267–269
litigators. *See also* attorneys; bankruptcy court
    access to depends on client, 141–144
    attorneys compared, 45–46
    core problems not addressed by, 12
    good ones, 109–115
    initial meetings with, 19–20
    outsourcing of legal work by, 53–54, 75–76
    personalities of, 71–72, 109
    quality versus money as focus of, 47–48
    researching filings in previous cases to
        select, 63–64
    role of, 7
    settlement and, 287, 299, 317–318, 319,
        323–324
    swarming on clients by, 241–242
    using e-court system for accountability of,
        152
loans, 173–174, 179–182.
    See also bankruptcy court
lodestar analysis, 99
Loeb & Loeb LLP
    chapters within bills, 91–92
    getting reduction of bill from, 97–100
    huge bill from, 85–86
    inflation of time charged, 93–96
    One-Page Summary Matrix for chapter
        billing, 101–102
losses, cutting, 325–327

M
malpractice, 144–145, 267–268
markup of documents, 57–58, 73–74
mediation, 250, 309, 319
mediators as advisors, 333–335
medical insurance, 196
medical malpractice stress syndrome (MMSS),
    267–268
medicine, law and, 11–13
Medved, Michael, 16
memory, reconstruction process for, 119
mental and physical examinations, defined, 170
message apps, review prior to discovery phase,
    21–22
mirage, attorney, 75–76
Morrison Cohen LLP, 356n13
Murphy's Law, 190

N
Nakash, Joseph, 356n13
negotiation, 33–35, 104–105, 307–308.
    See also settlement
New York Wheel, 356n13
New York Wheel LLC, 356n13
nutrition, 276
nutritional training, lacking in doctors, 12

O
objectivity, 301–303
One-Page Summary Matrix, 101–102
Ouchi, Hiroshi, 305
outsourcing, 53–54, 75–76

P
paranoia, strategic, 189–190
parasite stage, 232
Paul, Weiss, Rifkind, Wharton & Garrison
    LLP, 356n13
personal injury cases, contingency fees and, 41
personalities, 71–72, 109
pet custody, 197
pharmaceutical industry, 12

365

Reviews

§

Dear Reader,

Thank you for delving into the insights shared in The Terrible Truth About Litigation: An Insider's Guide How To Manage Your Litigation and Negotiate A Settlement. Your commitment to learning and growth is truly commendable!

If you found the advice and strategies beneficial, I would be immensely grateful if you could take a moment to share your thoughts by leaving a review on Amazon and or Goodreads. Your feedback not only helps me but also assists other readers in discovering valuable insights.

To leave a review, simply visit Amazon and Goodreads and share your thoughts on the practical advice, real-world examples, or any specific strategies that resonated with you.

Your honest review is not only appreciated but contributes to the broader conversation around business, dispute resolution, and success. Thank you for being a crucial part of this knowledge-sharing journey!

Warm regards,

Nik Lavrinoff